ISLĀM

BELIEFS AND TEACHINGS

Ghulam Sc

THE MUSLIM EDUCATIONAL TRUST

1st Edition	London 1980 (10,000) reprinted in India 1983 (2,000)
2nd Edition	London 1982 (12,000) reprinted in India twelve times 1989-1999 (24,000)
3rd Edition	London 1984 (20,000) reprinted in Kuwait 1985 (10,000) reprinted in London 1987 (20,000)
4th Edition	London 1989 (20,000) reprinted in Pakistan 1992 (5,000) reprinted in London 1992 (20,000), 1994 (20,000), 1996 (20,000)
5th Edition	London 1998 (21,000) reprinted in India 2000 (2,000)
6th Edition	London 2000 (21,000) reprinted in India 2001 (2,000), 2002 (4,000)
7th Edition	London 2003 (21,000)

Overseas Editions: French, Norwegian, Romanian, Chinese and Bengali

Published by
The Muslim Educational Trust
130 Stroud Green Road
London N4 3RZ, UK
TEL: 020 7272 8502 FAX: 020 7281 3457
WEB: http://www.muslim-ed-trust.org.uk EMAIL: info@muslim-ed-trust.org.uk

British Library Cataloguing in Publication Data:
Sarwar, Ghulam
Islām: beliefs and teachings – 7th Ed.
1. Islām
l. Title
297 BP161.2

ISBN 0 907261 38 8

Printed and bound in Great Britain by
Midland Regional Printers
Jubilee House, Nottingham Road
Basford
Nottingham
NG7 7BT

Contents

بســــم الله الرحمن الرحيم

Author's preface to the 7th edition

Alhamdulillāh (praise be to Allāh), our only Creator, Sustainer and Watcher of all our deeds; and peace and blessings of Allāh be upon *Muhammad* ﷺ, the final messenger of Allāh and the best example for us to follow. I feel humbled to note that 251,000 copies of my book *Islām: Beliefs and Teachings* have been printed in English since 1980. This has been possible due entirely to the mercy of Almighty Allāh, Whom I always beg to accept my efforts and grant me *Najāh* (salvation) in the *Ākhirah* (life after death). This is and has been my only aim in writing this book.

This edition has been thoroughly revised, with additions and improvements in language and content. I have now included the Arabic for words in the Glossary. I have also added the Arabic verses of the *Qur'ān* to chapter 12. A number of corrections, including Arabic words and names, have been made. Nonetheless, there may still be mistakes. I shall greatly appreciate if any remaining errors are brought to my attention.

The book is widely used in the English-speaking world, and is increasingly used in maintained schools in England to teach Islām as a part of the Religious Studies curriculum. This book has also motivated a number of non-Muslims to come to the eternal bliss of Islām. This trend, *alhamdulillāh*, continues.

I am indebted to *Usamah K. Ward, Prof Dr Muhammad Abdul Jabbar Beg, Dr Faruq Nurul Arefin, Dr Muhammad Qamarul Hasan* and *Nasreen Sarwar* for their suggestions and comments which have helped me to correct errors and improve the quality of the book. I pray to Allāh to reward *Farhat Yasmeen Sarwar* for redrafting all the exercises and notes for parents and teachers. I am grateful to *Ruqaiyyah Waris Maqsood (Rosalyn Kendrick)*, a former Head of Religious Studies, who has improved the exercises. *Syed Dohan Nuh* has enhanced the book by designing the cover; may Allāh reward him for his contribution. I beseech Allāh to bless and reward my wife, who has patiently supported me in the discharge of my Islāmic duties since the day we were bonded together in wedlock. Lastly, I am grateful to readers who have contacted me with their own suggestions.

It is sad to note that the book has been pirated in the USA, India and the Far East. We do not know how many thousands of copies have been pirated, but the estimated number is quite substantial. We would urge publishers, booksellers, teachers and all readers not to sell or buy pirated copies of the book. Piracy is a menace and dealing in pirated books is like dealing in stolen goods. We hope the combined efforts of honest publishers, booksellers and readers will help us stop the cancer of piracy.

I hope and pray that the book will continue to receive support from teachers, parents and young people, Muslims and non-Muslims.

I implore Allāh, my Creator, to accept my sincere efforts. I beg Him to guide and help me to dedicate everything I have for His sake. May He pardon my countless lapses and favour me with His mercy and blessings. *Āmīn.*

"And my success in my task can only come from Allāh. In Him I trust and unto Him I turn." (The Qur'ān, 11:88)

London
Muharram 1424 AH
March 2003 CE

Ghulam Sarwar

A Saying of Prophet Muḥammad ﷺ

Khālid bin al-Walīd narrated the following hadīth:

A Bedouin came one day to the Prophet ﷺ and said to him, "O Messenger of Allāh! I've come to ask you a few questions about the affairs of this Life and the Hereafter."

He ﷺ replied. *"Ask what you wish."*

"I'd like to be the most learned of men."

"Fear Allāh, and you will be the most learned of men."

"I wish to be the richest man in the world."

"Be contented, and you will be the richest man in the world."

"I'd like to be the most just man."

"Desire for others what you desire for yourself, and you will be the most just of men."

"I want to be the best of men."

"Do good to others and you will be the best of men."

"I wish to be the most favoured by Allāh."

"Engage much in Allāh's praise, and you will be most favoured by Him."

"I'd like to complete my faith."

"If you have good manners you will complete your faith."

"I wish to be among those who do good."

"Adore Allāh as if you see Him. If you don't see Him, He sees you. In this way you will be among those who do good."

"I wish to be obedient to Allāh."

"If you observe Allāh's commands you will be obedient."

"I'd like to be free from all sins."

"Bathe yourself from impurities and you will be free from all sins."

"I'd like to be raised on the Day of Judgement in the light."

"Don't wrong yourself or any other creature, and you will be raised on the Day of Judgement in the light."

"I'd like Allāh to bestow His mercy on me."

"If you have mercy on yourself and others, Allāh will grant you mercy on the Day of Judgement."

"I'd like my sins to be very few."

"If you seek the forgiveness Allāh as much as you can, your sins will be very few."

"I'd like to be the most honourable man."

"If you do not complain to any fellow creature, you will be the most honourable of men."

"I'd like to be the strongest of men."

"If you put your trust in Allāh, you will be the strongest of men."

"I'd like to enlarge my provision."

"If you keep yourself pure, Allāh will enlarge your provision."

"I'd like to be loved by Allāh and His messenger."

"If you love what Allāh and His messenger love, you will be among their beloved ones."

"I wish to be safe from Allāh's wrath on the Day of Judgement."

"If you do not lose your temper with any of your fellow creatures, you will be safe from the wrath of Allāh on the Day of Judgement."

"I'd like my prayers to be responded."
"If you avoid forbidden actions, your prayers will be responded."
"I'd like Allāh not to disgrace me on the Day of Judgement."
"If you guard your chastity, Allāh will not disgrace you on the Day of Judgement."
"I'd like Allāh to provide me with a protective covering on the Day of Judgement."
"Do not uncover your fellow creatures faults, and Allāh will provide you with a covering protection on the Day of Judgement."
"What will save me from sins?"
"Tears, humility and illness."
"What are the best deeds in the eyes of Allāh?"
"Gentle manners, modesty and patience."
"What are the worst evils in the eyes of Allāh?"
"Hot temper and miserliness."
"What assuages the wrath of Allāh in this life and in the Hereafter?"
"Concealed charity and kindness to relatives."
"What extinguishes Hell's fires on the Day of Judgement?"
"Patience in adversity and misfortunes"

(Related by Aḥmad ibn Ḥanbal)

Declaration of faith

Transliteration

Correct pronunciation of Arabic words is very important. Incorrect pronunciation changes the meaning of an Arabic word.

Transliteration marks are shown below as a guide to correct pronunciation. These marks help to show how the words should sound, but it is not possible to show on a printed page exactly how to pronounce words.

For example, the word *Allāh* should be pronounced correctly with the two *Ls* sounded distinctly, and the last *A* has to be a long sound. The name *Muḥammad* should be pronounced with a glottal sound of *H* rather than the normal *H* sound, with the two *Ms* sounded clearly.

I have used phonetic transliteration for the benefit of younger learners, e.g. *Sūratul Fātiḥah* rather than *Sūrah al-Fātiḥah*, *at-Tashahhud* rather than *al-Tashahhud*, etc.

Ideally, it is best to listen to an Arabic-speaking person, or someone who has learned how to say Arabic words correctly. Audio and video resources can be immensely helpful.

Arabic symbol	**Transliteration symbol**	**English sound**	**Example**	**Arabic symbol**	**Transliteration symbol**	**English sound**	**Example**
ا	a	add	*Akbar*	ف	f	far	*Fāṭimah*
ب	b	bit	*Bilāl*	ق	q	–	*Qur'ān*
ت	t	tap	*Tirmidhī*	ك	k	king	*Ka'bah*
ث	th	think	*'Uthmān*	ل	l	list	*Luqmān*
ج	j	just	*Jannah*	م	m	mist	*Mūsā*
ح	ḥ	–	*Muḥammad*	ن	n	name	*Nūḥ*
خ	kh	loch	*Khalīfah*	و	w	wait	*Wuḍū'*
د	d	dawn	*Dāwūd*	ه ه	h	rehash	*Ibrāhīm*
ذ	dh	worthy	*Tirmidhī*	ي	y	year	*Yāsīn*
ر	r	rip	*Raḥmān*	ة	t *if followed*, h *otherwise*		*Ṣalāh*
ز	z	zip	*Zakāh*	ء	'	–	*Qur'ān*
س	s	sat	*Sunnah*	َ *(fatḥa)*	a	tap	*Rajab*
ش	sh	shape	*Shahādah*	ـَا	ā	Saab	*Dāwūd*
ص	ṣ	–	*Ṣawm*	ِ *(kasra)*	i	grin	*Jinn*
ض	ḍ	–	*Ramaḍān*	ـِي	ī	deed	*Khadījah*
ط	ṭ	–	*Ṭahārah*	ُ *(ḍamma)*	u	pull	*Jumu'ah*
ظ	ẓ	–	*Ẓuhr*	ـُو	ū	food	*Dāwūd*
ع	'	–	*'Aṣr*	ـَوْ	aw	how	*Ṣawm*
غ	gh	–	*Maghrib*	ـَيْ	ai	tie	*Sulaimān*

Arabic Symbols

ﷺ	*Ṣallallāhu 'alaihi wasallam* Peace and blessings of Allāh be upon him	should be said when Prophet *Muḥammad* ﷺ is mentioned
عليه السلام	*Alaihis salām* Peace be upon him	may be said when a prophet of Allāh is mentioned
رضي الله عنه	*Raḍiyallāhu 'anhu* May Allāh be pleased with him	may be said when a male companion of Prophet *Muḥammad* ﷺ is mentioned
رضي الله عنها	*Raḍiyallāhu 'anhā* May Allāh be pleased with her	may be said when a female companion of Prophet *Muḥammad* ﷺ is mentioned

Arabic Dates

The Islāmic calendar is lunar (based on the cycle of the moon). The Islāmic year has twelve lunar months, and is about 354 days long, 11 days shorter than the Western solar year. Islāmic years are dated from the *Hijrah* (migration) of Prophet *Muḥammad* ﷺ in 622 CE (Christian or Common Era), so the first year of the Islāmic calendar is 1 AH (After Hijrah).

Formula to change AH to CE

$$CE = \frac{32}{33}(AH) + 622$$

Example: $1421\ AH = \frac{32}{33}(1421) + 622 = 2000\ CE$ (approx.)

Formula to change CE to AH

$$AH = \frac{33}{32}(CE - 622)$$

Example: $2000\ CE = \frac{33}{32}(2000 - 622) = 1421\ AH$ (approx.)

The Islāmic months are: *Muḥarram, Ṣafar, Rabī'ul Awwal, Rabī'ul Ākhir, Jumādal Ūlā, Jumādal Ākhirah, Rajab, Sha'bān, Ramaḍān, Shawwāl, Dhul Qa'dah, Dhul Ḥijjah.*

References from the Qur'ān

Quotations and references from the Qur'ān are followed by the number of the *Sūrah* (chapter) then the number of the verse, e.g. (2:177) means *Sūrah* 2, verse 177.

Verses in the same chapter are separated by a comma, e.g. (2:36, 47–49) means *Sūrah* 2, verse 36 and verses 47 to 49.

Verses quoted from different chapters are separated by a semicolon, e.g. (2:255; 5:56–59) means *Sūrah* 2, verse 255 and *Sūrah* 5, verses 56 to 59.

Dedication & Duā'

I dedicate this book to those sincere and selfless slaves of Almighty Allāh, especially the youth, who voluntarily decide to sacrifice everything they have to seek His pleasure.

O Almighty Allāh,
my Creator, Owner and Sustainer,
Watcher of all my deeds,
I implore You, beseech You, beg You
to accept this humble effort of mine,
help the readers of this book to the Light of Guidance
and grant me pardon on the Day of Judgement
When nothing except Your Mercy and Blessings
will be of any help.
Āmīn.

Introduction and Basic Beliefs 1

In the name of Allāh, the most Merciful, the most Kind

Islām: Introduction

Islām is a complete way of life. It is the guidance for all mankind from Allāh, the Creator of the Universe. It covers all the things people do in their lifetime. Islām tells us the purpose of our creation, our final destiny and our place among other creatures. It shows us the best way to conduct our private and public affairs, including social, political, economic, moral and spiritual activities.

Islām is an Arabic word which means submission and obedience. Submission is acceptance of Allāh's commands. Obedience means putting Allāh's commands into practice. Submission and obedience to Allāh bring peace, which is why Islām also means peace. A person who accepts the Islāmic way of life and acts upon it is a Muslim.

Allāh, another Arabic word, is the proper name of God. Muslims prefer to use the word Allāh rather than the word God. Allāh does not mean 'the God of the Muslims', as some people wrongly believe. Rather, it is the name the Creator has chosen for Himself. Allāh is the Creator of everyone and everything. He is unique and has no son or daughter. Muslims should begin their actions by saying *Bismillāh*, which means 'in the name of Allāh'.

Islām is the way of peace and harmony. If we look around, we see that all things — the sun, the moon and the stars, the high mountains and the mighty oceans — obey a law: *the Law of Allāh*. We find no disorder or chaos in them. Everything is in its right place. We see perfect order and total harmony in the system of Nature that Allāh has created. The sun rises in the east and sets in the west and there has been no exception to this rule. The moon and the stars shine at night. Night passes, a new day comes, and so the process goes on. Flowers blossom and the trees have green leaves in the spring. Everything has a set course that cannot be violated. Have you ever noticed any violation in the Law of Allāh by these objects of Nature? No, of course not. Why? Simply because they are made to obey Allāh. They have no choice but to obey.

Innad dīna 'indallāhil Islām
"Surely, the way of life acceptable to Allāh is Islām." (3:19)

This is why we find eternal peace in the system of Nature. But human beings are different: Allāh has given us the knowledge and ability to choose between right and wrong. Not only this, in case we forget He has also sent us constant reminders, by sending His prophets and books for our guidance. The final messenger of Allāh is *Muḥammad* ﷺ, and the final book of guidance is the *Qur'ān*.

Yet He does not force us to obey Him. He has given us the choice either to obey or disobey Him. Why? Because He wants to test us. After this test there will be a Day of reward and punishment. This is the Day of Judgement *(Yawmuddīn)*. Those who pass the test will be rewarded with everlasting happiness and peace in Paradise *(al-Jannah)* and those who fail will suffer terrible punishment in Hell *(al-Jahannam)*. We can earn this reward and escape punishment by obeying and worshipping Allāh.

We know there is peace and harmony in all of Nature; because nothing ever disobeys Allāh. Neither the sun nor the moon, the mountains nor the trees, the animals on land or in the sea, can disobey Allāh — they just behave as He has created them to behave. They have no choice.

The only exceptions are human beings and the *Jinn* (creatures we can't see); they have free will, which means they can choose whether to obey or disobey Allāh. But if we follow the guidance given to us through the prophets, we are sure to have peace in the world we live in.

All human beings, by their very nature, like good things and dislike bad things. For example, we all like truthfulness and hate lies. Even a liar does not like to be called a liar! Why? Because we know in our hearts that telling lies is a bad thing. In the same way, helping others, showing kindness, politeness, respect for parents and teachers, honesty and all other forms of good conduct are always liked and appreciated; but rudeness, cruelty, lies, hurting others, disobedience to parents and teachers, using bad names and other bad conduct are disliked by everyone. So, we can say that human nature likes the *Right* and dislikes the *Wrong*. Right is *Ma'rūf* and wrong is *Munkar* in Arabic — the language of the *Qur'ān*.

It is also human nature to love peace and hate disorder. Peace comes from obedience to Allāh's Law, whilst disorder is the outcome of disobedience. Islām establishes this peace, which is part of man's nature; so, Islām is called the *Religion of Nature*; in Arabic this is *Dīnul Fiṭrah*.

To achieve peace in society, Islām calls upon Muslims to work together towards what is right and to keep away from what is evil. This joint effort to root out evil and establish truth is called *Jihād* which means to try one's utmost to see *Truth* prevail and *Falsehood* vanish from society. The aim of *Jihād* is to earn the pleasure of Allāh. You will learn more about *Jihād* later in this book.

The Purpose of Human Creation

Allāh created human beings to do what He wants and obey His commands. Allāh says in the *Qur'ān*, His final guidance for mankind:

"I have not created Jinn and mankind (for any other purpose) except to worship Me." (51:56)

'Worship' in this verse means total obedience to Allāh's commands. The Qur'ānic word for worship is *'Ibādah* (عِبَادَة). Every good thing we do is *'Ibādah*, if we do it for Allāh's sake. The purpose of our life is to please Allāh through *'Ibādah*.

'Ibādah is the way to achieve success and happiness in this life and in the life after death.

Islām or 'Mohammedanism'

Islām is sometimes incorrectly called 'Mohammedanism' and Muslims 'Mohammedans'. Other religions have been named after their founder or after the community in which the religion prospered. For example, *Christianity* has been named after *Christ*, *Buddhism* after *Buddha* and *Judaism* after the tribe of *Judah*. But Islām has not been named after *Muḥammad* ﷺ. It is the name of Allāh's Guidance for mankind revealed through all the prophets, the last of whom was *Muḥammad* ﷺ.

Islām and *Muslims* are words used in the *Qur'ān*. The *Qur'ān* says, *"Surely, the way of life acceptable to Allāh is Islām." (3:19) "He named you Muslims before and in this." (22:78)* The message of all the prophets from Ādam عليه السلام to *Muḥammad* ﷺ is the same: obey Allāh and none other. This message, sent through prophets, was completed at the time of *Muḥammad* ﷺ who was the last in the chain of prophethood. This is mentioned in the *Qur'ān*: *"This day I have perfected your religion for you, completed my favour upon you and have chosen for you Islām as your way of life." (5:3)* It is wrong, then, to call Islām 'Mohammedanism' and Muslims 'Mohammedans'.

What did you learn? (1a)

Key Stage 3 (11–14)

1. What is Islām?
2. Explain why the word 'religion' does not give the full meaning to the word Islām.
3. How do you think Islām can bring peace?
4. Why do you think Allāh does not force us to obey Him?
5. What does being a Muslim really mean?
6. What do we mean when we say that things in Nature are in complete harmony?
7. Give some everyday examples of *'Ibādah.*
8. What do the following Arabic words mean:
   a. *Islām* b. *'Ibādah* c. *Ma'rūf* d. *Munkar*

Key Stage 4 (15–16)

1. What is Islām?
2. What does being a Muslim really mean?
3. Why did Allāh create us?
4. What special characteristic has Allāh given to humans and why?
5. Why is Islām called *Dīnul Fiṭrah?*
6. Write a paragraph on why just having a Muslim name does not always make a person Muslim.
7. Write down in your own words why Islām should not be called Mohammedanism.
8. Briefly describe the ideals of the Islamic way of life and why we should try to live by them.
9. Discuss how observing Nature and how it works points to the existence of a Creator. Use verses from the *Qur'ān* to clarify your answer.

Key Stage 5 (17–18)

1. *"Living true Islām in the modern world is definitely a challenge."* Discuss this statement with regards to advancements in technology and the search for spirituality.
2. *"To live means continual submission. Some submit to hedonism, or to a political idea; and some to faith. We all submit to something but we are free to choose."* Explain the meaning of this statement in relation to Islamic teaching.

Basic Beliefs

The basic beliefs of Islām are:

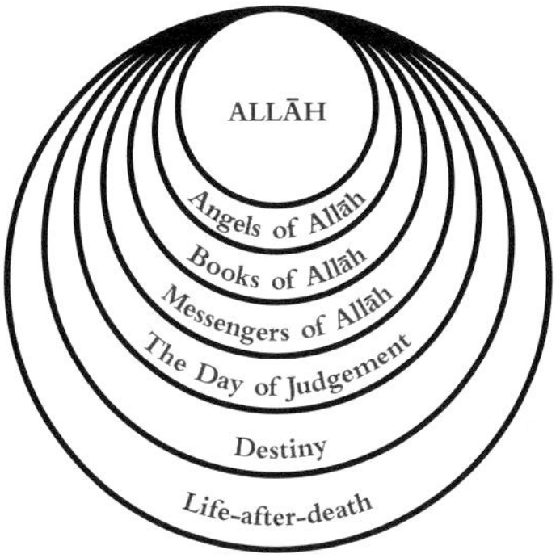

1 **Allāh**
2 **Angels of Allāh** *(Malā'ikah)*
3 **Books of Allāh** *(Kutubullāh)*
4 **Messengers of Allāh** *(Rusulullāh)*
5 **The Day of Judgement** *(Yawmuddīn)*
6 **Destiny** *(al-Qadr)*
7 **Life after death** *(Ākhirah)*⋆

These beliefs have been stated precisely in **al-Īmānul Mufaṣṣal**, the Faith in detail:

آمَنْتُ بِاللهِ وَمَلآئِكَتِهِ وَكُتُبِهِ وَرُسُلِهِ وَالْيَوْمِ الْآخِرِ وَالْقَدْرِ
خَيْرِهِ وَشَرِّهِ مِنَ اللهِ تَعَالَى وَالْبَعْثِ بَعْدَ الْمَوْتِ

Āmantu billāhi, wa malā'ikatihī, wa kutubihī, wa rusulihī,
wal yawmil ākhiri, wal qadri khairihī wa sharrihī minallāhi ta'ālā, wal ba'thi ba'dal mawt.

"I believe in Allāh, in His angels, in His books, in His messengers, in the Last Day *(Day of Judgement)* and in the fact that everything good or bad is decided by Allāh the Almighty, and in the life after death."

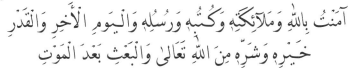

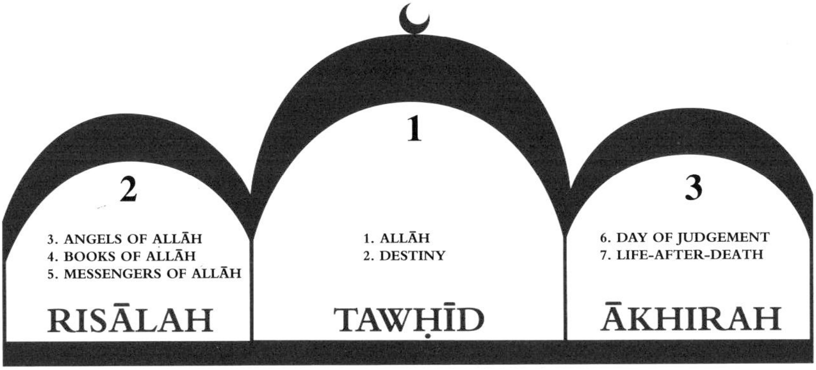

⋆ Note:
The basic beliefs appear as *six* in some texts where *The Day of Judgement* is included in *Life after death*.

The seven beliefs can be grouped into three:

Tawḥīd	(oneness and uniqueness of Allāh)	تَوْحِيد
Risālah	(prophethood)	رِسَالَة
Ākhirah	(life after death)	آخِرَة

Tawḥīd, *Risālah* and *Ākhirah* summarise the whole of the Islāmic system of life. So, we must understand them.

Tawḥīd

Allāh

Tawḥīd means the oneness of Allāh. It is the main part of *Īmān* (Faith) and is beautifully expressed in *Sūratul Ikhlāṣ* in the *Qur'ān:*

"Say, He is Allāh, the One. Allāh is Eternal and Absolute. None is born of Him, nor is He born. And there is none like Him." (Sūrah 112)

Tawḥīd is the most important Islāmic belief. It means that everything on this earth is created by Allāh, Who looks after and provides for all the needs of every creature. He is the only Source of our Guidance.

Tawḥīd is the belief in Allāh with all His powers. Allāh is All-Knowing, All-Wise and All-Powerful. He is the Merciful, the Kind and the Most-Loving. He is with us all the time. He sees us, but we do not see Him. He was, is and always will be. He is the First and the Last. He has no partner, son or daughter, nor was He born of anyone. He gives us life and takes it away. Everyone must return to Him after death.

The first duty of a Muslim is to declare his faith. To make this declaration a person must say in words and believe in his heart — *lā ilāha illallāhu Muḥammadur rasūlullāh* — (there is no god except Allāh; *Muḥammad* is Allāh's messenger). The saying of these Arabic words is called *ash-Shahādah* (Declaration of Faith). There are two parts of this declaration: (1) *Lā ilāha illallāh*, (2) *Muḥammadur rasūlullāh*.

The first part, *Lā ilāha illallāh*, has two aspects: **Negative** and **Positive**. *La ilāha* is the negative aspect, whilst *illallāh* is the positive one.

A believer must first cleanse his heart of the idea of any other god or any other object of worship; only then can faith in the Oneness of Allāh take root inside the heart.

Let us try to understand this with an example. Suppose we have a piece of land which is full of weeds and bushes where we want to grow wheat. Now, if we sow very good wheat seeds in the land without first cleaning it fully, we cannot hope to get a good wheat crop. So what must we do? We must cultivate the land, clear the weeds and bushes and prepare the soil before we sow the seeds. Then we can expect good crops.

Let us compare the land with the human heart. If the heart is full of belief in false gods, we cannot expect *Tawḥīd* to take root there. So it must be cleansed of any other god or object of worship; only then will *Tawḥīd* take root and the light of faith will shine.

Tawḥīd shapes and influences the entire course of our life. This is why we must have a clear understanding of its meaning.

The vast and majestic universe with its flawless system clearly indicates that there is one Creator and one Supreme Controller.

When we think about the unique system and perfect order of the universe, we find there is no chaos. The sun, the moon and the galaxy obey the same Supreme Authority. The whole universe obeys the laws of this Supreme Power. There is complete cooperation and harmony in the system. Everything is nicely set in its place. No improvement can be suggested and no defect detected. This superb and perfect combination of order and beauty is clear proof of the presence of an All-Wise and All-Powerful Creator and Regulator.

Had there been more than one Creator and Controller of the planets, for example, there would have been conflict and chaos (21:22). We notice no such disorder in the universe. The efficient running of a school and the steering of a car or a ship, calls for one headmaster, one driver or one captain. No single institution can be run problem-free with more than one leader, just as no vehicle can be driven by more than one person at the same time.

The universe, made up of many planets and stars, is a unit. All its components have a common origin and purpose because the universe was deliberately created by one Absolute Power. Everything in the universe works in harmony and co-operation as do the various parts of the human body. The limbs of the human body seem to have different functions, but they all serve the same purpose – keeping the body fit and functioning properly.

The Effect of Tawḥīd on Human Life

Belief in *Lā ilāha illallāh* or *Tawḥīd* has a far-reaching impact on our life:

a A believer in *Tawḥīd* surrenders himself completely to the Will of Allāh and becomes His true servant and subject. Allāh has created all that is on the earth and in the sky for the service of mankind. When a person surrenders himself to Allāh's commands, he understands and appreciates that Allāh has made all His Creation beneficial for him.

The *Qur'ān* confirms this when it says, *"Have you not seen how Allāh has made all that is in the earth subservient to you?" (22:65) "Do you not see how Allāh has harnessed whatever is in Heaven and whatever is on earth for you? He has lavished His bounties on you both apparent and hidden..." (31:20)*

These two verses clearly indicate that Allāh has created everything on the earth and in the sky for the service and comfort of humans. The blessing of being served by other objects and creatures is only apparent when we believe and practise *Tawḥīd*. This means we must be totally obedient to Allāh.

b It produces in the believer a high degree of self-respect, confidence and contentment. He knows that he depends on none but Allāh for the fulfilment of his needs. He firmly believes that Allāh alone has the power to provide all his requirements and no one else has any power to do good or harm him.

When can a believer be confident and develop self-respect? He can be so only when he feels that he depends on none but His Creator for the fulfilment of his needs. He does not become worried because he knows that Allāh will take care of all his needs if he is truly obedient.

c This belief makes a believer humble and modest. He is never arrogant or haughty. He is fully aware that everything on earth belongs to Allāh and he gains control over the rest of the creation only by being a subject of Allāh. He also knows very well that whatever he has is from Allāh. So there is no reason to be proud or arrogant.

d Belief in *Tawḥīd* makes a believer dutiful and upright. The believer knows that he must carry out the commands of his Creator to succeed in this life and the life hereafter. This awareness keeps him away from neglecting his duties and from other sins.

e It makes a person brave and courageous. It removes from his mind the fear of death or concern for safety. The believer knows that it is Allāh who will cause death at the appointed time and none but He can harm the believer's safety. So, if he obeys Allāh, he has nothing to worry about. He goes on doing his duty without any fear.

f A believer in *Tawḥīd* consciously feels himself to be part of the whole universe. He is the best of all creations of Allāh — the Powerful Master of the whole universe. This belief broadens his horizon and his outlook expands.

g It produces in a believer strong determination, patience and perseverance. The believer becomes single-minded and dedicates himself to seeking the pleasure of his Creator.

Think of a boat. It has a rudder which guides the boat's movement: with the rudder under control, the boat moves forward proudly over the waves, but if the boat is not controlled by the rudder, it is tossed in any direction by every wave.

Similarly, when a believer surrenders himself to Allāh alone, he can go forward in the affairs of life without fear. But if he does not obey Allāh, he has to obey false gods like the fear of losing his job, fear of danger, fear of hunger and the like. When someone believes in Allāh alone, his life is not ruled by such fears.

h The most important effect of the belief in *Lā ilāha illallāh* is that it makes a person obey Allāh's commands. A believer in *Tawḥīd* is sure that Allāh knows and sees everything and he cannot escape Allāh's ever-watchful eye for a single moment. In fact, Allāh is nearer to him than his own jugular vein (50:16). So, a true believer does not commit a sin either secretly or in the darkness of the night because he has a firm conviction that Allāh sees everything all the time.

A believer in *Tawḥīd* seeks the pleasure of Allāh by making his actions reflect his beliefs. Belief without practice has no place in Islām.

We Muslims are believers in *Tawḥīd*. We are Allāh's servants and subjects. Our faith must be reflected in our actions.

Al-Qadr

We believe that Allāh has created the universe and He is its Absolute Controller and Regulator. Allāh has fixed a set course for everything in the universe; this is called *al-Qadr.* Nothing can happen without the will and the knowledge of Allāh. The destiny of every creature is already known to Allāh. (25:2, 33:38)

But this does not mean that man has no freedom of will. We know that man is the *Khalīfah* (agent) of Allāh on this earth. We also know that Allāh does not force us to do anything. It is up to us to obey or disobey Him. Whether we will obey or disobey is known to Him. But the fact that Allāh knows what we are going to do does not affect our freedom of choice. Man does not know what his destiny is. He has the free will to choose the course he will take.

We will be judged on the basis of our intentions on the *Day of Judgement.* If we follow Allāh's guidance we will be rewarded; if not, we will be punished.

By believing in *al-Qadr* we testify that Allāh is the Absolute Controller of all the affairs of His universe. It is He Who decides what is good and what is bad.

Allāh knows already the fate of all human beings. This does not mean that we can do whatever we like, as if it would make no difference to what happens to us. We must pay attention to the Divine Guidance provided by Allāh the Almighty. He gave human beings free will. We can choose between right and wrong. We will be judged for our actions on earth on the *Day of Judgement.*

Allāh knows everything. He is the only One Who can judge His subjects. He commands mankind to follow the Divine Guidance He has prescribed for man's success in the life after death. But it depends entirely on the mercy of Allāh to judge who will be rewarded and who will not.

Allāh knows what will happen to everyone, but we do not know. This foreknowledge is one of His Divine qualities *(aṣ-Ṣifāt).*

Sometimes things happen that do not make sense to us. Why do floods, hurricanes and earthquakes happen? Why do people starve to death in many countries around the world? Why do people suffer? What makes one man good and another a criminal?

We do not know all the answers to these questions. We have only a little knowledge of the universe, but Allāh knows everything. We would be wasting time if we blamed Allāh for the problems or the bad things that happen, simply because we do not seem to see the reasons behind them.

We should have firm faith in the wisdom of our All-Knowing Creator, and help people in distress as much as we can.

We are unable to understand and interpret many of Allāh's actions. It is meaningless to argue that human beings act without freedom and that we are forced to act the way we do. We decide for ourselves what we will do, and what we will not, and we are responsible for our own actions. This freedom of action does not contradict the foreknowledge of Allāh.

What did you learn? (1b)

Key Stage 3 (11–14)

1. Look at the diagram of the basic beliefs on page 17. Can you design your own diagram to display the seven basic beliefs of a Muslim?
2. What do the following Arabic words mean:
   a. *Malā'ikah* b. *Kutubullāh* c. *Risālah* d. *Ākhirah*
3. What does the word *Tawḥīd* mean?
4. Carefully read the words of *Sūratul Ikhlāṣ*. What does it tell us about *Tawḥīd?*
5. Who is the Controller of the Universe?
6. Why do you think the presence of more than one Creator would cause problems?
7. Look at the diagram on page 19, and describe in your own words how it explains the belief in *Tawḥīd*.

Key Stage 4 (15–16)

1. *"Belief in Tawḥīd ought to change a person's life."* Explain this statement, giving practical examples to clarify your answer.
2. *"Tawḥīd, Risālah and Ākhirah, summarise the whole of the Islāmic system of life."* Discuss this statement.
3. Group the seven basic beliefs of Islām into the three basic concepts and create a diagram of your own.
4. What is the Arabic word for each of the words listed below:
   a. *Faith* b. *Prophethood* c. *The One* d. *Oneness of Allāh*
   e. *Angels* f. *Books of Allāh* g. *Declaration of Faith*
5. Explain why belief in *al-Qadr* is so important in the life of a Muslim.

Key Stage 5 (17–18)

1. Discuss the significance of the positive and negative aspects of *Tawḥīd*.
2. *"Belief in Tawḥīd has to result in action in order to be effective."* Justify this statement in your own words.
3. Give an outline of the Islāmic belief that *al-Qadr* does not contradict a person's free will to choose between right and wrong.

Risālah (Prophethood)

Risālah is a channel of communication between Allāh and mankind. Allāh, the Most Merciful, has provided man with Guidance to follow the right course and so make this world a happy and peaceful place to live in. There will be a great reward in the life after death for those who follow this Guidance.

Since the beginning of Creation, Allāh has sent His Guidance for mankind through His chosen agents. These chosen people are called prophets (sing. *nabī*, pl. *anbiyā'*). They asked the people of their time to obey and worship Allāh alone. They taught, guided and trained the people to follow the way of Allāh.

Prophets were human beings. We should never refer to them as the sons of Allāh. Allāh is One and He has no partner, son or daughter. It is a major sin to say that Allāh has a son, daughter or partner.

The message of all the prophets is one and the same. As Allāh is One, so is His message. The message is to worship Allāh alone and to reject all false gods. *"We did send Nūḥ (Noah) to his people, and he said 'My folk, worship Allāh, you have no other god than Him. I fear for you the torment of an awful day.'"* (7:59) In other words, all the prophets preached the message of:

Lā ilāha illallāh

(There is no god except Allāh)

You may ask why we need Guidance from Allāh. The answer is simple: we human beings are weak and frail; we have no knowledge of the future and the knowledge we do have is limited. Also, we are not perfect. You can see that with so many weaknesses, we are unable to make any Guidance for ourselves which can hold good for all times and all conditions. This is the reason why Allāh has blessed us with Guidance through prophets.

Not only this, Allāh has also sent books of Guidance through some of His prophets (2:213, 7:52). These prophets are also called messengers (sing. *rasūl*, pl. *rusul*). The *Qur'ān* is the last book of Allāh's Guidance. We will learn about it later.

Allāh sent prophets to every nation at different times (10:47, 13:7, 35:24). It was necessary to send prophets at different times to bring forgetful human beings back to the **right path** *(aṣ-Ṣirāṭul Mustaqīm).*

Prophets of Allāh

According to a saying of Prophet *Muḥammad* ﷺ, the number of prophets is *one hundred and twenty-four thousand.* As Muslims, we must believe in all the prophets and messengers (2:285). Allāh's guidance to mankind, which began with *Ādam* عليه السلام, was completed with *Muḥammad* ﷺ. The *Qur'ān* mentions only the twenty-five most prominent by name:

Prophets of Allāh
mentioned in the Qur'ān
ءادَم Ādam Adam
إدْرِيس Idrīs Enoch
نُوح Nūḥ Noah
هُود Hūd
صَالِح Ṣāliḥ
إبْرَاهِيم Ibrāhīm Abraham
إسْمَاعِيل Ismā'īl Ishmael
إسْحَاق Isḥāq Isaac
لُوط Lūṭ Lot
يَعْقُوب Ya'qūb Jacob
يُوسُف Yūsuf Joseph
شُعَيب Shu'aib
أيُّوب Ayyūb Job
مُوسَىٰ Mūsā Moses
هَارُون Hārūn Aaron
ذُوالْكِفْل Dhul Kifl Ezekiel
دَاوُد Dāwūd David
سُلَيمَان Sulaimān Solomon
إلْيَاس Ilyās Elias
اَلْيَسَع Al Yasa' Elisha
يُونُس Yūnus Jonah
زَكَرِيَّا Zakariyyā Zechariah
يَحْيَىٰ Yaḥyā John
عِيسَىٰ 'Īsā Jesus
مُحَمَّد Muḥammad
peace be upon them all

Angels

We have already mentioned belief in Angels *(Malā'ikah)* in *al-Īmānul Mufaṣṣal*. Who are the angels? What do they do? Can we see them? How are they different from man?

Angels are a special creation of Allāh. They have been created from divine light *(Nūr)* to perform specific duties. By comparison *Ādam*, the first man, was created from clay, and the *Jinn* from fire. *Iblīs*, the devil, is from the *Jinn*. Some people think *Iblīs* was the leader of the angels. This *Qur'ān* says *Iblīs* was from among the Jinn (18:50).

Angels have been given the qualities and powers necessary to carry out their duties, but they do not have free will. They always obey Allāh and can never disobey Him. Man, on the other hand, has been given free will and can choose between right and wrong. This is why man will have to account for his actions on the Day of Judgement.

Angels do what Allāh commands them to. They are the sinless servants of Allāh's will. They help men in the use of free will. Man decides what to do and angels help him to carry out the decision.

The duty of angels is to glorify and praise Allāh. They never get tired. They are always ready to obey Allāh. They do not need sleep, nor do they require the things a human being would need.

We cannot see angels unless they appear in human form. Angel *Jibrā'īl* once appeared in human form before a gathering of the companions of the Prophet ﷺ. He came to teach them, but only the Prophet ﷺ knew he was an angel. Angels can take any suitable appearance to carry out their duties.

There are many angels in the kingdom of Allāh. Prominent among them are:

Jibrā'īl or **Jibrīl** *(Gabriel)*	جِبْرَائِيْل ، جِبْرِيْل
Mikā'īl or **Mīkāl** *(Michael)*	مِكَائِيْل ، مِيْكَال
'Izrā'īl *(Malakul Mawt, also called Azrail)*	عِزْرَائِيْل (مَلَكُ الْمَوْت)
Isrāfīl	إِسْرَافِيْل

Jibrā'īl brought the revelation from Allāh to Prophet Muḥammad ﷺ and to all the other prophets. *'Izrā'īl* — also called the 'Angel of Death' *(Malakul Mawt)* — is responsible for ending our life. *Isrāfīl* will blow the trumpet at the time of the end of the world and on the Day of Judgement.

Some angels are busy recording all that we do. They are called the Honourable Recorders *(Kirāman Kātibūn)*. Not a single word we say goes unrecorded (50:18).

Allāh maintains His kingdom perfectly, and angels are His obedient servants. Angels will welcome in *Heaven* those of us who always obey Allāh's commands and will throw the wrong-doers into *Hell* (39:71–74).

The Books of Allāh

So far we have learned that we human beings are the servants of Allāh and His agents on earth. But we need guidance to carry out our duties as Allāh's agents. We are unable to guide ourselves because we have many weaknesses within us and we have very limited knowledge of the past, present and future. Only Allāh is above all these shortcomings and He alone has the power to give us guidance that is suitable for all times and places. We know that Allāh has not left us without guidance and that He has sent prophets to show us the right path in life. In addition to this, He has also sent books of guidance through some prophets — His messengers.

Allāh's blessings are countless. He provides us with all that we need. Just imagine how wonderfully He arranges our growth in the tender and affectionate care of our parents from birth to youth. Who provides us with food when we are in our mother's womb? Who fills our mother's breasts with milk to suckle as soon as we are born? Allāh, the Merciful, of course.

Allāh's greatest favour to mankind is His Guidance contained in the revealed books. The pure, perfect and most useful knowledge comes only from Allāh, the Wisest and the Greatest (2:146–147, 4:163, 53:1–6).

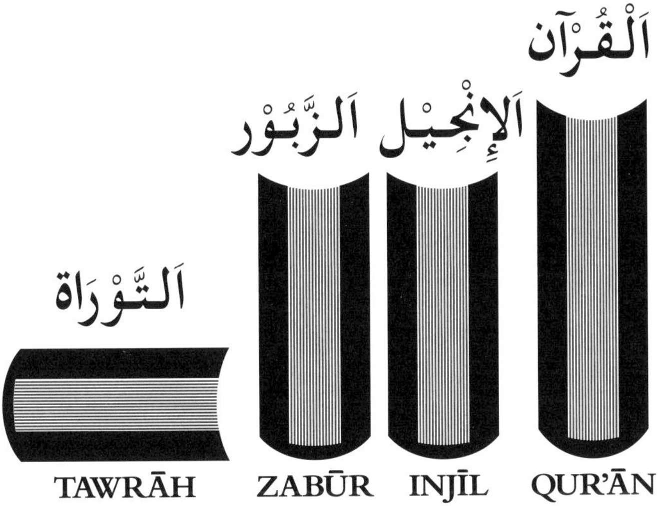

A Muslim believes in all the revealed books which are mentioned in the *Qur'ān*. They are: the **Tawrāh** *(Torah)* of *Mūsā* عليه السلام (Moses), the **Zabūr** *(Psalms)* of *Dāwūd* عليه السلام (David), the **Injīl** *(Gospel)* of *'Īsā* عليه السلام (Jesus) and the **Qur'ān** revealed to *Muḥammad* ﷺ. The *Qur'ān* also mentions the *Ṣuḥuf* of *Ibrāhīm* عليه السلام (Scripture of Abraham).

Of the divine books, only the *Qur'ān* remains unchanged, preserved in its original form. The original *Tawrāh*[1], *Zabūr* and *Injīl*[2] no longer exist. The texts available today were written by their followers many years after the death[3] of their prophets. The writers have changed and distorted Allāh's words. They have mixed divine words with those of human beings.

The *Bible*, which is a collection of the books of the *Old Testament* and the *New Testament*, has been translated into English from available Hebrew and Greek manuscripts. A careful reader can easily find some of the additions and alterations made to them.

The *Bible*, as it is available today, has many human additions which do not appear to be correct[4]. It is not a divine revelation. It contains numerous misleading misconceptions and false accounts of the prophets. The message of Allāh sent through them was either lost or distorted, because of the neglect or folly of their followers. On the other hand, the *Qur'ān* contains Allāh's guidance for mankind in its original form and language, unchanged and undistorted. It restates in clear and unambiguous language the message of Allāh which the followers of earlier prophets have lost. The message of the *Qur'ān* is valid for all times and climes.

Notes:

1 The *Tawrāh* was revealed in Hebrew and the *Injīl* most probably in the Aramaic (Syriac) language.

2 The *Bible* consists of the *Old Testament* and the *New Testament.*

The *Old Testament* includes the five books of the *Pentateuch (Genesis, Exodus, Leviticus, Numbers* and *Deuteronomy)*, the books of *Ezra*, *Psalms* and others.

The *New Testament* includes four gospels: *Matthew, Mark, Luke* and *John*. The *Gospel of Barnabas*, which appears to be the most authentic version of Prophet *'Īsā's* life, is not included in it.

3 The *Injīl* (Gospel) was compiled after Prophet *'Īsā* (Jesus) was taken up by Allāh. According to Christians, *'Īsā* was crucified and died as a result. The *Qur'ān* refutes this and states that *'Īsā* was taken up by Allāh (4:157–158).

4a Prophet *Nūḥ* (Noah) is described as drunk and naked in the book of *Genesis* (ch. 9, verses 20–22).

b Incest ascribed to *Lūṭ* (Lot) in *Genesis* (ch. 19, verses 31–37).

c Falsehood attributed to *Isḥāq* (Isaac) in *Genesis* (ch. 26, verses 7–11).

d A comparison of verses 16–17 in chapter 19 in *Matthew* with verses 17–18 of chapter 10 of *Mark* in the *New Testament* shows the method of distortion by individual compilers.

Source: The New English Bible, Oxford University Press, 1970.

What did you learn? (1c)

Key Stage 3 (11–14)

1. What is *Risālah?*
2. Why did Allāh need to send so many prophets and messengers?
3. How many prophets are named in the *Qur'ān?*
4. Write down the names of four great angels and briefly describe their jobs.
5. Draw the diagram of the Books of Allāh in your exercise book. To whom was each book revealed?

Key Stage 4 (15–16)

1. Who was the first Prophet of Allāh?
2. Who was the last Prophet of Allāh?
3. What is *aṣ-Ṣirāṭul Mustaqīm?*
4. *"Prophets and messengers have been sent since the beginning of time to guide us."* Why was this necessary?
5. In your own words write ten sentences about the angels of Allāh.
6. Name the revealed books mentioned in the *Qur'ān* and the form in which they can now be found.

Key Stage 5 (17–18)

1. Define the word *Risālah* and explain its significance for our lives.
2. Explain in your own words the status and duties of the angels of Allāh.
3. If humans possess free will, explain why they need guidance from Allāh. Why can't they just do as they like?

سُوْرَةُ الْفَاتِحَةِ مَكِّيَّةٌ وَهِيَ سَبْعُ اٰيَاتٍ

بِسْمِ اللّٰهِ الرَّحْمٰنِ الرَّحِيْمِ ﴿١﴾

اَلْحَمْدُ لِلّٰهِ رَبِّ الْعٰلَمِيْنَ ﴿٢﴾ الرَّحْمٰنِ
الرَّحِيْمِ ﴿٣﴾ مٰلِكِ يَوْمِ الدِّيْنِ ﴿٤﴾ اِيَّاكَ نَعْبُدُ
وَاِيَّاكَ نَسْتَعِيْنُ ﴿٥﴾ اِهْدِنَا الصِّرَاطَ
الْمُسْتَقِيْمَ ﴿٦﴾ صِرَاطَ الَّذِيْنَ اَنْعَمْتَ عَلَيْهِمْ
غَيْرِ الْمَغْضُوْبِ عَلَيْهِمْ وَلَا الضَّآلِّيْنَ ﴿٧﴾

Sūratul Fātiḥah

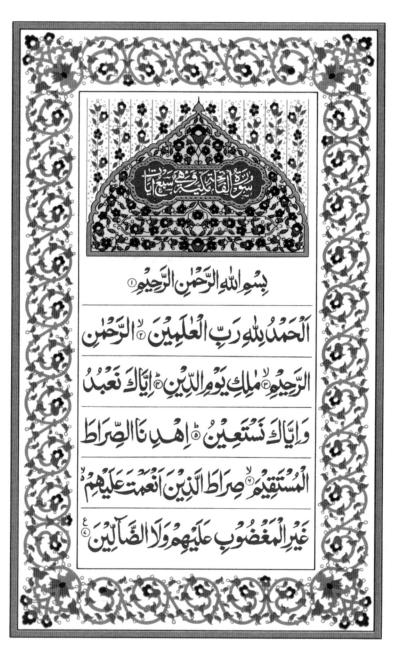

The Qur'ān

The *Qur'ān* is a unique book. It is the Guidance from our Creator for all of mankind. It is the sacred book of Muslims and the main source of Law in Islām. Every word of the *Qur'ān* is from Allāh.

The *Qur'ān* is the final revelation from Allāh to mankind. The revelation to Prophet *Muḥammad* ﷺ began in the cave of *Ḥirā'* in 610 CE. As we have said, the previous books sent to earlier prophets no longer exist in their original form. Only the *Qur'ān* remains unchanged. It is the Guidance for all of humanity until the end of the world. So, it is clearly very important that this book is preserved and kept free from human distortion.

No other book in the world can match the *Qur'ān* in respect of its recording and preservation. The astonishing fact about this book of Allāh is that it has remained unchanged even to a dot over the last fourteen hundred years. Allāh the Almighty has Himself taken the responsibility of preserving the *Qur'ān*. He says: *"Surely, We have revealed this reminder (Dhikr) and Lo, We verily are its Guardian."* (15:9) This verse shows that Allāh revealed the *Qur'ān* and He will protect it. Indeed, He has protected it from any change whatsoever, and His protection will continue until the end of the world.

None except the Creator could have produced the unique verses of the *Qur'ān*. Allāh challenges humans and *Jinn* together to produce anything similar to the *Qur'ān*, whilst informing them that they will never be able to do it (2:23; 10:37–38; 17:88). This challenge remains, and will continue to remain, unanswered.

The *Qur'ān* was recorded as soon as it was revealed under the personal supervision of Prophet *Muḥammad* ﷺ. The *Qur'ān* exists today in its original form, unaltered and undistorted. It is a living miracle in the sense that it has survived so many centuries without suffering even the smallest change. Every word of it — every single letter and sound — is in the hearts and minds of thousands of Muslims who continue to memorise and recite it every day. No variation of text can be found in it. You can check this for yourself by listening to and comparing the recitation of Muslims from different parts of the world.

Arabic, the language of the *Qur'ān*, unlike the languages of other revealed books, is a living, dynamic and very rich language. Millions of people all over the world use Arabic in their daily lives. This shows the relevance of the *Qur'ān* and its universal usefulness even in today's world.

Through the *Qur'ān* our Creator speaks to us. It is a clear proof of His Sovereignty over the universe, and that He is All-knowing, All-aware.

The subject matter of the *Qur'ān* is Man and his ultimate goal in life. Its teachings cover all areas of this life and the life after death. It contains principles, teachings and guidance for every area of human activity. The theme of the *Qur'ān* consists broadly of the three fundamental concepts of *Tawḥīd*, *Risālah* and *Ākhirah*. *Tawḥīd* is the basic theme of the *Qur'ān*. All the prophets of Allāh called people towards *Tawḥīd*. The *Qur'ān* gives a vivid description of the Paradise which will be awarded to the truly obedient servants of Allāh. The severe punishment to be meted out to the evildoers is also described vividly in the *Qur'ān*.

The *Qur'ān* urges people to follow its guidance and teachings. The success of human beings on this earth and in the life after death depends on obedience to the teachings of the *Qur'ān*. We cannot perform our duties as the servants of Allāh and His agents if we do not follow the *Qur'ān*. The *Qur'ān* urges us to use our energies and wealth to establish the supremacy of Allāh's Laws and remove all evils from the society in which we live.

The superb style of the *Qur'ān* has a tremendous effect on its readers. It totally changes the pattern of life of those who believe and practice its teachings. It leaves a soothing effect on the mind of its reader, even if he does not fully understand its meaning. The incredible effect is hard to describe, it has to be experienced to really appreciate it.

The revelation, collection and compilation of the Qur'ān

The *Qur'ān* was revealed to *Muḥammad* ﷺ through the angel *Jibrā'īl*. It was sent down in stages and completed over a period of twenty-three years.

Each and every word of the *Qur'ān* was recorded as soon as it was revealed by Allāh to the Prophet ﷺ through the angel *Jibrā'īl*. The verses of the *Qur'ān* were sent down at different times according to the needs of the early Muslims. *Jibrā'īl* carefully instructed the Prophet ﷺ in which order the verses should be put together. The *Qur'ān* is not put together in the order the verses were revealed, nor according to subject matter. Its order is according to the plan of Allāh, and is yet another of its striking and unique characteristics.

The Prophet's secretary, *Zaid bin Thābit*, used to record them exactly as the Prophet ﷺ told him. He would read back to the Prophet ﷺ what he had recorded.

The *Qur'ān* consists of 114 chapters (sing. *Sūrah*, pl. *Suwar*). The short opening chapter, *Sūratul Fātiḥah* (shown on page 32) is followed by the longest chapter of the *Qur'ān*, *Sūratul Baqarah* (The Cow), with 286 verses. The chapters gradually get shorter. The shortest chapter is the 108th chapter, *Sūratul Kawthar* (The Abundance), which has just 3 verses. There are 6236 verses (sing. *Āyah*, pl. *Āyāt*) altogther. Chapters revealed when the Prophet was living in *Makkah* are known as *Makkī (Makkan)* and those revealed in *Madīnah* are called *Madanī (Madinan)*.

The *Qur'ān* is also divided into 30 parts (sing. *Juz'*, pl. *Ajzā'*) of roughly equal size, which is convenient for recitation purposes.

Many of the early Muslims memorised the *Qur'ān* immediately after the verses were revealed. Some of the famous *Ḥuffāẓ* (plural: persons who memorised the *Qur'ān*; singular: *Ḥāfiẓ*) were: *Mu'ādh bin Jabal*, *'Ubādah bin aṣ-Ṣāmit*, *Abud Dardā'*, *Abū Ayyūb al-Anṣārī* and *Ubayy bin Ka'b*.

Shortly after the death of the Prophet ﷺ in 632 CE, *'Umar* suggested to the *Khalīfah, Abū Bakr*, that the *Qur'ān* be compiled in one volume. Up until then, the *Qur'ān* was written down in separate sections. A committee was formed under *Zaid bin Thābit* to gather the material of the *Qur'ān* into one volume.

Great care was taken to compile the *Qur'ān* exactly as it had been recorded during the time of the Prophet ﷺ. After careful checking and rechecking the work was completed. During the *Khilāfah* of *'Umar*, the copy was kept with *Ḥafṣah*, one of the widows of the Prophet ﷺ.

Later, many schools were established for the teaching of the *Qur'ān* throughout the Muslim territories. During *'Umar's* time, one such school in Damascus had sixteen hundred pupils under *Abud Dardā'*, one of the famous *Ḥuffāẓ*.

As the Islāmic state expanded, people in various places recited the *Qur'ān* in their local dialect and accent. To avoid the possibility of any confusion or misunderstanding, the *Khalīfah, 'Uthmān*, ordered the preparation of one standard version of the *Qur'ān* to be written in the dialect of the *Quraish*. Prophet *Muḥammad* ﷺ was from the *Quraish* tribe. *Zaid bin Thābit, 'Abdullāh bin az-Zubair, Sa'īd bin al-'Āṣ* and *'Abdur Raḥmān bin al-Ḥārith* were asked to prepare copies from the copy of *Ḥafṣah*.

This far-sighted action by *'Uthmān* made the uniform recitation of the *Qur'ān* possible. Two original copies from the time of the *Khilāfah* of *'Uthmān* still exist today — one in

the *Topkapi Museum* in Istanbul, Turkey and the other in Tashkent, Uzbekistan. The *National Library* of Karachi, Pakistan has a photocopy of the Tashkent original.

The revelation of the *Qur'ān* began in 610 CE at the cave *Ḥirā'* on Mount *Nūr* in *Makkah*. The first revealed verses are:

اِقْرَأْ بِاسْمِ رَبِّكَ الَّذِى خَلَقَ .
خَلَقَ الْإِنسَٰنَ مِنْ عَلَقٍ .
اِقْرَأْ وَرَبُّكَ الْأَكْرَمُ .
الَّذِى عَلَّمَ بِالْقَلَمِ .
عَلَّمَ الْإِنسَٰنَ مَا لَمْ يَعْلَمْ .

Iqra' bismi rabbikal ladhī khalaq,
Khalaqal insāna min 'alaq.
Iqra' wa rabbukal akram,
Alladhī 'allama bil qalam.
'Allamal insāna mālam ya'lam.

"Read in the name of your Lord Who created,
Created man from something that clings.
Read, and your Lord is most generous,
Who taught by the pen,
Taught man what he did not know." (96:1–5)

The *Qur'ān* was revealed over 22 years, 5 months and 14 days. The last verse of the *Qur'ān* was revealed shortly before the Prophet's ﷺ death:

الْيَوْمَ أَكْمَلْتُ لَكُمْ دِينَكُمْ
وَأَتْمَمْتُ عَلَيْكُمْ نِعْمَتِى
وَرَضِيتُ لَكُمُ الْإِسْلَٰمَ دِينًا .

Al yawma akmaltu lakum dīnakum,
wa atmamtu 'alaikum ni'matī,
wa raḍītu lakumul islāma dīnan.

"This day I have perfected your religion for you,
and completed My favour upon you,
and chosen for you Islām as your way of life." (5:3)

Many Arabic words used in the *Qur'ān* are almost impossible to translate into other languages, including English. However, with the help of the *Aḥādīth* and *Sīrah* (biography of the Prophet ﷺ and his companions) translations of the *Qur'ān* have been produced in many languages.

Muslims scholars have devoted years of study to explain and interpret the *Qur'ān* in Arabic and other languages. These explanations and interpretations are called *Tafāsīr* (sing. *Tafsīr*). They help us to understand the *Qur'ān*. We seek Allāh's help to understand His words and act on them.

Death

Death is a natural event for all living things. It comes to every one of us. We will all die. The *Qur'ān* says:

"Everyone shall taste death." (3:185; 21:35; 29:57)

Death brings an end to our temporary life on this earth. It is an occasion of sorrow and grief for the loved ones of the deceased. In Islām, people mourn for the dead person by reciting the *Qur'ān* and saying prayers *(du'ā')*.

Islām asks us to keep in mind that death can arrive at any time. Only Allāh knows when His servants will die. Death puts an end to our human body but it does not destroy our soul *(rūḥ)*. The soul is taken away by the angel *Malakul Mawt ('Izrā'īl* or *Azrail)* to Allāh (32:11).

A person is sure to behave well and follow Allāh's commands if he remains conscious of death and the life after death.

In Islām, a dead body is ritually washed before it is buried. It is then covered with white sheets and fragrance is spread all over it. A funeral prayer is conducted before the burial. This prayer is called *Ṣalātul Janāzah*.

Ākhirah

We have already mentioned the three most important beliefs in Islām: *Tawḥīd* (oneness of Allāh), *Risālah* (prophethood) and the *Ākhirah* (life after death). Now we will look at the *Ākhirah*.

Belief in *Ākhirah* is vital for all Muslims. Our life on this earth is temporary. It is meant to prepare us for the *Ākhirah*, which is never-ending. Life on this earth is meaningless if good actions are not rewarded and bad conduct not punished. Why attend school if bad behaviour goes unpunished and there's nothing at the end to reward all our efforts? In the same way, life on earth is meaningless if we don't face the consequences of our actions after death, standing in the majestic Court of Justice of Almighty Allāh on the Day of Judgement *(Yawmul Ākhir* or *Yawmuddīn)*.

To prepare ourselves for this day, we need to follow the Guidance given through the prophets. There would have been no need for prophets if there were no life after death.

There are people who do not care whether there is a life after death. Some do not even believe in it at all. These people will suffer terribly for their disbelief. A sensible person cannot possibly say there is no life after death. He can be doubtful but he will always be at a loss if his doubt proves untrue.

So, the safe course to follow is to believe in all that the prophets told people to believe. Not to care about *Ākhirah* is a serious failing. We are certain that all human beings die, so it is quite reasonable to prepare for that eternal life which, no doubt, will follow death.

Doubts have been expressed by unbelievers about life after death. They cannot understand how Allāh can raise men and women after death. But Allāh can make human beings out of nothing so it is not difficult for Him to raise them after death (22:5–7; 36:77–79).

The *Qur'ān* says:

"Does man think that we shall not assemble his bones? Yes, surely, yes, we are able to restore the very shape of his fingertips." (75:3–4)

Life on this earth would not be peaceful, rather it would be horrible, if all people thought that there would be no life after death. There would be no restraint or control on what we do. Belief in *Ākhirah* has a tremendous influence on the life of a Muslim. He knows that Allāh is watching all his actions and he will have to account for them on the Day of Judgement. His conduct and behaviour will therefore be responsible, controlled and careful. He will always try to do those things which Allāh will favour and give up those actions which will incur His punishment.

A Muslim believes that he will be rewarded in the life after death for all his good actions. He will live in *Heaven*, a place of eternal happiness and peace.

Wrong-doers will be punished on the Day of Judgement and will be sent to *Hell*, a place of severe punishment and suffering.

To prepare for that day and to be rewarded by Allāh, the Merciful and the Kind, we need to do all that Allāh demands of us and give up all bad habits and wrong actions. We can do this if we follow the Guidance given to *Muḥammad* ﷺ by Allāh. This is the safest course for our success in this world and in the *Ākhirah*.

What did you learn? (1d)

Key Stage 3 (11–14)

1. What is the Qur'ān?
2. How many parts are there in the *Qur'ān?*
3. When were the first verses of the *Qur'ān* revealed?
4. What does the *Qur'ān* say about death?
5. What is a *Ḥāfiẓ* of the *Qur'ān?*
6. What is *Yawmuddīn*, and how should we prepare for it?
7. Describe how the *Qur'ān* came to be in its present form.

Key Stage 4 (15–16)

1. Through whom was the *Qur'ān* revealed to *Muḥammad* ﷺ?
2. Who suggested the compilation of the *Qur'ān*, and why?
3. How long did it take for the revelation of the *Qur'ān* to be completed?
4. Which verse of the *Qur'ān* was revealed first?
5. *"Belief in the Ākhirah helps to keep everything in perspective."* Justify this statement in relation to your understanding of Islām.
6. What is the basic message of the *Qur'ān* and how can it shape our lives in a modern world?

Key Stage 5 (17–18)

1. *"The message of the Qur'ān is universal even though it was revealed over 1400 years ago."* Justify this statement in the form of a newspaper or magazine article.
2. *"Enjoy today with no thought for tomorrow."* Explain the disadvantages of this kind of outlook, and discuss why belief in the *Ākhirah* puts a check on this attitude to life.
3. *"Remembering death helps to keep us from being hypnotised by the glitter of worldly things."* What does this sentence mean? Discuss.

Basic Duties of Islām 2

Islām has five basic duties which Muslims must do. They are known as the five pillars of Islām *(Arkānul Islām)*. These pillars are mentioned in the following *Ḥadīth* (a saying of Prophet *Muḥammad* ﷺ):

بُنِيَ الْإِسْلَامُ عَلَى خَمْسٍ : شَهَادَةِ أَنْ لَا إِلٰهَ إِلَّا اللّٰهُ وَأَنَّ مُحَمَّدًا رَسُولُ اللّٰهِ ، وَإِقَامِ الصَّلَاةِ ، وَإِيتَاءِ الزَّكَاةِ ، وَالْحَجِّ ، وَصَوْمِ رَمَضَانَ .

"Buniyal islāmu 'alā khamsin: shahādati an lā ilāha illallāhu wa anna muḥammadan rasūlullāhi, wa iqāmiṣ ṣalāti, wa ītā'iz zakāti, wal ḥajji, wa ṣawmi ramaḍān."

"Islām is based on five things: declaring that there is no god except Allāh and that *Muḥammad* is the Messenger of Allāh, the establishment of *Ṣalāh*, the payment of *Zakāh*, the *Ḥajj* and *Ṣawm* in the month of *Ramaḍān*." *(al-Bukhārī)*

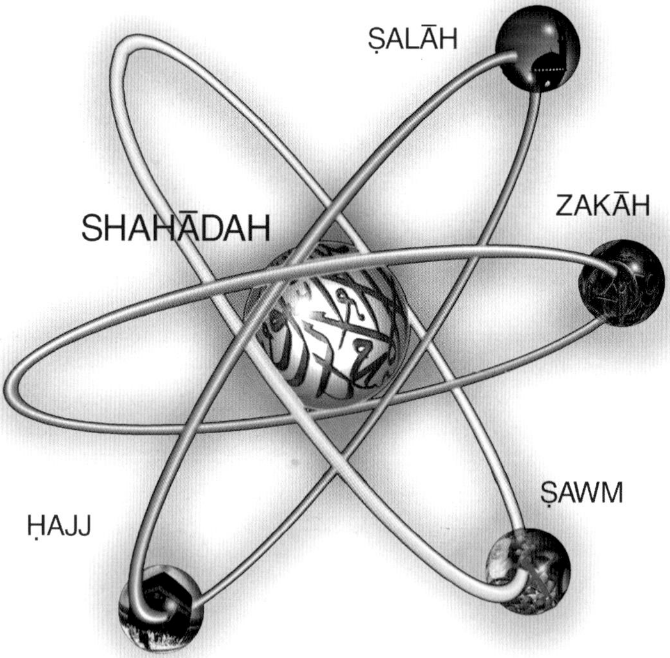

The five pillars as mentioned in the *Ḥadīth* are:

Shahādah	*(declaration of faith)*	اَلشَّهَادَة
Ṣalāh	*(five compulsory daily prayers)*	اَلصَّلاَة
Zakāh	*(welfare contribution)*	اَلزَّكَاة
Ḥajj	*(pilgrimage to Makkah)*	اَلْحَجّ
Ṣawm	*(fasting during Ramaḍān)*	اَلصَّوْم

Shahādah

A Muslim declares his faith by reciting:

لَآ إِلٰهَ إِلَّا اللهُ مُحَمَّدٌ رَسُولُ اللهِ

Lā ilāha illallāhu Muḥammadur rasūlullāh.

These Arabic words mean: *"There is no god except Allāh; Muḥammad is the messenger of Allāh."* This declaration is called *al-Kalimatuṭ Ṭaiyibah*. It contains the whole of Islāmic belief. There are two parts. The first part *(Lā ilāha illallāh)* is about the Oneness of Allāḥ (*Tawḥīd* in Arabic) while the second part *(Muḥammadur rasūlullāh)* concerns the prophethood *(Risālah)* of Muḥammad ﷺ. The four Arabic words of the first part are: *Lā* which means no; *ilāha* meaning god; *illa* meaning except; and *Allāh*. The second part has three words: *Muḥammad*; *rasūl* meaning messenger; and *Allāh*.

The first pillar of Islām is *Shahādah*, which is about belief in *Tawḥīd* and *Risālah* of *Muḥammad* ﷺ. The other four pillars are the main duties in Islām, called *'Ibādah*. *'Ibādah*, an Arabic term, includes any activity which is done to gain Allāh's favour. *Ṣalāh*, *Zakāh*, *Ṣawm* and *Ḥajj* are the main forms of worship or *'Ibādah*. If we perform them regularly and correctly we come closer to Allāh, our Creator and Sustainer.

These four basic duties of *Ṣalāh*, *Zakāh*, *Ṣawm* and *Ḥajj* make up the training programme which is required to shape our life around *Shahādah*. We already know that we belong to Allāh and He is our Master. So, in order to behave like the servants of our Creator, we must practise *Ṣalāh*, *Zakāh*, *Ṣawm* and *Ḥajj* honestly and faithfully.

Ṣalāh

Ṣalāh is the second pillar of Islām. It refers to the five compulsory daily prayers. *Ṣalāh* is offered five times a day individually or preferably, for men and older boys, in congregation. Women and girls may also join in congregation whenever possible. We offer *Ṣalāh* to remember Allāh. It brings us closer to Him. The *Qur'ān* says:

"Indeed, I am Allāh; there is no god except Myself; so worship Me and establish Ṣalāh to remember Me." (20:14)

Ṣalāh is the practical proof of our faith in Allāh and Islām. It has been made compulsory at certain fixed times. Allāh says in the *Qur'ān*:

"Ṣalāh at fixed times has been enjoined on the believers." (4:103)

The five daily prayers are:

Fajr	*From dawn until just before sunrise*	صَلَاةُ الْفَجْر
Ẓuhr	*After midday until afternoon*	صَلَاةُ الظُّهْر
'Aṣr	*From late afternoon until just before sunset*	صَلَاةُ الْعَصْر
Maghrib	*After sunset until daylight ends*	صَلَاةُ الْمَغْرِب
'Ishā'	*Night until midnight or dawn*	صَلَاةُ الْعِشَاء

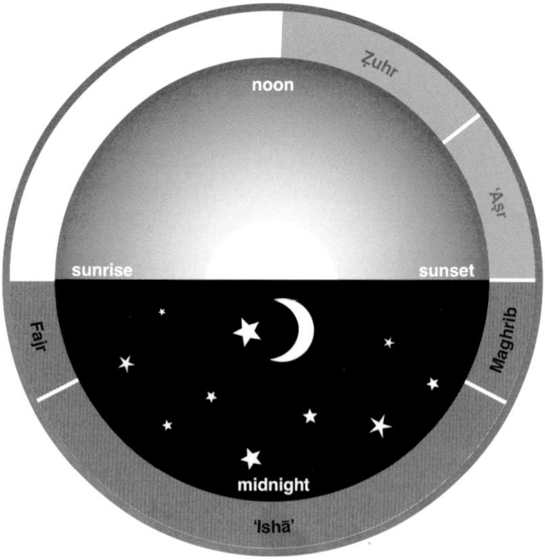

Timings of the five daily Ṣalāh

You should know at this stage how to say *Ṣalāh*. First, try to understand clearly why we need to offer *Ṣalāh*. We offer *Ṣalāh* to remember Allāh our Creator and to be close to Him and to gain His favour.

To say your *Ṣalāh* you must be pure and clean. The *Qur'ān* says: *"Indeed Allāh loves those who turn to Him in repentence and loves those who purify themselves." (2:222)* Purification of the body and clothes is called *Ṭahārah*, and cleanliness is called *Naẓāfah*. They are not the same, but they are connected to one another. You may be clean outwardly and still not be pure — it is especially important to remove all traces of urine or excrement from the clothes worn for *Ṣalāh*.

How can we have cleanliness? We can fully wash the whole body with pure and clean water or we can have a part-wash, cleaning only parts of the body. The full wash or bath is called *Ghusl* and the part wash is *Wuḍū'* (ablution).

Keep in mind that Muslims are not allowed to have a bath or a shower in the nude in the presence of others.

Wuḍū' اَلْوُضُوْءُ

Prophet *Muḥammad* ﷺ said: *"Indeed, on the Day of Resurrection, my followers will be called 'al-Ghurrul Muḥajjalūn' from the traces of Wuḍū', so whoever can increase the area of his radiance should do so (i.e. by performing ablution regularly)." (al-Bukhārī)*

Before we can begin to say *Ṣalāh*, we must first prepare ourselves. This preparation includes making sure we are clean. We do this by carrying out *Wuḍū'*.

Wuḍū' is essential for performing *Ṣalāh*. We must not say *Ṣalāh* without first making *Wuḍū'*. Allāh says in the *Qur'ān:*

"O you who believe, when you prepare for Ṣalāh, wash your faces and your hands to the elbows; wipe over your heads and wash your feet up to the ankles." (5:6)

This verse refers to the compulsory *(Farḍ)* parts of *Wuḍū'*. The additional actions performed by Prophet *Muḥammad* ﷺ are recommended *(Sunnah)*, and are mentioned in the books of *Aḥādīth*.

The steps to take are:

1 Make *Niyyah* (intention) saying the *Tasmiyah* (*Basmalah* or *Bismillāh*):

بِسْمِ اللّٰهِ الرَّحْمٰنِ الرَّحِيْمِ

Bismillāhir raḥmānir raḥīm

In the name of Allāh, the Most Merciful, the Most Kind.

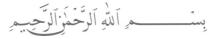

2 Then wash both hands up to the wrists three times making sure that water has reached between the fingers.

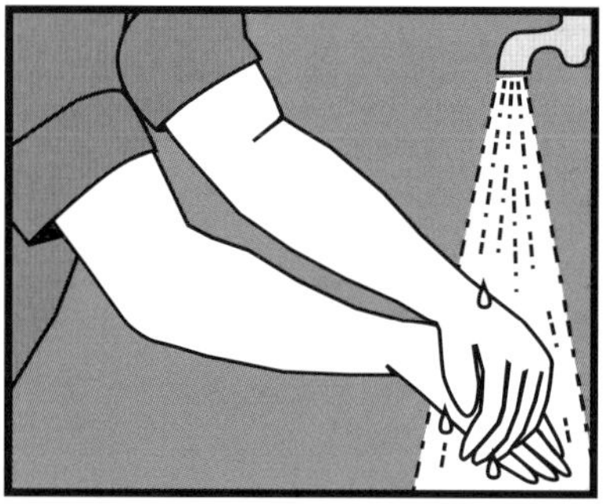

3 Put a handful of water into the mouth and rinse it thoroughly three times.

4 Sniff water into the nostrils three times to clean them and then wash the tip of the nose.

5 Wash the face three times from right ear to left ear and from forehead to throat.

6 Wash the right arm, and then left arm, thoroughly from hand to elbow three times.

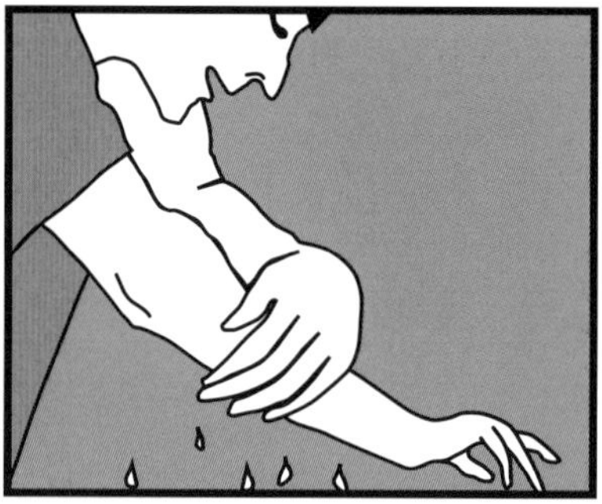

7 Move the wet palms of both hands over the head, starting from the top of the forehead to the neck.

8 Rub the wet fingers into the grooves and holes of both ears and also pass the wet thumbs behind the ears.

9 Pass the backs of the wet hands over the nape.

(See *Nailul Awṭār* by 'Allāmah Shawkāni, 1973, vol. 1, p. 203)

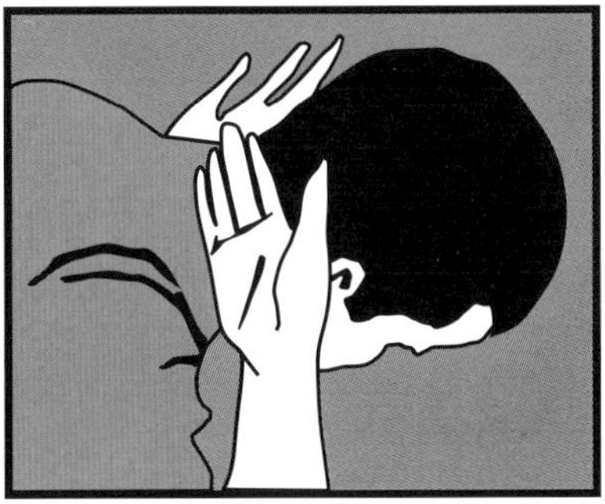

10 Wash both feet to the ankles starting from the right foot and making sure that water has reached between the toes and all other parts of the feet.

If you made a full *Wuḍū'* before putting on your socks, it is not necessary to take them off every time you repeat your *Wuḍū'*; it is enough to wipe the upper part of the socks with wet fingers. Leather socks are better for this, but any durable, untorn thick socks will also do. This type of wiping is valid for twenty-four hours only (three days in the case of a journey).

At the end of all the steps, recite:

أَشْهَدُ أَنْ لَّآ إِلٰهَ إِلَّا اللّٰهُ وَحْدَهُ لَا شَرِيْكَ لَهُ
وَأَشْهَدُ أَنَّ مُحَمَّدًا عَبْدُهُ وَرَسُوْلُهُ

Ash-hadu allā ilāha illallāhu waḥdahu lā sharīka lahu
wa ash-hadu anna Muḥammadan 'abduhu wa rasūluh.

I testify that there is no god but Allāh and He is One and has no partner and I testify that Muḥammad is His servant and messenger.

You should repeat your Wuḍū' after:

1 Natural discharges (e.g. urine, stool, wind and the like).
2 Flow of blood or pus from any part of the body.
3 Full mouth vomiting.
4 Falling asleep or losing consciousness.
5 Touching the sexual organs.

Tayammum (Dry Ablution) اَلتَّيَمُّم

You can perform your *Ṣalāh* with *Tayammum* (4:43) when:
1 water is not available at all,
2 the water available is insufficient (e.g. available water is enough for drinking only), or
3 use of water is harmful (e.g. in sickness)

For *Tayammum* you are required to:
1 (a) Make *Niyyah* by saying: *Bismillāhir raḥmānir raḥīm*, then (b) place both your hands lightly on earth, sand, stone or any other object having dust on it.
2 Blow the dust off your hands and wipe your face with the hands once the same way as you do in *Wuḍū'*.
3 Repeat 1(b) and wipe the right arm from wrist to elbow with the left hand and the left arm with the right hand.

Adhān (Call to Prayer) اَلْأَذَان

Prophet *Muḥammad* ﷺ, by his practice and sayings, showed that Muslim men and older boys should offer their compulsory *(Farḍ) Ṣalāh* in congregation in a mosque *(Masjid)*. Women and girls may offer their *Ṣalāh* in a mosque if they wish. All other *Ṣalāh* can be offered privately at home.

To call Muslims to *Ṣalāh*, Prophet *Muḥammad* ﷺ introduced the *Adhān* to signal that the time of *Ṣalāh* has arrived. The person who calls the *Adhān* is called the *Mu'adhdhin* (Caller). While doing so he faces the *Qiblah* (the direction towards the *Ka'bah* in *Makkah*). He raises his hands up to his ears and calls out:

اَللّٰهُ أَكْبَرُ	اَللّٰهُ أَكْبَرُ	اَللّٰهُ أَكْبَرُ	اَللّٰهُ أَكْبَرُ
Allāhu akbar	*Allāhu akbar*	*Allāhu akbar*	*Allāhu akbar*
Allāh is the Greatest	Allāh is the Greatest	Allāh is the Greatest	Allāh is the Greatest

أَشْهَدُ أَنْ لَّآ إِلٰهَ إِلَّا اللّٰهُ	أَشْهَدُ أَنْ لَّآ إِلٰهَ إِلَّا اللّٰهُ
Ash-hadu allā ilāha illallāh	*Ash-hadu allā ilāha illallāh*
I testify that there is no god except Allāh	I testify that there is no god except Allāh

أَشْهَدُ اَنَّ مُحَمَّدًا رَسُوْلُ اللهِ

Ash-hadu anna Muḥammadar rasūlullāh

I testify that Muḥammad is Allāh's messenger

أَشْهَدُ اَنَّ مُحَمَّدًا رَسُوْلُ اللهِ

Ash-hadu anna Muḥammadar rasūlullāh

I testify that Muḥammad is Allāh's messenger

حَيَّ عَلَى الصَّلٰوةِ

Ḥaiya 'alaṣ ṣalāh

Rush to Ṣalāh

حَيَّ عَلَى الصَّلٰوةِ

Ḥaiya 'alaṣ ṣalāh

Rush to Ṣalāh

حَيَّ عَلَى الْفَلَاحِ

Ḥaiya 'alal falāḥ

Rush to success

حَيَّ عَلَى الْفَلَاحِ

Ḥaiya 'alal falāḥ

Rush to success

اَللهُ أَكْبَرُ

Allāhu akbar

Allāh is the Greatest

اَللهُ أَكْبَرُ

Allāhu akbar

Allāh is the Greatest

لَآ إِلٰهَ إِلَّا اللهُ

Lā ilāha illallāh

There is no god except Allāh

During the *Adhān* for *Fajr Ṣalāh* the following words are added after *Ḥaiya 'alal falāḥ:*

اَلصَّلٰوةُ خَيْرٌ مِّنَ النَّوْمِ

Aṣ-ṣalātu khairum minan nawm

Ṣalāh is better than sleep

اَلصَّلٰوةُ خَيْرٌ مِّنَ النَّوْمِ

Aṣ-ṣalātu khairum minan nawm

Ṣalāh is better than sleep

Iqāmah اَلْإِقَامَةُ

Iqāmah is the second call to *Ṣalāh* said inside the mosque at the beginning of *Ṣalāh* in congregation *(Jama'ah)*. When the *muṣallis* (persons saying *Ṣalāh*) stand in rows, the *Mu'adhdhin* says *Iqāmah* which is the same as the *Adhān* except that after *Ḥaiya 'alal falāḥ*, the following words are added:

قَدْ قَامَتِ الصَّلٰوةُ

Qad qāmatiṣ ṣalāh

Ṣalāh has begun

قَدْ قَامَتِ الصَّلٰوةُ

Qad qāmatiṣ ṣalāh

Ṣalāh has begun

Usually, the *Iqāmah* is said in a lower voice than the *Adhān*.

Farḍ (Compulsory) Ṣalāh

A Muslim must pray five times a day. The compulsory prayers are called *Farḍ* in Arabic. Each unit of prayer is called a *rak'ah* (رَكْعَة). *Farḍ rak'ahs* are:

Fajr	....	**2** *rak'ahs*
Ẓuhr	....	**4** *rak'ahs*
'Aṣr	....	**4** *rak'ahs*
Maghrib	....	**3** *rak'ahs*
'Ishā'	....	**4** *rak'ahs*
		17 *rak'ahs*
Jumu'ah	....	**2** *rak'ahs* (in place of *Ẓuhr* on Friday)

Sunnah Ṣalāh

Prophet *Muḥammad* ﷺ prayed extra *rak'ahs* in addition to *Farḍ* prayers. These prayers are called *Sunnah*. Prophet *Muḥammad* ﷺ always prayed two *rak'ahs* before the *Farḍ* of *Fajr* and three *rak'ahs* after the *Farḍ* of *'Ishā'* even on a journey. The three *rak'ahs* after *'Ishā'* are called *Witr* (odd number). Muslims also pray additional *rak'ahs* other than *Farḍ* and *Sunnah*. These are called *Nāfilah* (optional).

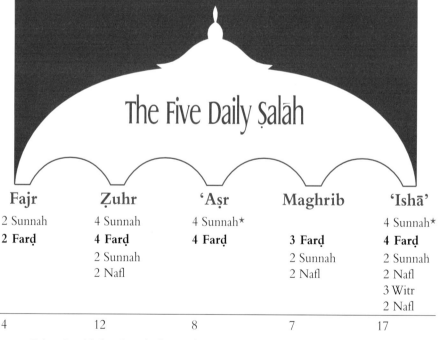

Fajr	Ẓuhr	'Aṣr	Maghrib	'Ishā'
2 Sunnah	4 Sunnah	4 Sunnah*		4 Sunnah*
2 Farḍ	**4 Farḍ**	**4 Farḍ**	**3 Farḍ**	**4 Farḍ**
	2 Sunnah		2 Sunnah	2 Sunnah
	2 Nafl		2 Nafl	2 Nafl
				3 Witr
				2 Nafl
4	12	8	7	17

(* these *Sunnah* before *'Aṣr* and *'Ishā'* are *Ghair Mu'akkadah*, not done regularly, only occasionally.)

In addition to the five daily *Ṣalāh*, there are *Ṣalāh* for other occasions, e.g. *Ṣalātul Jumu'ah* every Friday, *Ṣalātul 'Īdul Fiṭr*, *Ṣalātul 'Īdul Aḍḥā* and *Ṣalātut Tarāwīḥ* in the month of *Ramaḍān*. The number of *rak'ahs* in these *Ṣalāh* are:

Jumu'ah	'Īdul Fiṭr	'Īdul Aḍḥā	Tarāwīḥ
4 Sunnah			20 Sunnah
2 Farḍ	**2 Wājib**	**2 Wājib**	
4 Sunnah			
2 Sunnah			
2 Nafl			
14	2	2	20

Wājib is a term used in *Ḥanafī fiqh* for something compulsory to a degree less than *Farḍ*. Those who follow *Ḥanafī fiqh* consider *Ṣalātul Janāzah*, *Ṣalātul 'Īdul Fiṭr*, *Ṣalātul 'Īdul Aḍḥā* and *Witr Ṣalāh* as *Wājib*.

Tarāwīḥ is offered after the two *Sunnah rak'ahs* of *'Ishā'* but before the three of *Witr*.

Between *'Ishā'* and *Fajr*, a prayer called *Tahajjud* was regularly offered by the Prophet ﷺ. It was obligatory for the Prophet ﷺ. Devout Muslims try to follow the practice. Only those who wish to taste the sweetness of being closer to Allāh can appreciate the benefits of the *Tahajjud* prayer.

Times when you must not pray:

1 From the beginning of sunrise until 15–20 minutes after full sunrise.
2 When the sun is at its height (zenith or meridian).
3 From the beginning of sunset until it is fully set.
4 For women during menstruation, and for up to 40 days during post-childbirth bleeding.

How to perform Ṣalāh

At this stage you should be ready to start saying your *Ṣalāh*. Make sure you have *Wuḍū'*, a clean body, clean clothes and a clean place. This is how you should do your *Ṣalāh:*

1 Stand upright in a clean place (like a prayer mat) facing the direction of the *Ka'bah*. This is called *Qiyām* and the direction is called the *Qiblah* in Arabic. In the UK the *Qiblah* is towards the south-east. In other countries the direction will be different. You will have to find out its direction before doing your *Ṣalāh*.

2 Say your *Niyyah* (intention) either verbally or in your mind. *Niyyah* is said with the words:

			Fajr★	
	two★	*Farḍ*★	*Ẓuhr*	
"I intend to say	three	*Sunnah* *rak'ahs* of *Ṣalātul*	*'Aṣr*	for Allāh facing the *Ka'bah*."
	four		*Maghrib*	
	(★say the one which is relevant)		*'Ishā'*	

3 Raise your hands up to your ears (women and girls up to their shoulders) and say:

اَللّٰهُ أَكْبَرُ

Allāhu Akbar

Allāh is the Greatest

This is called *Takbīratul Iḥrām*, meaning that all wordly things are now forbidden to you.

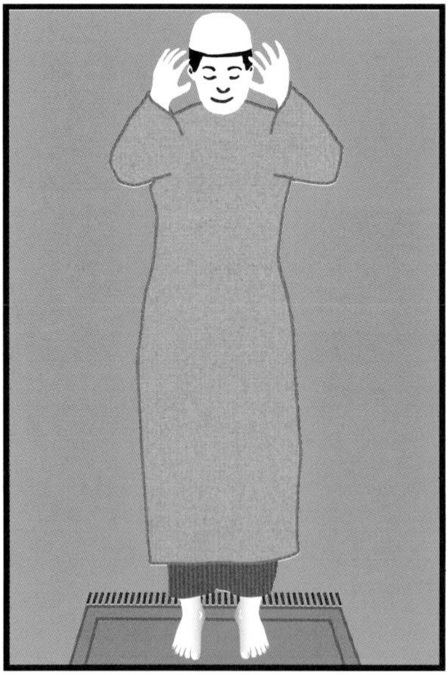

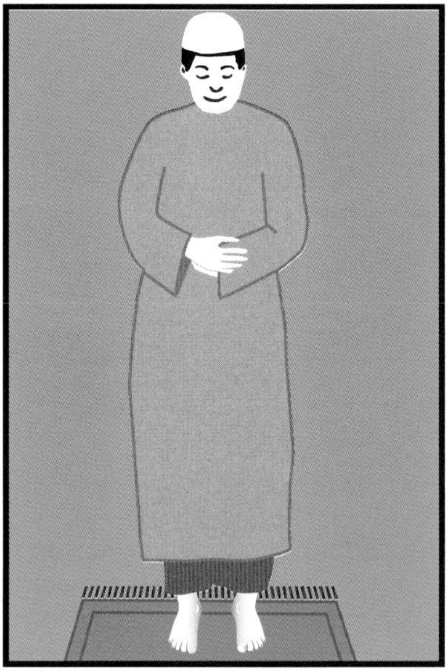

4 Place your right hand on your left hand just below the navel or on the chest (women and girls put their hands on their chest) and recite *Thanā':*

سُبْحَانَكَ اللّٰهُمَّ وَبِحَمْدِكَ وَتَبَارَكَ اسْمُكَ وَتَعَالٰى جَدُّكَ
وَلَآ إِلٰهَ غَيْرُكَ

Subḥānakallāhumma wa biḥamdika,
wa tabārakasmuka,
wa ta'ālā jadduka,
wa lā ilāha ghairuk.
(or you may read *ghairuka)*

O Allāh, glory and praise are for You,
and blessed is Your name,
and exalted is Your Majesty;
there is no god but You.

أَعُوذُ بِاللّٰهِ مِنَ الشَّيْطَانِ الرَّجِيمِ

A'ūdhu billāhi minash shaiṭānir rajīm

I seek refuge in Allāh from the cursed Satan *(Shaiṭān).*

بِسْمِ ٱللّٰهِ ٱلرَّحْمَٰنِ ٱلرَّحِيمِ

Bismillāhir raḥmānir raḥīm

In the name of Allāh, the Most Merciful, the Most Kind.

5 Recite the rest of *Sūratul Fātiḥah* (the opening chapter) of the *Qur'ān*:

ٱلْحَمْدُ لِلّٰهِ رَبِّ ٱلْعَٰلَمِينَ .
ٱلرَّحْمَٰنِ ٱلرَّحِيمِ .
مَٰلِكِ يَوْمِ ٱلدِّينِ .
إِيَّاكَ نَعْبُدُ وَإِيَّاكَ نَسْتَعِينُ .
ٱهْدِنَا ٱلصِّرَٰطَ ٱلْمُسْتَقِيمَ .
صِرَٰطَ ٱلَّذِينَ أَنْعَمْتَ عَلَيْهِمْ
غَيْرِ ٱلْمَغْضُوبِ عَلَيْهِمْ وَلَا ٱلضَّآلِّينَ .

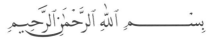

Alḥamdu lillāhi rabbil 'ālamīn.	All praise is for Allāh, the Lord of the Universe.
Arraḥmānir raḥīm.	The Most Merciful, the Most Kind.
Māliki yawmid dīn.	Master of the Day of Judgement.
Iyyāka na'budu wa iyyāka nasta'īn.	You alone we worship, from You alone we seek help.
Ihdinaṣ ṣirāṭal mustaqīm.	Guide us along the straight path.
Ṣirāṭal ladhīna an'amta 'alaihim, ghairil maghḍūbi 'alaihim wa laḍ ḍāllīn.	The path of those whom You have favoured, not of those who earned Your anger nor of those who went astray (or who are misguided).

Then say, quietly or loudly:

آمين

Āmīn

Amen

The recitation of *al-Fātiḥah* is a must in all prayers.

6 Recite any other *Sūrah* or some verses from the *Qur'ān*. For example:

بِسْمِ ٱللَّهِ ٱلرَّحْمَٰنِ ٱلرَّحِيمِ

Bismillāhir raḥmānir raḥīm

In the name of Allāh, the Most Merciful, the Most Kind.

قُلْ هُوَ ٱللَّهُ أَحَدٌ

ٱللَّهُ ٱلصَّمَدُ

لَمْ يَلِدْ وَلَمْ يُولَدْ

وَلَمْ يَكُن لَّهُۥ كُفُوًا أَحَدٌۢ

Qul huwallāhu aḥad.	Say, He is Allāh, the One.
Allāhuṣ ṣamad.	Allāh is Eternal and Absolute.
Lam yalid walam yūlad.	None is born of Him nor is He born.
Walam yakul lahu kufuwān aḥad.	And there is none like Him.
	(Sūratul Ikhlāṣ 112*)*

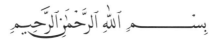

7 Bow down saying *Allāhu Akbar,* then place your hands on your knees and say three times:

سُبْحَانَ رَبِّيَ الْعَظِيمِ

Subḥāna rabbiyal 'aẓīm

Glory to my Lord, the Great

This position is called *Rukū'* (رُكُوع).

8 Stand up from *Rukū'* saying:

سَمِعَ اللّٰهُ لِمَنْ حَمِدَهُ

Sami' allāhu liman ḥamidah

Allāh hears those who praise Him

followed by:

رَبَّنَا لَكَ الْحَمْدُ

Rabbanā lakal ḥamd

Our Lord, praise be to You

This is called *I'tidāl* as you return to the position of *Qiyām* (قِيَام) (standing).

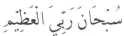

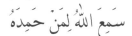

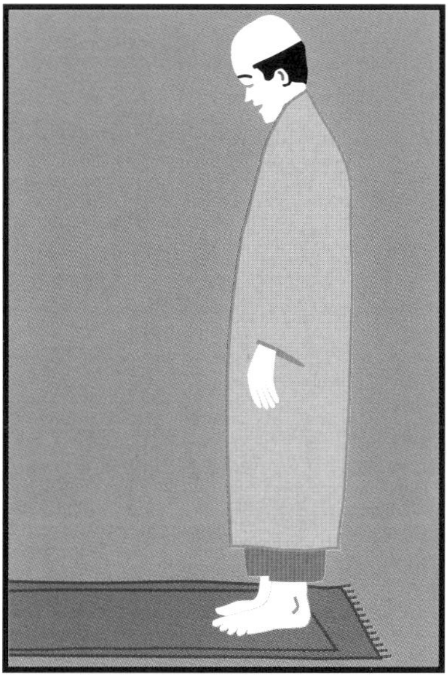

9 Prostrate saying *Allāhu akbar*, with your forehead, nose, palms of both hands, your knees and your toes touching the floor. Recite three times:

سُبْحَانَ رَبِّيَ الأَعْلَى

Subḥāna rabbiyal a'lā

Glory to my Lord, the Highest

This position is called *Sujūd*. Your arms should not touch the floor.

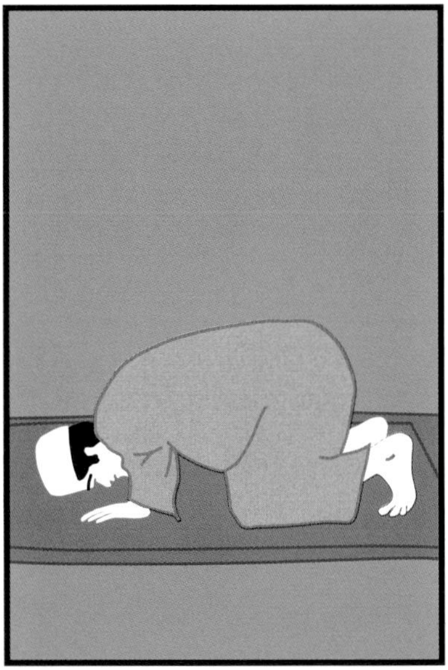

10 Get up from the floor saying *Allāhu akbar* and sit upright with your knees bent and palms placed on them. After a moment's rest* prostrate again saying *Allāhu akbar* and recite *Subḥāna rabbiyal a'lā* three times. Get up from this position saying *Allāhu akbar*.

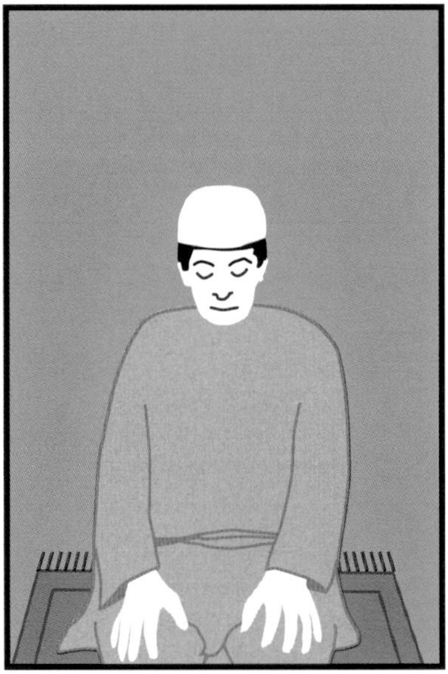

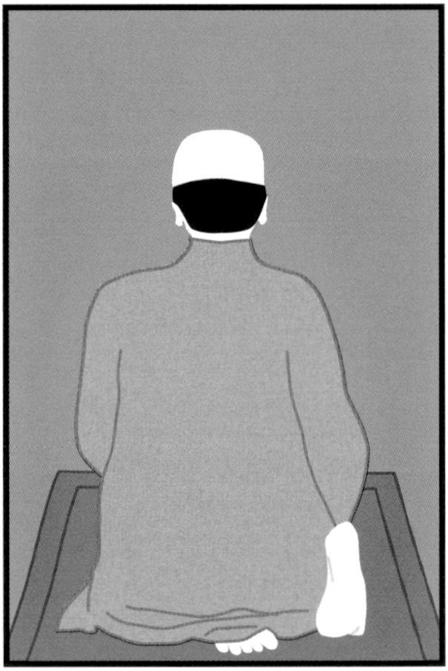

* Here you may say the *du'ā'*:

رَبِّ اغْفِرْ لِي وَارْحَمْنِي وَاهْدِنِي وَعَافِنِي وَارْزُقْنِي

Rabbighfir lī warḥamnī wahdinī wa'āfinī warzuqnī

My Lord forgive me, have mercy upon me, guide me, give me health and grant me sustenance.

This completes one *rak'ah* of *Ṣalāh*. The second *rak'ah* is performed in the same way, except you do not recite *Subḥānaka*, *Ta'awwudh* (*A'ūdhu billāhi…*) or *Tasmiyah* (*Bismillāh…*), then after the second prostration you sit upright and recite quietly *at-Tashahhud*:

اَلتَّحِيَّاتُ لِلّٰهِ وَالصَّلَوٰتُ وَالطَّيِّبَاتُ . اَلسَّلَامُ عَلَيْكَ أَيُّهَا النَّبِيُّ
وَرَحْمَةُ اللّٰهِ وَبَرَكَاتُهُ . اَلسَّلَامُ عَلَيْنَا وَعَلٰى عِبَادِ اللّٰهِ الصَّالِحِيْنَ .
أَشْهَدُ أَنْ لَّآ إِلٰهَ إِلَّا اللّٰهُ وَأَشْهَدُ أَنَّ مُحَمَّدًا عَبْدُهُ وَرَسُوْلُهُ .

At-taḥiyyātu lillāhi	All compliments are for Allāh,
waṣ ṣalawātu waṭ ṭaiyibāt.	and prayers and goodness.
As-salāmu 'alaika aiyuhan nabiyyu	Peace be upon you, O Prophet,
wa raḥmatullāhi wa barakātuh.	and the Mercy of Allāh and His blessings.
As-salāmu 'alainā	Peace be upon us
wa 'alā 'ibādillāhiṣ ṣāliḥīn.	and on the righteous servants of Allāh.
Ash-hadu allā ilāha illallāhu	I testify that there is no god except Allāh
wa ash-hadu anna Muḥammadan	and I testify that Muḥammad
'abduhu wa rasūluh.	is His servant and messenger.
	(al-Bukhārī, Muslim)

If the *Ṣalāh* has three *rak'ahs* (*Maghrib*) or four *rak'ahs* (*Ẓuhr*, *'Aṣr* and *'Ishā'*), stand up for the remaining *rak'ah* after *Tashahhud*. But for a two-*rak'ah Ṣalāh* remain seated after the second *rak'ah* and recite *aṣ-Ṣalāh 'alan nabiyy* (blessings for the Prophet) or *Darūd* (a Persian word):

اَللّٰهُمَّ صَلِّ عَلٰى مُحَمَّدٍ وَّعَلٰى آلِ مُحَمَّدٍ كَمَا صَلَّيْتَ عَلٰى إِبْرَاهِيْمَ
وَعَلٰى آلِ إِبْرَاهِيْمَ إِنَّكَ حَمِيْدٌ مَّجِيْدٌ . اَللّٰهُمَّ بَارِكْ عَلٰى مُحَمَّدٍ وَّعَلٰى آلِ
مُحَمَّدٍ كَمَا بَارَكْتَ عَلٰى إِبْرَاهِيْمَ وَعَلٰى آلِ إِبْرَاهِيْمَ إِنَّكَ حَمِيْدٌ مَّجِيْدٌ .

Allāhumma	O Allāh,
ṣalli 'alā Muḥammadiw	let Your blessings come on Muḥammad
wa 'alā āli Muḥammadin,	and the family of Muḥammad
kamā ṣallaita 'alā Ibrāhīma	as You blessed Ibrāhīm
wa 'alā āli Ibrāhīma,	and the family of Ibrāhīm.
innaka ḥamīdum majīd,	Truly You are Praiseworthy and Glorious.
Allāhumma bārik 'alā Muḥammadiw	O Allāh, bless Muḥammad
wa 'alā āli Muḥammadin,	and the family of Muḥammad
kamā bārakta 'alā Ibrāhīma	as You blessed Ibrāhīm
wa 'alā āli Ibrāhīma,	and the family of Ibrāhīm.
innaka ḥamīdum majīd.	Truly You are Praiseworthy and Glorious.
	(*Muslim*)

After this say any of the following *du'ā's* (supplications):

اَللّٰهُمَّ إِنِّى ظَلَمْتُ نَفْسِي ظُلْمًا كَثِيرًا وَلَا يَغْفِرُ الذُّنُوبَ إِلَّا أَنْتَ فَاغْفِرْ
لِي مَغْفِرَةً مِنْ عِنْدِكَ وَارْحَمْنِي إِنَّكَ أَنْتَ الْغَفُورُ الرَّحِيمُ .

Allāhumma innī ẓalamtu nafsī ẓulmān kathīrān
wa lā yaghfirudh dhunūba illā anta
faghfir lī maghfiratan min 'indika
warḥamnī
innaka antal ghafūrur raḥīm.

O Allāh, I have been very unjust to myself
and no one grants pardon for sins but You,
so forgive me with Your forgiveness
and have mercy on me.
Surely, You are the Forgiver, the Merciful.
(*al-Bukhārī, Muslim*)

رَبِّ اجْعَلْنِي مُقِيمَ الصَّلٰوةِ وَمِنْ ذُرِّيَّتِي رَبَّنَا وَتَقَبَّلْ دُعَآءِ .
رَبَّنَا اغْفِرْ لِي وَلِوَالِدَيَّ وَلِلْمُؤْمِنِينَ يَوْمَ يَقُومُ الْحِسَابُ .

Rabbij'alnī muqīmaṣ ṣalāti
wa min dhurriyyatī,
rabbanā wa taqabbal du'ā'.
Rabbanaghfir lī wa liwālidaiya
wa lilmu'minīna yawma yaqūmul ḥisāb.

My Lord, make me steadfast in Ṣalāh
and also my descendents;
our Lord, and accept my prayer.
Our Lord, forgive me and my parents
and the believers on the Day of Judgement.
(*Sūrah Ibrāhīm* 14:40–41)

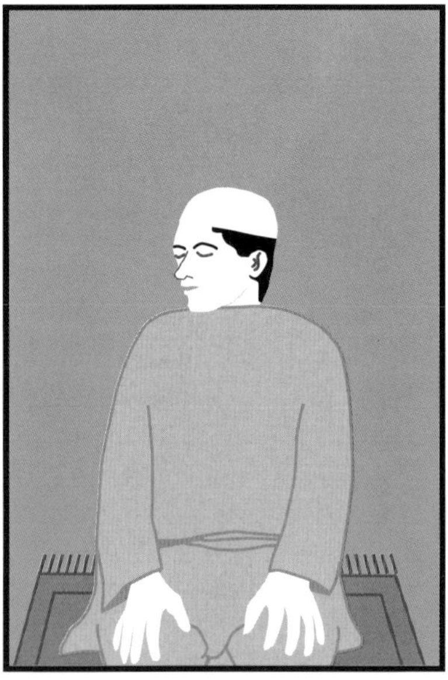

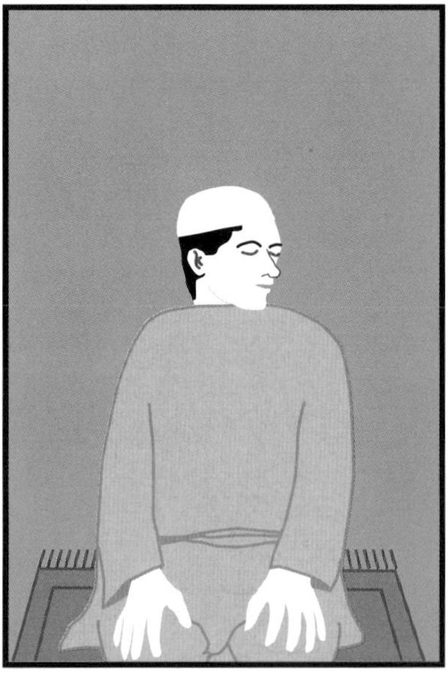

11 Now turn your face to the right saying:

اَلسَّلَامُ عَلَيْكُمْ وَرَحْمَةُ اللّٰهِ

Assalāmu 'alaikum wa raḥmatullāh

peace and the mercy of Allāh be upon you

and then to the left repeating the words.

This completes the two-*rak'ah Ṣalāh*. In the four-*rak'ah Ṣalāh* of *Ẓuhr*, *'Aṣr* and *'Ishā'*, the whole procedure is repeated except that when you get up to complete the remaining two *rak'ahs* (one *rak'ah* in *Maghrib* and *Witr*) after *Tashahhud*, you only recite *al-Fātiḥah* in *Farḍ* prayers and no other *Sūrah*. In a four-*rak'ah Sunnah Ṣalāh* you should recite another *Sūrah* or some verses of the *Qur'ān* after *al-Fātiḥah*.

In the first two *rak'ahs* of the *Farḍ* prayer of *Fajr*, *Maghrib* and *'Ishā'* the *Qur'ān* is recited aloud while in *Ẓuhr* and *'Aṣr* it is recited silently. In all prayers, *Tasbīḥ (Subḥāna rabbiyal 'aẓīm* and *Subḥāna rabbiyal a'lā)*, *Tashahhud* and *Darūd* are said quietly. When the *Fajr*, *Maghrib* and *'Ishā'* prayers are said in congregation, only the *Imām* (one who leads the prayer) recites the *Qur'ān* aloud. This also applies to اَلْجُمُعَة *Jumu'ah* prayer (Friday prayer in place of *Ẓuhr*).

Some du'a' after Ṣalah بَعْضُ الْأَدْعِيَة بَعْدَ الصَّلَاة

It is good practice to ask for forgiveness and mercy from Allāh at the end of your *Ṣalāh*. You can make *du'ā'* in your own words and in your own language but it is better for you to memorise some *du'ā's* in Arabic.

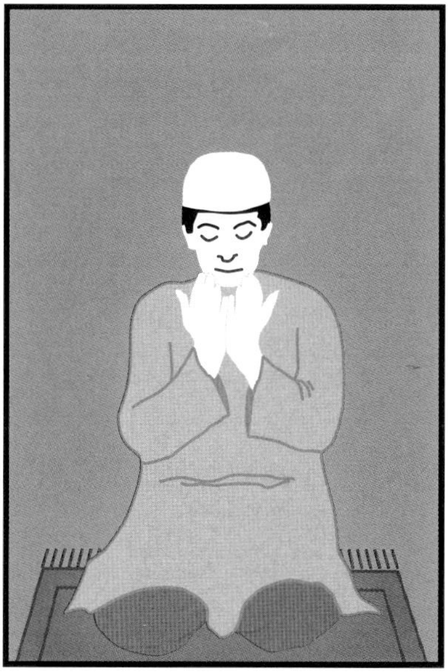

رَبَّنَآ ءَاتِنَا فِي ٱلدُّنْيَا
حَسَنَةً وَفِي ٱلْأٓخِرَةِ حَسَنَةً
وَقِنَا عَذَابَ ٱلنَّارِ.

Rabbanā ātinā fiddunyā ḥasanah,
wa fil ākhirati ḥasanah,
wa qinā 'adhābannār.

Our Lord, grant us good in this world,
and good in the Hereafter,
and save us from the punishment of
Hellfire. (*Sūratul Baqarah* 2:201)

رَبَّنَا ظَلَمْنَآ أَنْفُسَنَا وَإِن لَّمْ تَغْفِرْ لَنَا وَتَرْحَمْنَا لَنَكُونَنَّ مِنَ الْخَٰسِرِينَ.

Rabbanā ẓalamnā anfusanā
wa illam taghfirlanā
wa tarḥamnā
lanakūnanna minal khāsirīn.

Our Lord, we have wronged ourselves
and if You do not forgive us
and have no mercy upon us,
surely we will be among the losers.
(*Sūratul A'rāf* 7:23)

اَللّٰهُمَّ أَنْتَ السَّلَامُ وَمِنْكَ السَّلَامُ تَبَارَكْتَ يَا ذَا الْجَلَالِ وَالْإِكْرَامِ.

Allāhumma antas salāmu
wa minkas salāmu
tabārakta
yādhal jalāli wal ikrām.

O Allāh, You are the source of peace
and from You comes peace,
exalted You are,
O Lord of Majesty and Honour.
(Muslim)

لَآ إِلٰهَ إِلَّا اللّٰهُ وَحْدَهُ لَا شَرِيكَ لَهُ، لَهُ الْمُلْكُ وَلَهُ الْحَمْدُ وَهُوَ عَلَىٰ كُلِّ شَيْءٍ قَدِيرٌ، اَللّٰهُمَّ لَا مَانِعَ لِمَا أَعْطَيْتَ، وَلَا مُعْطِيَ لِمَا مَنَعْتَ، وَلَا يَنْفَعُ ذَا الْجَدِّ مِنْكَ الْجَدُّ.

Lā ilāha illallāhu
waḥdahu lā sharīka lah,
lahul mulku wa lahul ḥamdu
wa huwa 'alā kulli shai'in qadīr.
Allāhumma lā māni'a
limā a'ṭait,
wa lā mu'ṭiya limā mana't,
wa lā yunfa'u dhal jaddi minkal jadd.

There is no god except Allāh
and He is One and has no partner,
sovereignty is His, all praise is His
and He has power over all things.
O Allāh, none can stop You giving
what You want to give,
nor give what You do not want given,
and none with means can do anything
with their means against You.
(*al-Bukhārī* and *Muslim*)

Ṣalātul Witr صَلَاةُ الْوِتْر

The *Witr* (odd number) prayer has three *rak'ahs*. The first two *rak'ahs* are said like the first two *rak'ahs* of the *Maghrib* prayer. Then, after *Tashahhud* in the second *rak'ah*, stand up saying *Allāhu akbar* for the third *rak'ah*. Recite *Sūratul Fātiḥah* and some other verses from the *Qur'ān* but before going to *Rukū'* raise your hands up to the ears saying *Allāhu akbar* and recite the following *du'ā'* after placing your hands below your navel or on the chest. This *du'ā'* is called *al-Qunūt*:

اَللّٰهُمَّ إِنَّا نَسْتَعِينُكَ وَنَسْتَغْفِرُكَ وَنُؤْمِنُ بِكَ وَنَتَوَكَّلُ عَلَيْكَ وَنُثْنِي
عَلَيْكَ الْخَيْرَ وَنَشْكُرُكَ وَلَا نَكْفُرُكَ وَنَخْلَعُ وَنَتْرُكُ مَنْ يَّفْجُرُكَ.
اَللّٰهُمَّ إِيَّاكَ نَعْبُدُ وَلَكَ نُصَلِّي وَنَسْجُدُ وَإِلَيْكَ نَسْعٰى وَنَحْفِدُ وَنَرْجُوْ
رَحْمَتَكَ وَنَخْشٰى عَذَابَكَ إِنَّ عَذَابَكَ بِالْكُفَّارِ مُلْحِقٌ.

Allāhumma innā nasta'īnuka
wa nastaghfiruka
wa nu'minu bika wa natawakkalu 'alaika
wa nuthnī 'alaikal khaira
wa nashkuruka wa lā nakfuruka
wa nakhla'u wa natruku
man yafjuruk.
Allāhumma iyyāka na'budu
wa laka nuṣallī wa nasjudu
wa ilaika nas'ā wa naḥfidu
wa narjū raḥmataka
wa nakhshā 'adhābaka.
Inna 'adhābaka bil kuffāri mulḥiq.

O Allāh, we seek Your help
and ask Your forgiveness
and we believe in You and trust in You,
and we praise You in the best way
and we thank You and we are not ungrateful
and we cast off and forsake
him who disobeys You.
O Allāh, You alone we worship
and to You we pray and we prostrate,
and to You we turn in haste,
and hope for Your mercy
and we fear Your punishment.
Your punishment overtakes the
unbelievers. *(al-Baihaqī)*

Then say *Allāhu akbar* and bow down in *Rukū'* and complete the rest of the prayer like the *Maghrib* prayer.

The above *du'ā'* is used by Muslims who follow *Ḥanafī fiqh*. Another *du'ā'* used by some Muslims is:

اَللّٰهُمَّ اهْدِنِي فِيمَنْ هَدَيْتَ، وَعَافِنِي فِيمَنْ عَافَيْتَ وَتَوَلَّنِي فِيمَنْ
تَوَلَّيْتَ، وَبَارِكْ لِي فِيمَا أَعْطَيْتَ، وَقِنِي شَرَّ مَا قَضَيْتَ، فَإِنَّكَ تَقْضِي
وَلَا يُقْضٰى عَلَيْكَ، إِنَّهُ لَا يَذِلُّ مَنْ وَالَيْتَ، تَبَارَكْتَ رَبَّنَا وَتَعَالَيْتَ.

Allāhummahdinī fīman hadait,	O Allāh, guide me with those You have guided,
wa 'āfinī fīman 'āfait,	pardon me with those You have pardoned,
wa tawallanī fīman tawallait,	be an ally to me with those whom You are an ally to,
wa bārik lī fīmā a'ṭait,	bless me for what You have bestowed,

wa qinī sharra mā qaḍait,	and protect me from the evil You have decreed,
fa'innaka taqḍī wa lā yuqḍā 'alaik,	for verily You decree and none can decree over You,
innahu lā yadhillu man wālait,	indeed to he whom You show allegiance is never abased,
tabārakta rabbanā wa ta'ālait.	O Our Lord blessed and Exalted are You. *(Abū Dāwūd, at-Tirmidhī, Ibn Mājah)*

Sajdatus Sahw (prostration of forgetfulness) سَجْدَةُ السَّهو

Since we are human beings, we are not above mistakes and errors. If we forget to do something in our *Ṣalāh*, we can make up for it by making two extra *sujūd* (prostrations) as we do in any *rak'ah* of *Ṣalāh*. This is called *Sajdatus Sahw*. This is done at the end of the last *rak'ah* of *Ṣalāh*. What you have to do is:

1 Say *Tashahhud* (but not *Darūd*), then turn your face to the right and say *Assalāmu 'alaikum wa raḥmatullāh*;
2 Turn your face to the front, make two extra *sujūd* (with *Tasbīḥ – Subḥāna rabbiyal a'lā*);
3 Then recite *Tashahhud* again with *Darūd* and *du'ā'*;
4 Then turn your face, first to the right and then to the left, saying *Assalāmu 'alaikum wa raḥmatullāh*.

A slightly different sequence is followed by some Muslims: at the end of the last *rak'ah* you say *Tashahhud* and *Darūd*. Then turn your face to the right and say *Assalāmu 'alaikum wa raḥmatullāh*. Turn your face to the front, make two extra *sujūd* (with *Tasbīḥ – Subḥāna rabbiyal a'lā*). Then turn your face, first to the right and then to the left, saying *Assalāmu 'alaikum wa raḥmatullāh*.

Sajdatus Sahw is necessary if you forget to do any essentials of *Ṣalāh*, for example, the recitation of parts of the *Qur'ān* after *al-Fātiḥah*, forgetting to say the first *Tashahhud* in a four-*rak'ah Ṣalāh*, or saying *salām* after two *rak'ahs* in a four-*rak'ah Ṣalāh*.

Your *Ṣalāh* will not be valid if you do any of the following:

1 Miss out *Niyyah* (intention).
2 Miss out *Takbīratul Iḥrām*.
3 Forget to recite *al-Fātiḥah*.
4 Forget or do not make *rukū'* or *sujūd*.
5 Do not face the *Qiblah*.
6 Do not have *Wuḍū'*.
7 Talk during *Ṣalāh*.
8 Eat or drink during *Ṣalāh*.
9 Do not sit for *Tashahhud*.

Under these circumstances, you must repeat your *Ṣalāh*. *Sajdatus Sahw* will not be enough.

Qaḍā' (قَضَاء): making up for missed Ṣalāh

We must always try to offer *Ṣalāh* at the right time and make every effort not to miss our *Ṣalāh*. If you miss your *Ṣalāh*, you must do it at the first opportunity. Performing a missed *Ṣalāh* after its proper time is called *Qaḍā'*. We must make up our *Farḍ Ṣalāh*.

Ṣalātul Jumu'ah (Friday Prayer) صَلَاةُ الْجُمُعَة

Ṣalātul Jumu'ah or Friday Prayer (not *Jumma* or *Juma*, as some Muslims incorrectly say) is offered in congregation. All adult Muslim men must take part. It is offered on Friday during *Ẓuhr* time. It is not a must for women, but they can join this prayer if it does not upset their household duties.

People assemble for this *Ṣalāh* immediately after noon. Upon arrival at the mosque or the prayer hall, they offer four or more *rak'ahs Sunnah* prayer and then the *Imām* (prayer leader) delivers a *Khuṭbah* (sermon). After the *Khuṭbah*, the *Imām* leads two *rak'ahs Farḍ* prayer. After the *Farḍ* prayer, six or more *rak'ahs* of *Sunnah* and *Nafl* prayers are offered individually by each person.

Muslims are a community. *Ṣalātul Jumu'ah* is a community prayer. Every week, on Friday, Muslims living in an area get together to offer this prayer. This day is likened to a weekly *'Īd* (festival) for Muslims.

Mosques were the centre of all Islāmic activity during our Prophet's ﷺ time, but this is not so nowadays.

Friday prayer is an occasion for the assembly of Muslims in any given area. It gives them an opportunity to meet, discuss and solve their community problems. It develops unity, cooperation and understanding.

In an Islāmic state, the Head of State or his representative or the local leader is supposed to lead the five daily prayers and the Friday prayer at the central mosque of the capital city or the central mosque of the locality. Prophet *Muḥammad* ﷺ, the first head of the Islāmic state in *Madīnah*, used to lead all the prayers in *al-Masjidun Nabawī*.

How nice it would be to live in a country where the Head of State or his representative or the local leader leads the prayer in the central mosque of the capital city or of the area! May Allāh help us to revive this practice in all Muslim countries. *Āmīn!*

Ṣalātul Janāzah (Funeral Prayer) صَلَاةُ الْجَنَازَة

We have already briefly mentioned death and *Ṣalātul Janāzah*. We shall all die. When a Muslim dies, the body is given a simple ritual wash and then a funeral prayer called *Ṣalātul Janāzah* is offered in congregation. This *Ṣalāh*, unlike other *Ṣalāh*, has neither any *rukū'* (bowing) nor any *sujūd* (prostration) and you don't have to recite *Tashahhud*.

It is a collective duty *(Farḍu Kifāyah)* on all the Muslims of the locality of the dead person. If a number of them join in, the duty is discharged on behalf of all. If no one joins in everyone of the locality will be considered sinful before Allāh. This is how the prayer is offered:

1 Make *Niyyah* (intention) that you are saying this prayer to Allāh for the dead person.

2 Stand in rows facing the *Qiblah*. The coffin is placed in front of the congregation on a bier.

3 Say *Allāhu akbar* after the *Imām* (this is *Takbīratul Iḥrām*; there are three more *takbīrāt* after this), raising your hands up to your ears. Then lower them, placing them on or below your chest, putting the right hand on the left, and recite the following:

سُبْحَانَكَ اَللّٰهُمَّ وَبِحَمْدِكَ وَتَبَارَكَ اسْمُكَ وَتَعَالٰى جَدُّكَ وَجَلَّ
ثَنَآءُكَ وَلَآ إِلٰهَ غَيْرُكَ.

Subḥānakallāhumma wa biḥamdika	O Allāh, glory and praise are for You,
wa tabārakasmuka	and blessed is Your Name,
wa ta'ālā jadduka	and exalted is Your Majesty,
wa jalla thanā'uka	and Glorious is Your Praise
wa lā ilāha ghairuk	and there is no god but You.
(or you may read *ghairuka*).	

(Some Muslims recite Ṣūratul Fātiḥah instead of this.)

4 Now the *Imām* will say *Allāhu akbar* loudly; you follow him repeating the words quietly. There is no need to raise your hands up to your ears this time. Then, recite *Darūd*.

5 After this, the third *takbīr* will be said loudly by the *Imām* and those in the congregation will repeat it quietly. Then, if the dead person is an adult male Muslim, recite the following *du'ā'*:

اَللّٰهُمَّ اغْفِرْ لِحَيِّنَا وَمَيِّتِنَا وَشَاهِدِنَا وَغَآئِبِنَا وَصَغِيْرِنَا وَكَبِيْرِنَا
وَذَكَرِنَا وَأُنْثَانَا . اَللّٰهُمَّ مَنْ أَحْيَيْتَهُ مِنَّا فَأَحْيِهِ عَلَى الْإِسْلَامِ وَمَنْ
تَوَفَّيْتَهُ مِنَّا فَتَوَفَّهُ عَلَى الْإِيْمَانِ.

Allāhummaghfir liḥaiyinā	O Allāh, forgive those of us who are alive
wa maiyitinā	and those who have passed away,
wa shāhidinā wa ghā'ibinā	those present and those absent,
wa ṣaghīrinā wa kabīrinā	and our young and elderly,
wa dhakarinā wa unthāna.	the males and the females.
Allāhumma	O Allāh,
man aḥyaitahu minnā	he whom You keep alive from among us,
fa'aḥyihi 'alal islāmi	make him live according to Islām,
wa man tawaffaitahu minnā	and he whom You wish to die from among us,
fatawaffahu 'alal īmān.	let him die in the state of *Īmān* (faith).
	(at-Tirmidhī, Abū Dāwūd)

If the dead person is an adult female Muslim, then the second part of this *du'ā'* is replaced by:

اَللّٰهُمَّ مَنْ أَحْيَيْتَهَا مِنَّا فَأَحْيِهَا عَلَى الْإِسْلَامِ وَمَنْ تَوَفَّيْتَهَا مِنَّا
فَتَوَفَّهَا عَلَى الْإِيْمَانِ.

Allāhumma	O Allāh,
man aḥyaitahā minnā	she whom You keep alive from among us,
fa'aḥyihā 'alal islāmi,	make her live according to Islām,
wa man tawaffaitahā minnā	and she whom You wish to die from among us,
fatawaffahā 'alal īmān.	let her die in the state of *īmān*.

If the deceased is a boy, then recite the following:

اَللّٰهُمَّ اجْعَلْهُ لَنَا فَرَطًا وَّاجْعَلْهُ لَنَآ أَجْرًا وَّذُخْرًا وَّاجْعَلْهُ لَنَا
شَافِعًا وَّمُشَفَّعًا.

Allāhummaj'alhu lanā faraṭan	O Allāh, make him our forerunner
waj'alhu lanā ajran wa dhukhran	and make him for us a reward and a treasure
waj'alhu lanā shāfi'an	and make him one who will plead for us
wa mushaffa'ā.	and accept his pleading.

If the deceased is a girl, then recite the following:

اَللّٰهُمَّ اجْعَلْهَا لَنَا فَرَطًا وَّاجْعَلْهَا لَنَآ أَجْرًا وَّذُخْرًا وَّاجْعَلْهَا لَنَا
شَافِعَةً وَّمُشَفَّعَةً.

Allāhummaj'alhā lanā faraṭan	O Allāh, make her our forerunner
waj'alhā lanā ajran wa dhukhran	and make her for us a reward and a treasure
waj'alhā lanā shāfi'atan	and make her one who will plead for us
wa mushaffa'ah.	and accept her pleading.

6 After reciting whichever *du'ā'* is appropriate for the dead person, the *Imām* says the fourth *takbīr* loudly and those in the congregation repeat it quietly.

7 Then the *Imām* turns his face first to the right saying *Assalāmu 'alaikum wa raḥmatullāh*, and then to the left repeating the same words. Follow the *Imām*, repeating the words quietly.

This completes *Ṣalātul Janāzah*.

What did you learn? (2a)

Key Stage 3 (11–14)

1. Name the five basic duties of Islām and explain why they are so important in the life of a Muslim.
2. Write out the declaration of faith.
3. Name the five daily prayers, and explain the reason behind their spacing?
4. What does *Farḍ* mean? Add up how many *Farḍ rak'ahs* there are in the five daily prayers?
5. What is *Ṭahārah?*
6. What are the times in which we should not pray?
7. Write the meanings of:
   a. *Qiblah* b. *Qiyām* c. *Rukū'* d. *Sujūd*

Key Stage 4 (15–16)

1. *"Islam is based on five things:..."* Read the *Ḥadīth* stated on page 40 about the five pillars of Islam, and explain how they are intended to transform a Muslim's life.
2. If performing regular *Ṣalāh* does not affect our lives, there must be something wrong in our awareness of Allāh. Why? Explain in detail.

Key Stage 5 (17–18)

1. *"Our Ṣalāh is the first thing we will be asked about when we die and stand before Allāh."* Explain the significance of this statement in relation to the benefits of *Ṣalāh*.
2. Making *Niyyah* (intention) is vital at the start of *Ṣalāh*. Why is a *Niyyah* so important in every action of a Muslim?

What did you learn? (2b)

Key Stage 3 (11–14)

1. Write the names of the five daily prayers with their timings.
2. What should you recite after you finish your *Wuḍū'*? Write its meaning in English.
3. When does *Wuḍū'* need to be done again?
4. Why is *Ṭahārah* important in the life of a Muslim?
5. What is *Tayammum*, and why would a Muslim do this?
6. Write the meaning of:
   a. *Bismillāhir raḥmānir raḥīm.*
   b. *A'ūdhu billāhi minash shaiṭānir rajīm.*

What did you learn? (2c)

Key Stage 3 (11–14)

1. What is the meaning of *Tasbīḥ* which is recited in *Rukū'*?
2. What do we recite in *Sujūd?*
3. What is *Sajdatus Sahw?* Give two examples of instances when *Sajdatus Sahw* could be done.
4. Give four examples of things which invalidate your *Ṣalāh.*
5. What is the importance of *Ṣalātul Jumu'ah?*
6. When are you not allowed to say your *Ṣalāh?*
7. What is *Ṣalātul Janāzah?* When would you be guilty if you did not join it?

إِحْدَى عَشَرَ سُورَةً مِنَ الْقُرْآنِ

1 Sūratul Fātiḥah (1) سُورَةُ الْفَاتِحَة

بِسْمِ ٱللَّهِ ٱلرَّحْمَٰنِ ٱلرَّحِيمِ
ٱلْحَمْدُ لِلَّهِ رَبِّ ٱلْعَٰلَمِينَ
ٱلرَّحْمَٰنِ ٱلرَّحِيمِ
مَٰلِكِ يَوْمِ ٱلدِّينِ
إِيَّاكَ نَعْبُدُ وَإِيَّاكَ نَسْتَعِينُ
ٱهْدِنَا ٱلصِّرَٰطَ ٱلْمُسْتَقِيمَ
صِرَٰطَ ٱلَّذِينَ أَنْعَمْتَ عَلَيْهِمْ غَيْرِ ٱلْمَغْضُوبِ عَلَيْهِمْ وَلَا ٱلضَّآلِّينَ

Bismillāhir raḥmānir raḥīm.
Alḥamdu lillāhi rabbil 'ālamīn.
Arraḥmānir raḥīm.
Māliki yawmid dīn.
Iyyāka na'budu wa iyyāka nasta'īn.
Ihdinaṣ ṣirāṭal mustaqīm.
Ṣirāṭal ladhīna an'amta 'alaihim, ghairil maghḍūbi 'alaihim wa laḍ ḍāllīn.

In the name of Allāh, the Most Merciful, the Most Kind.
All praise is for Allāh, the Lord of the Universe.
The Most Merciful, the Most Kind.
Master of the Day of Judgement.
You alone we worship, from You alone we seek help.
Guide us along the straight path.
The path of those whom You have favoured, not of those who earned Your anger nor of those who went astray (or who are misguided).

2 Sūratun Nās (114) سُورَةُ النَّاس

بِسْمِ ٱللَّهِ ٱلرَّحْمَٰنِ ٱلرَّحِيمِ

قُلْ أَعُوذُ بِرَبِّ ٱلنَّاسِ. مَلِكِ ٱلنَّاسِ. إِلَٰهِ ٱلنَّاسِ. مِن شَرِّ ٱلْوَسْوَاسِ
ٱلْخَنَّاسِ. ٱلَّذِي يُوَسْوِسُ فِي صُدُورِ ٱلنَّاسِ. مِنَ ٱلْجِنَّةِ وَٱلنَّاسِ.

Bismillāhir raḥmānir raḥīm.
Qul a'ūdhu birabbin nās,
Malikin nās,
Ilāhin nās,
Min sharril waswāsil khannās,
Alladhī yuwaswisu fī ṣudūrin nās,
Minal jinnati wan nās.

In the name of Allāh, the Most Merciful, the Most Kind.
Say, I seek refuge in the Lord of mankind,
the King of mankind,
the God of mankind,
from the mischief of the sneaking whisperer (who whispers secretly),
who whispers into the hearts of mankind,
from among Jinn and mankind.

3 Sūratul Falaq (113) سُورَةُ الْفَلَق

بِسْمِ ٱللَّهِ ٱلرَّحْمَٰنِ ٱلرَّحِيمِ

قُلْ أَعُوذُ بِرَبِّ ٱلْفَلَقِ. مِن شَرِّ مَا خَلَقَ. وَمِن شَرِّ غَاسِقٍ إِذَا
وَقَبَ. وَمِن شَرِّ ٱلنَّفَّٰثَٰتِ فِي ٱلْعُقَدِ. وَمِن شَرِّ حَاسِدٍ إِذَا حَسَدَ.

Bismillāhir raḥmānir raḥīm.
Qul a'ūdhu birabbil falaq,
Min sharri mā khalaq,
Wa min sharri ghāsiqin idhā waqab,
Wa min sharrin naffāthāti fil 'uqad,
Wa min sharri ḥāsidin idhā ḥasad.

In the name of Allāh, the Most Merciful, the Most Kind.
Say, I seek refuge in the Lord of the Daybreak,
from the evil of what He has created,
and from the evil of the darkness when it is intense,
and from the evil of those who blow on knots (practise witchcraft),
and from the evil of the envier when he envies.

4 Sūratul Ikhlāṣ (112) سُورَةُ الإِخْلَاص

بِسْمِ ٱللَّهِ ٱلرَّحْمَٰنِ ٱلرَّحِيمِ

قُلْ هُوَ ٱللَّهُ أَحَدٌ . ٱللَّهُ ٱلصَّمَدُ . لَمْ يَلِدْ وَلَمْ يُولَدْ . وَلَمْ يَكُن
لَّهُۥ كُفُوًا أَحَدٌۢ .

Bismillāhir raḥmānir raḥīm.
Qul huwallāhu aḥad.
Allāhuṣ ṣamad.
Lam yalid wa lam yūlad.
Wa lam yakul lahū kufuwan aḥad.

In the name of Allāh, the Most Merciful, the Most Kind.
Say, He is Allāh, the One.
Allāh is Eternal and Absolute (lives forever and is above all needs).
None is born of Him nor is He born.
And there is none like Him.

5 Sūratul Lahab (111) سُورَةُ اللَّهَب / سُورَةُ المَسَد

بِسْمِ ٱللَّهِ ٱلرَّحْمَٰنِ ٱلرَّحِيمِ

تَبَّتْ يَدَآ أَبِي لَهَبٍ وَتَبَّ . مَآ أَغْنَىٰ عَنْهُ مَالُهُۥ وَمَا كَسَبَ .
سَيَصْلَىٰ نَارًا ذَاتَ لَهَبٍ . وَٱمْرَأَتُهُۥ حَمَّالَةَ ٱلْحَطَبِ .
فِي جِيدِهَا حَبْلٌ مِّن مَّسَدٍۭ .

Bismillāhir raḥmānir raḥīm.
Tabbat yadā abī lahabin watabb.
Mā aghnā ‘anhu māluhū wa mā kasab.
Sayaṣlā nāran dhāta lahab,
Wamra’atuhū ḥammālatal ḥaṭab,
Fī jīdihā ḥablum mim masad.

In the name of Allāh, the Most Merciful, the Most Kind.
May the hands of Abū Lahab perish—doomed he is.
His wealth and his gains shall not help him.
He shall enter a blazing fire,
and his wife, the carrier of firewood,
shall have a rope of palm fibre around her neck.

6 Sūratun Naṣr (110) سُورَةُ النَّصْر

بِسْمِ ٱللَّهِ ٱلرَّحْمَٰنِ ٱلرَّحِيمِ

إِذَا جَآءَ نَصْرُ ٱللَّهِ وَٱلْفَتْحُ . وَرَأَيْتَ ٱلنَّاسَ يَدْخُلُونَ فِي
دِينِ ٱللَّهِ أَفْوَاجًا . فَسَبِّحْ بِحَمْدِ رَبِّكَ وَٱسْتَغْفِرْهُ إِنَّهُۥ كَانَ تَوَّابًا .

Bismillāhir raḥmānir raḥīm.
Idhā jā'a naṣrullāhi wal fatḥ.
Wa ra'aitan nāsa yadkhulūna fī dīnillāhi afwājā.
Fasabbiḥ biḥamdi rabbika wastaghfirh,
Innahū kāna tawwābā.

In the name of Allāh, the Most Merciful, the Most Kind.
When the help of Allāh comes and the conquest,
and you see the people accepting the religion of Allāh in large numbers,
then glorify the praises of your Lord, and seek His forgiveness.
He is ever ready to forgive.

7 Sūratul Kāfirūn (109) سُورَةُ الكَافِرُون

بِسْمِ ٱللَّهِ ٱلرَّحْمَٰنِ ٱلرَّحِيمِ

قُلْ يَٰٓأَيُّهَا ٱلْكَٰفِرُونَ . لَآ أَعْبُدُ مَا تَعْبُدُونَ .
وَلَآ أَنتُمْ عَٰبِدُونَ مَآ أَعْبُدُ . وَلَآ أَنَا۠ عَابِدٌ مَّا عَبَدتُّمْ .
وَلَآ أَنتُمْ عَٰبِدُونَ مَآ أَعْبُدُ . لَكُمْ دِينُكُمْ وَلِىَ دِينِ .

Bismillāhir raḥmānir raḥīm.
Qul yā'aiyuhal kāfirūn,
Lā a'budu mā ta'budūn, wa lā antum 'ābidūna mā a'bud,
Wa lā ana 'ābidum mā 'abattum, wa lā antum 'ābidūna mā a'bud,
Lakum dīnukum wa liya dīn.

In the name of Allāh, the Most Merciful, the Most Kind.
Say: O unbelievers!
I do not worship what you worship,
and you do not worship what I worship.
Nor will I worship what you worship,
and you will not worship what I worship.
You have your own religion and I have mine.

8 Sūratul Kawthar (108) سُورَةُ ٱلْكَوْثَر

بِسْمِ ٱللَّهِ ٱلرَّحْمَٰنِ ٱلرَّحِيمِ

إِنَّآ أَعْطَيْنَٰكَ ٱلْكَوْثَرَ . فَصَلِّ لِرَبِّكَ وَٱنْحَرْ .

إِنَّ شَانِئَكَ هُوَ ٱلْأَبْتَرُ

Bismillāhir raḥmānir raḥīm.
Innā a'ṭainākal kawthar.
Faṣalli lirabbika wanḥar.
Inna shāni'aka huwal abtar.

In the name of Allāh, the Most Merciful, the Most Kind.
Indeed we have given you the Kawthar (Fountain of Abundance).
So pray to your Lord and make sacrifice.
Surely your hater is the one cut off (i.e. without an heir).

9 Sūratul Mā'ūn (107) سُورَةُ ٱلْمَاعُون

بِسْمِ ٱللَّهِ ٱلرَّحْمَٰنِ ٱلرَّحِيمِ

أَرَءَيْتَ ٱلَّذِي يُكَذِّبُ بِٱلدِّينِ . فَذَٰلِكَ ٱلَّذِى يَدُعُّ ٱلْيَتِيمَ .

وَلَا يَحُضُّ عَلَىٰ طَعَامِ ٱلْمِسْكِينِ . فَوَيْلٌ لِّلْمُصَلِّينَ .

ٱلَّذِينَ هُمْ عَن صَلَاتِهِمْ سَاهُونَ . ٱلَّذِينَ هُمْ يُرَآءُونَ . وَيَمْنَعُونَ ٱلْمَاعُونَ.

Bismillāhir raḥmānir raḥīm.
Ara'aital ladhī yukadhdhibu biddīn.
Fadhālikal ladhī yadu'-'ul yatīm.
Wa lā yaḥuḍḍu 'alā ṭa'āmil miskīn.
Fawailul lil muṣallīn.
Alladhīna hum 'an ṣalātihim sāhūn.
Alladhīna hum yurā'ūn.
Wa yamna'ūnal mā'ūn.

In the name of Allāh, the Most Merciful, the Most Kind.
Have you seen him who denies the religion (the judgement)?
It is he who (harshly) pushes aside the orphan,
and does not urge others to feed the poor and the needy.
Woe to those who do their Ṣalāh
but are forgetful of their Ṣalāh,
who show off
but refuse to give even the smallest help to others.

10 Sūrah Quraish (106) سُورَةُ قُرَيْشٍ

بِسْمِ ٱللَّهِ ٱلرَّحْمَٰنِ ٱلرَّحِيمِ

لِإِيلَٰفِ قُرَيْشٍ . إِۦلَٰفِهِمْ رِحْلَةَ ٱلشِّتَآءِ وَٱلصَّيْفِ . فَلْيَعْبُدُوا۟ رَبَّ هَٰذَا ٱلْبَيْتِ . ٱلَّذِىٓ أَطْعَمَهُم مِّن جُوعٍ وَءَامَنَهُم مِّنْ خَوْفٍۭ.

Bismillāhir raḥmānir raḥīm.
Li īlāfi quraish.
Īlāfihim riḥlatash shitā'i waṣ-ṣaif.
Falya'budū rabba hādhal bait.
Alladhī aṭ'amahum min jū'in wa āmanahum min khawf.

In the name of Allāh, the Most Merciful, the Most Kind.
For the tradition of the Quraish;
their tradition of travelling in winter and summer.
So they should worship the Lord of this house,
Who has fed them and protected them from hunger, and made them safe from fear.

11 Sūratul Fīl (105) سُورَةُ الْفِيلِ

بِسْمِ ٱللَّهِ ٱلرَّحْمَٰنِ ٱلرَّحِيمِ

أَلَمْ تَرَ كَيْفَ فَعَلَ رَبُّكَ بِأَصْحَٰبِ ٱلْفِيلِ . أَلَمْ يَجْعَلْ كَيْدَهُمْ فِى تَضْلِيلٍ . وَأَرْسَلَ عَلَيْهِمْ طَيْرًا أَبَابِيلَ . تَرْمِيهِم بِحِجَارَةٍ مِّن سِجِّيلٍ . فَجَعَلَهُمْ كَعَصْفٍ مَّأْكُولٍۭ.

Bismillāhir raḥmānir raḥīm.
Alam tara kaifa fa'ala rabbuka bi aṣḥābil fīl.
Alam yaj'al kaidahum fī taḍlīl.
Wa arsala 'alaihim ṭairan abābīl.
Tarmīhim biḥijāratim min sijjīl.
Faja'alahum ka'aṣfim ma'kūl.

In the name of Allāh, the Most Merciful, the Most Kind.
Have you not seen how your Lord dealt with the people of the elephant?
Did He not make their schemes to be nothing,
and send against them flocks of birds,
which pelted them with stones of hard-baked clay?
Thus he made them like eaten straw.

Lessons of Ṣalāh

Ṣalāh is the most important of the five basic duties of Islām after *Shahādah*. We come closer to Allāh by performing it correctly, regularly and with full awareness of its significance and meaning. At this stage, refresh your memory about the purpose of our creation and the need for performing Islāmic duties. Allāh has created us to worship Him. He says in the Qur'ān: *"Indeed I created Jinn and human beings for no other purpose but to worship Me."* (*Sūratudh Dhāriyāt* 51:56) So, whatever duty we carry out, we must bear in mind that we are doing it for the sake of Allāh. Only then can we expect to gain the desired benefits of the performance of *Ṣalāh*.

The lessons of *Ṣalāh* are:

1. *It brings men and women closer to Allāh.*
2. *It keeps human beings away from indecent, shameful and forbidden activities. (Sūratul 'Ankabūt 29:45)*
3. *It is a training programme designed to control evil desires and passions.*
4. *It purifies the heart, develops the mind and comforts the soul.*
5. *It is a constant reminder of Allāh and His greatness.*
6. *It develops discipline and willpower.*
7. *It is a guide to the most upright way of life.*
8. *It is a proof of true equality, solid unity and universal brotherhood.*
9. *It is the source of patience, courage, hope and confidence.*
10. *It is a means of cleanliness, purity and punctuality.*
11. *It develops gratitude, humility and refinement.*
12. *It is the demonstration of our obedience to our Creator.*
13. *It is a programme which prepares us to match our actions with our words.*
14. *It is the solid programme of preparing oneself for Jihād — striving one's utmost to please Allāh.*

If our *Ṣalāh* does not improve our conduct we must think seriously about where we are going wrong.

Zakāh

Zakāh (welfare contribution) is the third pillar of Islām. The Arabic word *Zakāh* means "to purify or cleanse". *Zakāh* is to be paid once a year on savings at the rate of two and a half per cent. This rate applies to cash, bank savings and gold and silver jewellery. The rate for cattle and agricultural produce is different.

Payment of *Zakāh* is a means of keeping our wealth clear of greed and selfishness. It also encourages us to be honest in our earnings and expenditure.

Zakāh is a compulsory payment and is neither charity nor a tax. Charity is optional and taxes can be used by the state for any purpose, but *Zakāh* has to be spent under fixed headings like helping the poor, the needy, payment of salaries to its collectors,

Niṣāb and Rate of Zakāh

Wealth on which *Zakāh* is payable	Amount which determines the payment of *Zakāh* (*Niṣāb*)	Rate of *Zakāh*
1. Agricultural produce	5 *Awsuq* (also *Awsāq*, 653 kg) per harvest*	5% in case of irrigated land; 10% of produce from rain-fed land
2. Gold, silver, ornaments of gold and silver	85 grams of gold or 595 grams of silver*	2.5% of value
3. Cash in hand or at the bank	Value of 595 grams of silver*	2.5% of amount
4. Merchandise	Value of 595 grams of silver*	2.5% of value of goods
5. Cows and buffaloes	30 in number	For every 30, one 1-year-old; for every 40, one 2-year-old.
6. Goats and sheep	40 in number	One for the first 40; two for 120; three for 300; one more for every 100.
7. Produce of mines	Any quantities	20% of value of produce
8. Camels	5 in number	a) up to 24, one sheep or goat for each five camels b) 25-35, one 1-year-old she-camel c) 36-45, one 2-year-old she-camel d) 46-60, one 3-year-old she-camel e) 61-75, one 4-year-old she-camel f) 76-90, two 2-year-old she-camels g) 91-120, two 3-year-old she-camels h) 121 or more, one 2-year-old she-camel for each additional 40, or one 3-year-old she-camel for each additional 50

* *Fiqhuz Zakāh* — Yūsuf al-Qaraḍāwī, vol. 1, pages 360, 372-373 (Beirut, 1977). English translation by Monzer Kahf, pages 232-236 (London, 1999).

to free captives and debtors, for travellers in need, to win over hearts of new converts and for the cause of Allāh (9:60).

Zakāh is an act of *'Ibādah*. *'Ibādah* is an Arabic term which means worship and obedience. It includes all activities of life, if we do them to please Allāh. We pay *Zakāh* to gain Allāh's favour.

Zakāh provides us with the opportunity of sharing our excess wealth with those less fortunate than ourselves. In fact, we and our wealth belong to Allāh. He is the real owner and we are merely the trustees of His wealth. We do our duty as trustees if we pay *Zakāh* as an obligatory part of *'Ibādah*. The words *Zakāh* and *Ṣadaqah* are used interchangeably in the *Qur'ān*.

We learned earlier that Islām is a complete code of life which includes, among other things, the economic side of life. Islām has its own economic principles. *Zakāh* is one of the basic principles of the Islāmic economy, based on social welfare and the fair distribution of wealth. In addition to the compulsory payment of *Zakāh*, Muslims are encouraged to make voluntary contributions to help the poor and needy, and for other social welfare purposes. This voluntary contribution is called *Ṣadaqah* (charity).

Through the payment of *Zakāh*, the rich share their wealth with the poor and thus the process of concentration of wealth is checked and a fair distribution of wealth is ensured. The categories for the use of *Zakāh* are mentioned in the *Qur'ān* (*Sūratut Tawbah* 9:60).

Ṣawm

Ṣawm (fasting), the fourth pillar of Islām, is another act of *'Ibādah*. All adult Muslims must fast from dawn to sunset every day of *Ramaḍān*, the ninth month of the Islāmic calendar. This means abstaining from eating, drinking and conjugal relations during the hours of fasting. Travellers and the sick can defer fasting during *Ramaḍān* and make up for it later.

Ṣawm develops self-control and helps us to overcome selfishness, greed, laziness and other faults. It is an annual training programme to refresh us for doing our duties for Allāh, our Creator and Sustainer. *Ṣawm* enables us to experience the pangs of hunger and thirst. We feel for ourselves what it is like to be hungry. We can begin to appreciate what it must be like for the poor and the unfortunate — the millions who go hungry every day. Fasting develops self-control, and teaches us not to think just about comfort. It also helps us to restrain our sexual passions. We must learn to control our appetite for food, love of comfort and sexual desires if we would like to be true servants of Allāh.

Ṣawm helps us to remain truly obedient to Allāh's commands. That is why the *Qur'ān* says: *"O you who believe, fasting is prescribed for you as it was prescribed for those before you that you are expected to be truly obedient." (2:183)* A truly obedient Muslim is called a *muttaqī* (a person with *taqwā*) and his true obedience or piety — developed through *Ṣawm* — is known as *taqwā* in Islām. *Taqwā* keeps a person away from sins and vices.

Ramaḍān is a month of blessings, mercy of Allāh and His forgiveness. It helps us to avoid the punishment of Hell in the life after death.

The duty of fasting is only for Allāh's sake and there is a very delightful and attractive reward for this in the life after death.

The following acts will break the fast if they occur during the fasting hours:

a. Deliberate eating or drinking.
b. Anything entering the body through the nose or mouth; this includes smoking or sniffing any powdered substance.
c. Having any conjugal relations (sex between husband and wife).

An injection in the muscle is allowed during fasting but not a nutritional injection. Unintentional eating or drinking due to forgetfulness or rinsing out the mouth or bathing and putting drops in the eye do not make the fast invalid.

A Muslim is expected to keep away from all bad actions during his fast. He should not tell a lie, break a promise or do any deceitful act.

The very purpose of fasting is to make a Muslim able to control his passions, so that he becomes a person of good deeds and intentions. Anger — a common human weakness — can also be brought under control by fasting.

In addition to the compulsory fasting in *Ramaḍān*, a Muslim may fast during other times of the year. These fasts will be treated as *Sunnah*.

Women are not allowed to fast during menstruation or post-childbirth bleeding. They are required to make up the days lost during this period at some other time. A Muslim must not fast:

a. On the day of *'Īdul Fiṭr*.
b. On the day of *'Īdul Aḍḥā*.

The *Qur'ān* was first revealed in the month of *Ramaḍān*. There is a night in the month which is "better than a thousand months" (97:3). This night is called *Lailatul Qadr* (Night of Power). According to *Ḥadīth*, this night occurs during the last ten days of *Ramaḍān* (most probably the odd-numbered nights). It is a night of great importance; we should worship as much as we can on this night.

An additional prayer known as *Tarāwīḥ* (20 *rak'ahs* or 8 *rak'ahs*) is offered during *Ramaḍān* after *'Ishā'*. This is a *sunnah* prayer in which efforts are made to recite as much of the *Qur'ān* as possible. In many mosques, the whole *Qur'ān* is recited in *Tarāwīḥ* prayer. This prayer is generally offered in congregation. Those who cannot join a congregation should offer *Tarāwīḥ* at home. A pre-dawn meal known as *Saḥūr* is taken in *Ramaḍān*.

At the end of *Ramaḍān* Muslims celebrate *'Īdul Fiṭr*, a day of thanksgiving and happiness. It is one of the great occasions for the Muslim community. On this day, Muslims offer special prayers in congregation and thank Allāh for His blessings and mercy.

Al-Ka'bah — The 'House of Allāh' at Makkah — ٱلْكَعْبَة

Ḥajj

Ḥajj is the fifth pillar of Islām. It is a visit to *al-Ka'bah*, the house of Allāh in *Makkah*, once in a lifetime by those Muslims who can afford to make the journey. It is performed during the period 8–13 *Dhul Ḥijjah*, the twelfth month of the Islāmic calendar (3:97; 22:27–30; 2:197).

Al-Ka'bah, also known as *Baitullāh* (House of Allāh), is a cube-like one-storey building which was built originally by Prophet *Ibrāhīm* (Abraham) and his son *Ismā'īl* (Ishmael). It is the first house ever built for the sole purpose of the worship of Allāh (3:96). Allāh has blessed *al-Ka'bah*. Muslims who can afford to make the journey and are physically fit come here every year from all over the world.

The occasion may rightly be called the *Annual International Muslim Assembly*. During *Ḥajj*, Islāmic brotherhood becomes particularly evident and can be experienced in a special way by everyone who takes part. Barriers of language, territory, colour and race disappear and the bond of faith is uppermost. Everyone has the same status in the House of Allāh — the status of His servant.

Ḥajj has a number of important rituals associated with it, including:

1. *Putting on Iḥrām (2:200).*
2. *Going around al-Ka'bah seven times (2:200).*
3. *A fast walk between aṣ-Ṣafā and al-Marwah near al-Ka'bah (2:158).*
4. *Visiting and staying at Minā, 'Arafāt and Muzdalifah (2:198).*
5. *Throwing pebbles at three fixed places in Minā (2:200).*
6. *Shaving or trimming hair (2:200; 48:27).*
7. *Sacrifice of an animal (2:196, 200).*

At the time of *Ḥajj*, while approaching *Makkah*, a pilgrim must put on *Iḥrām* before reaching a point called *Mīqāt* (station). For men, *Iḥrām* consists of two sheets of unsewn white cloth. This is the very simple form of dress a pilgrim must wear in place of his normal everyday clothes. For a woman, *Iḥrām* is her ordinary dress.

This change is very significant. It reminds the pilgrim of his position in relation to Allāh. He is a humble servant of his Creator. It also reminds him that after death he will be wrapped in white sheets and his favourite or expensive clothes will be left behind.

When putting on *Iḥrām*, pilgrims express their intention *(Niyyah)* by saying: "I intend to put on *Iḥrām* for *Ḥajj*."

There are then some restrictions on the pilgrim while in the state of *Iḥrām*. He or she *must not:*

a. use perfume	—	*to help forget enjoyment of ordinary daily life*
b. kill or harm animals, even insects	—	*to feel that everything belongs to Allāh*
c. break or uproot plants	—	*to kill one's urge for aggression and feel a love for nature*
d. hunt	—	*to develop mercy*
e. marry or take part in a wedding	—	*to forget normal life and think of the Creator*
f. do anything dishonest or arrogant	—	*to behave like a servant of Allāh*
g. carry arms	—	*to give up aggressive attitudes*
h. cover the head (males)	—	*to express humbleness*
i. cover the face (females)	—	*to feel a pure atmosphere*
j. wear shoes covering ankles	—	*to express simplicity*
k. cut hair or clip nails	—	*to express non-interference with nature*
l. have conjugal relations	—	*to forget worldly pleasure*

All these restrictions make a pilgrim think of Allāh and his ultimate goal in life — success in the life after death — and nothing else. While in *Iḥrām* the pilgrim recites *Talbiyah* as follows:

لَبَّيْكَ اللَّهُمَّ لَبَّيْكَ، لَبَّيْكَ لَا شَرِيْكَ لَكَ لَبَّيْكَ،

إِنَّ الْحَمْدَ وَالنِّعْمَةَ لَكَ وَالْمُلْكُ، لَا شَرِيْكَ لَكَ

Labbaikallāhumma labbaik, labbaika lā shaīka laka labbaik,
innal ḥamda wan ni'mata laka wal mulk, lā sharīka lak.

Here I am O Lord, here I am, here I am, You have no partner, here I am,
surely praise, blessings and the kingdom are for You, You have no partner.

One of the important things pilgrims do is to drink from the well of *Zamzam*, located to the south of *al-Ka'bah*. *Hājar* (Hagar), the mother of Prophet *Ismā'īl* (Prophet *Ibrāhīm's* eldest son), discovered the well as she ran between *aṣ-Ṣafā* and *al-Marwah*, desperately searching for water for baby *Ismā'īl*.

Ḥajj has in it all the lessons of *Ṣalāh*, *Zakāh* and *Ṣawm*. Do you remember why we offer *Ṣalāh*, pay *Zakāh* and fast? We offer *Ṣalāh* to remember Allāh, pay *Zakāh* to please Him and fast only for His sake. During *Ṣalāh* we present ourselves to Allāh five times a day, but during *Ḥajj* we have to think of Allāh all the time. At the time of *Ṣalāh*, we face towards *al-Ka'bah*, but during *Ḥajj* we go there in person. *Zakāh* teaches us to pay part of our savings for welfare and other good causes for Allāh's sake, but during *Ḥajj* we sacrifice much more of our money for the pleasure of Allāh.

Muslims from all parts of the world perform a lesser pilgrimage called *'Umrah* (2:158). It can be performed at any time of the year. For *'Umrah*, a person has to put on *Iḥrām* and do rituals 1, 2, 3 and 6 only (see page 79).

Ṣawm teaches us to control ourselves during daylight hours from eating, drinking or smoking or having conjugal relations. But in the state of *Iḥrām* there are many more restrictions. (Eating and drinking are not prohibited in the state of *Iḥrām* though.)

What do we learn from all these exercises during *Ḥajj?* We learn that we belong to Allāh, we will return to Him and we must do as He commands us. If we do, we will surely be successful in this life and in the *Ākhirah*.

Jihād

Jihād is the use of all our energies and resources to establish the Islāmic system of life, in order to gain Allāh's favour. *Jihād* is an Arabic word which means "to try one's utmost". It is a continuous process. In its first phase a Muslim learns to control his own passions and intentions. We need to strive hard to achieve this. This is *Jihād* within ourselves and is the basis for the comprehensive *Jihād* which is concerned with establishing *Ma'rūf* (right) and removing *Munkar* (evil) from our lives and from society. It demands the use of all our material and mental resources. Eventually we may be required to give our life for the cause of Islām.

The aim of *Jihād* is to seek the pleasure of Allāh. This must not be forgotten because this purpose is the basis of all Islāmic endeavours.

Earlier, we learned about the basic duties of *Shahādah*, *Ṣalāh*, *Zakāh*, *Ṣawm* and *Ḥajj*. All these duties teach us to obey Allāh and gain His favour so that we pass the test on the Day of Judgement and receive the reward of entering Paradise — the place of permanent happiness, joy and peace.

Regular and conscious performance of the four basic duties should motivate us to live and die for the cause of Islām, which we believe to be the only sure way to success in this life and in the hereafter. In other words, all Islāmic duties should prepare us to engage in *Jihād*. *Jihād* is the end result of our efforts in *Ṣalāh*, *Zakāh*, *Ṣawm* and *Ḥajj*. We cannot think of Islām without *Jihād*.

We would like to see truth prevail and falsehood vanish, but we are aware that this cannot happen on its own; we have to do our utmost to achieve it. The performance of other Islāmic duties will be meaningless if they do not motivate us to engage in *Jihād*.

The method of *Jihād* is the one practised by Prophet *Muḥammad* ﷺ. His life is the perfect example for us and we will learn about it later.

Our duty as Muslims is to practise Allāh's commands and to urge others to do the same. This duty has been given to us by Allāh in His own words in the *Qur'ān:*

"You are the best Ummah (community); you have been raised for mankind so that you command what is right and forbid what is evil, and you believe in Allāh." (3:110)

We should ask others to be obedient to Allāh in a persuasive and convincing way. Our own lifestyle will count for much here. It is most important that we try hard to practise what we say. Allāh does not like those who say something but do something different. The *Qur'ān* says: *"Why do you ask of others the right conduct and you yourselves forget?" (2:44)* In another place in the *Qur'ān*, Allāh says, *"O you who believe! Why do you say that which you do not do? It is most hateful to Allāh that you say that which you do not." (61:2–3)*

These verses clearly direct us to compare our own deeds with our words. To achieve this, we must do good ourselves and also urge others to do the same. This will enable us to remove our weaknesses and deficiencies. None of us is perfect, but our imperfections will gradually decrease if we do our very best to pursue our duty of *Jihād*.

What did you learn? (2d)

Key Stage 3 (11–14)

1. What does the word *Zakāh* mean, and how often should it be paid?
2. What is the rate of *Zakāh* on your cash savings?
3. What are the times during which we fast in *Ramaḍān?*
4. Why is *Lailatul Qadr* such an important night?
5. Write a letter telling a non-Muslim friend about *'Īdul Fiṭr*.
6. What is the *Ḥajj* and what is it intended to teach us?

Key Stage 4 (15–16)

1. What lesson do we learn from the payment of *Zakāh?*
2. Which people are helped by our giving *Zakāh?*
3. What does *Ṣawm* develop in us and how is it a training programme?
4. What actions make our fasting invalid?
5. *Ḥajj* is called the Annual International Muslim Assembly. Explain why, discussing the whole concept of Islāmic Brotherhood (and Sisterhood).
6. Does the phrase 'Holy War' correctly explain the full meaning of *Jihād?* Give examples to explain your answer.

Key Stage 5 (17–18)

1. Explain the importance of *Zakāh* in the context of social welfare in an Islāmic society.
2. What are the moral and social lessons of *Ṣawm?* Give examples of how this month of training should improve our conduct for the rest of the year.
3. What is the significance of putting on *iḥrām* during *Ḥajj?*
4. *"Living as a Muslim in a non-Muslim society can be described as Jihād."* Explain this statement with practical examples from your own experiences.

The Life of Muḥammad ﷺ 3

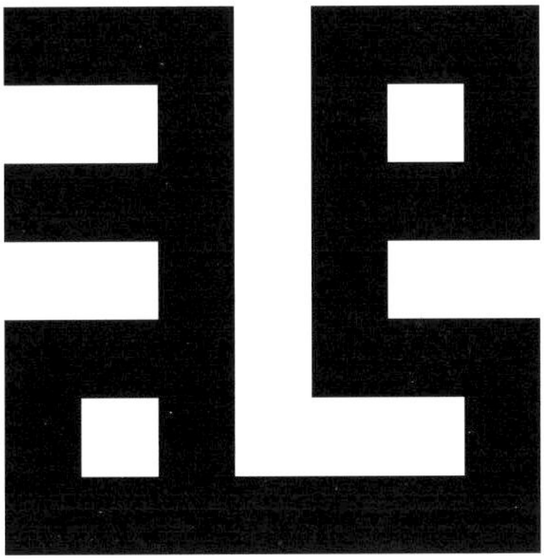

Muḥammad ﷺ

Introduction

"Indeed, in the Messenger of Allāh, you have for you an excellent model (uswatun ḥasanah), for all who hope (to meet) Allāh and the Last Day and remember Allāh very much." (33:21)
"We sent you (Muḥammad) not but as a mercy for the Universe." (21:107)
"He it is who has sent His Messenger with the guidance and the religion of truth, that He may make it victorious over all religions, however much idolators may hate it." (61:9)

So far you have been learning the basics of Islām. Now it is time to learn about our great and dear Prophet, *Muḥammad* ﷺ. It is through *Muḥammad* ﷺ that Allāh has completed the Islāmic way of life.

No other person in the history of mankind has left so great an impact on the life of his followers as *Muḥammad* ﷺ, the last and final messenger of Allāh. His life is the best example *(uswatun ḥasanah)* for us to follow. He has shown us how to obey Allāh, the Lord of the Universe. Allāh says in the *Qur'ān:*

"Say (O Muḥammad), if you love Allāh, follow me; Allāh will love you and forgive your sins, Allāh is Forgiving and Merciful." (3:31)

It means that Allāh will be pleased with us only if we practise Islām as practised by *Muḥammad* ﷺ. He has been described in the *Qur'ān* as *"a mercy for the universe (raḥmatul lil 'ālamīn)"* (21:107).

Muḥammad's ﷺ duty, according to the *Qur'ān*, was to make Islām supreme over all other systems of life (61:9, 48:28, 9:33). In other words, you can say that *Muḥammad's* ﷺ duty as the final messenger of Allāh was to establish the truth and remove falsehood from society. As Muslims, we must also work towards the establishment of the supremacy of Allāh's Law and the removal of evil from the society in which we live. This is *Jihād*, which we learned about earlier.

The difference between *Muḥammad* ﷺ and us is that he received guidance direct from Allāh through revelation *(Waḥī)*, but we have not. He was the final messenger of Allāh (18:110; 33:40). *Muḥammad* ﷺ was not only a messenger but a human as well. He was not a super-human being, but a mortal man. Yet he had extraordinary qualities that distinguished him as the very best human being in the whole history of mankind, a shining example for all to follow.

Birth and Childhood

Muḥammad ﷺ was born into the noble tribe of the *Quraish* in Makkah, Arabia, in 571 CE (Christian/Common Era)*. His father, *'Abdullāh*, died before his birth and *Āminah*, his mother died when he was only six. A few days after his birth he was given to *Ḥalīmah*, who took care of him until he was five years and one month old, when he was returned to the care of his mother. It was the custom of the *Quraish* to give their new-born babies to foster-mothers (wet nurses) for breast-feeding.

After the death of his mother, his grandfather, *'Abdul Muṭṭalib*, looked after him. From early childhood *Muḥammad* ﷺ suffered one shock after another. His grandfather died when he was only eight years old. *Muḥammad* ﷺ was then looked after by his uncle, *Abū Ṭālib*, a leader of the *Quraish* and a businessman. The name *Muḥammad* means 'praiseworthy'.

Business Trip to ash-Shām (now Syria)

Muḥammad ﷺ was growing up in the affectionate care of his uncle, *Abū Ṭālib*, when at the age of twelve he accompanied him on a business trip to *ash-Shām*. When their caravan reached *Buṣrā* in *ash-Shām*, a Christian monk called *Baḥīrā* invited them to a dinner. This was unusual. *Abū Ṭālib* and his caravan had passed this way before, several times, but had never been asked in by the monk. All members of the caravan went to the dinner except *Muḥammad* ﷺ who stayed behind, probably to look after the camels and their baggage. *Baḥīrā* insisted on *Muḥammad's* ﷺ joining in the dinner. When he did, *Baḥīrā* asked him a few questions, and *Muḥammad* ﷺ answered precisely and to the point.

When he heard the answers, *Baḥīrā* — a person knowledgeable about Christianity and the *Bible* — recognised from what he knew that the boy, *Muḥammad* ﷺ, was going to be a prophet in the future. He advised *Abū Ṭālib* to take special care of his nephew. When they finished their trading, *Abū Ṭālib* lost no time in returning to *Makkah* with *Muḥammad* ﷺ.

---

* The Prophet's biographers have differed about the exact year of his birth. Some give 569 CE or 570 CE, but I have preferred *Shiblī Nu'mānī's* view from his famous *Sīratun Nabī*: 571 CE.

Young Shepherd

Whilst still a boy *Muḥammad* ﷺ tended sheep, so he had plenty of time to think and reflect upon the situation around him. He moved around with his flock in the vast expanse of the Arabian desert. It provided him with a unique opportunity to have a clear vision of nature and to see the wonders of the creation of Allah. *Muḥammad* ﷺ was very proud of having spent his boyhood as a shepherd. He used to say, *"Allāh sent no prophet who was not a shepherd. Mūsā (Moses) was a shepherd, Dāwūd (David) was also a shepherd." (al-Bukhārī)*

The reason for this might be that Allāh wanted His prophets to gain the experience of life as a shepherd, to help deal with human beings with rare patience whilst preaching Allāh's message. It is very difficult to control a flock of sheep, goats or camels which do not have any understanding or sense of right and wrong. It needs a lot of patience to handle animals. This experience was very useful for the prophets in carrying out their real duty of preaching the message of Allāh.

Teenager, Ḥarbul Fijār and Ḥilful Fuḍūl

When *Muḥammad* ﷺ was fifteen, a local war broke out during the *Ḥajj* season between the tribes of *Quraish* and *Hawāzin*. According to Makkan tradition, war was forbidden in the pilgrimage season (known as 'sacred months'). Despite this, the war lasted for four years, with intervals, and caused tremendous hardship to people on both sides. Life was becoming intolerable because of the unnecessary bloodshed. Hence it was called the Sacrilegious War *(Ḥarbul Fijār)*.

The reason for the war seemed silly to *Muḥammad* ﷺ and he felt quite disgusted at the senseless bloodshed. It made people think. It inspired many of them to take steps to stop the war and make peace.

Upon the initiative of *az-Zubair bin 'Abdul Muṭṭalib, Muḥammad's* ﷺ uncle, a meeting was called at the house of *'Abdullāh bin Jud'ān*, who was a person of influence and wealth. A society called *Ḥilful Fuḍūl* (Alliance for Charity) was formed at this meeting to help those affected by this senseless war, the oppressed, the poor and the needy. *Muḥammad* ﷺ was present at the meeting and took the following oath: *"I uphold the pact concluded in my presence when Ibn Jud'ān gave us a great banquet. Should it ever be invoked, I shall immediately rise to answer the call."*

The participation of *Muḥammad* ﷺ in this alliance is a proof of his concern and interest in welfare activities, even when he was a youth. There is a lesson for you here. As young people, when you study the life of *Muḥammad* ﷺ, you should decide to take part in the welfare of people in general and the welfare of your fellow youngsters in particular. You should study the life of *Muḥammad* ﷺ, take lessons from it and put them into practice. If you look around you, you will find many unjust and wrong things are taking root in society. You should do whatever you can to remedy injustices and wrongdoings. If you do so, Allāh will reward you in this life and in the life after death *(Ākhirah)*.

Marriage

As *Muḥammad* ﷺ grew up, he helped in running the business of his uncle, *Abū Ṭālib*, who was managing his family with some difficulty. During this time, *Muḥammad* ﷺ received an offer from a noble lady named *Khadījah* to look after her business affairs. *Muḥammad's* ﷺ fame as an honest and upright young man had now become well known in *Makkah* which is why *Khadījah* made the proposal.

Muḥammad ﷺ accepted the offer and set out for *ash-Shām* with the merchandise of *Khadījah*, accompanied by her slave called *Maisarah*. This was *Muḥammad's* ﷺ second business trip to *ash-Shām*. He sold the goods and bought what he was told to before returning to *Makkah*. He made big profits for *Khadījah* on this trip because of his intelligence, skill and honesty. It was almost double what anyone else had earned for *Khadījah* before. During the journey, his companion *Maisarah* noticed that *Muḥammad* ﷺ was protected from the heat of the sun by clouds. On their return, *Maisarah* hurried to *Khadījah* and told her about this unusual experience of *Muḥammad* ﷺ and the big profits he had made for her.

Khadījah, the daughter of *Khuwailid*, was a determined, intelligent and noble woman. She was impressed by the ability, noble character and fine performance of *Muḥammad* ﷺ. *Khadījah* decided to send a proposal of marriage to *Muḥammad* ﷺ. On the advice of his uncle, *Abū Ṭālib*, *Muḥammad* ﷺ agreed to the proposal and the wedding ceremony went ahead. Now *Muḥammad* ﷺ was a family man and the marriage marked the beginning of a new phase in his life. He was twenty-five years of age and *Khadījah* was forty and a widow.

From the marriage, they had six children — two boys, *al-Qāsim* and *'Abdullāh* (also known as *Ṭāhir* and *Ṭaiyib*), and four girls, *Zainab*, *Ruqaiyah*, *Umm Kulthūm* and *Fāṭimah*. Both sons died before his prophethood but the daughters lived into Islām, embraced it and later migrated to *Madīnah*.

Physical Features

Muḥammad ﷺ was a handsome man of medium build — neither very tall nor short. He had a large head, thick black hair, a wide forehead, heavy eyebrows and large dark eyes with long eyelashes. He had a fine nose, well placed teeth, a thick beard, a long handsome neck and a wide chest and shoulders. His skin was light coloured and he had thick palms and feet. He walked steadily with firm steps. His appearance had the mark of deep thought and contemplation. His eyes gave the feeling of the authority of a commander and a natural leader.

Rebuilding of the Ka'bah

The *Ka'bah* needed repairs or rather rebuilding after a sudden flood had damaged it and cracked its walls. The task was divided among the four clans of the *Quraish*. *Muḥammad* ﷺ took an active part in the work. The rebuilding progressed and the walls were raised until it was time to place the Black Stone, *al-Ḥajarul Aswad*, on the south eastern corner of the *Ka'bah*. The Black Stone was regarded as very sacred by the Makkans and it is still regarded as sacred by Muslims. At the time of *Ḥajj*, the pilgrims kiss this stone as a mark of respect and as the *Sunnah* (practice) of *Muḥammad* ﷺ.

There were arguments about who should have the honour of placing this holy stone in its place. The situation became tense and there was the possibility of a civil war over the issue. To avoid bloodshed, an idea put forward by *Abū Umaiyah*, the oldest man in *Makkah*, was accepted. He proposed to all the people present, "Let the first man to enter the gate of the mosque next morning decide the matter in dispute among us."

What a pleasant surprise! The first man to enter the mosque was *Muḥammad* ﷺ! All the people shouted in a chorus, "This is the trustworthy one *(al-Amīn)*, this is *Muḥammad*. We accept his judgement."

When he came to them, they asked him to decide the matter and he agreed. He said, "Give me a cloak." When they brought him a cloak, he spread it on the ground, placed the Black Stone over it and said, "Let the elders of each clan hold on to one edge of the cloak." They did so and carried the stone to its place. *Muḥammad* ﷺ then picked up the stone and put it in its place on the wall of the *Ka'bah*. In this way he acted as an umpire (arbiter) among his people and averted a bloody civil war. The rebuilding continued and was completed by the *Quraish*. *Muḥammad* ﷺ was then thirty-five years old.

This event shows beyond any doubt that even before his prophethood, *Muḥammad* ﷺ was regarded as a judge and a referee for the *Quraish* at the time of their disputes and crises. He earned the titles of *al-Amīn* (the trustworthy) and *aṣ-Ṣādiq* (the truthful). The irony was that after his prophethood, many of those same people turned against him because of their ignorance and arrogance which made them too stone-hearted to respond to the call of the truth.

Search for the Truth

Muḥammad ﷺ was a soft spoken, gentle person who loved to think and meditate. He was not like others of his age, in that he had no interest in the attractions of the worldly life, a characteristic suited to a person destined to be the guide and teacher for the whole of mankind.

Muḥammad ﷺ very often used to retreat in seclusion and solitude to a cave, *Ḥirā'*, in mount *Nūr*. There he passed his time in meditation and devotion. He used to pass the month of *Ramaḍān* in this cave, where he immersed himself deep into thoughts about the mysteries of nature. He had an eager longing in his heart and searched seriously for the truth.

Why did he do this? He did it because he did not find the answers to the questions agitating his inquisitive mind about man, his creation and his ultimate goal. He was also unhappy about the feuds, conflicts, strife and divisions in the society around him.

He was fed up with existing social and political systems. The religions of the Jews and the Christians at that time were so corrupted by the rabbis and priests that they no longer had any appeal to reason and wisdom. He was unable to adjust himself to the senseless bloodshed, tribal disputes, oppression of the helpless by the powerful, idol worship and the low status of women.

The Makkans worshipped idols made by themselves. *Muḥammad* ﷺ used to think about the stupidity of idol worship. The idols could not move, talk or do anything. How could they respond to the prayers of human beings?

All these appeared nonsensical to *Muḥammad's* ﷺ thinking mind. The retreat in the cave was to find answers to these deep-rooted feelings in his own heart. It was a search for comfort, consolation, peace, tranquillity and right guidance. Could it be anything else? Of course not. *Muḥammad's* ﷺ mind was full of feelings, sympathy, and concern for the welfare of the people of *Makkah*. How could his upright mind rest while anarchy, injustice, falsehood and exploitation were rife in the city?

These idols, including the three biggest, *Hubal*, *al-Lāt*, and *al-'Uzzā*, were lifeless stones unable to help themselves if somebody happened to break them. But the Makkans worshipped them, asked their help, took oaths in their name and fought for them. *Muḥammad's* ﷺ curious mind was searching for the truth, to get rid of the social misdeeds and change the existing social and political order. It was during the days of his retreat in the month of *Ramaḍān* that Allāh, the Lord of the Universe, favoured *Muḥammad* ﷺ with His blessing — the first revelation of the *Qur'ān*.

Mount Ḥirā' — the first place of revelation

Receiving the Truth

Muḥammad ﷺ had reached the age of forty when one night, while meditating in his mountain retreat in *Ḥirā'* during *Ramaḍān*, an angel appeared before him.

"Read!" said the angel. *"I am not a reader,"* replied *Muḥammad* ﷺ. At this, the angel hugged him and squeezed him so hard that he thought he would die of suffocation. He was then released and the angel again said, *"Read!"* *Muḥammad* ﷺ gave the same reply. The angel squeezed him harder and then released him. The angel asked him a third time, *"Read!"* *Muḥammad* ﷺ repeated his reply, *"I am not a reader."* The angel hugged him again even harder for the third time. *Muḥammad's* ﷺ fear of suffocation increased, so he asked, *"What shall I read?"* The angel then released him, saying:

اِقْرَأْ بِاَسْمِ رَبِّكَ اَلَّذِى خَلَقَ .

خَلَقَ اَلْإِنْسَـٰنَ مِنْ عَلَقٍ .

اِقْرَأْ وَرَبُّكَ اَلْأَكْرَمُ .

اَلَّذِى عَلَّمَ بِاَلْقَلَمِ .

عَلَّمَ اَلْإِنْسَـٰنَ مَالَمْ يَعْلَمْ .

"Read in the name of your Lord Who created,
Created man from something that clings.
Read, and your Lord is most generous,
Who taught by the pen,
Taught man what he did not know."
(96:1–5)

Muḥammad ﷺ recited the verses and felt as though the words were written on his heart. These are the first revealed verses of the *Qur'ān*.

How wondrous that Allāh should choose for His messenger an *ummiyy* — someone who could neither read nor write (7:157–158; 29:48–49; 62:2). In those days only very few people in Arabia learnt to read or write. The verses of the *Qur'ān* surpassed all literature of the time, and have never been matched since. Indeed, they cannot be equalled (17:88; 2:23; 10:37–38). Imagine the astonishment of the Arabs to hear such powerful, perfect words coming from *Muḥammad* ﷺ.

Muḥammad ﷺ was greatly troubled by this strange happening. He looked around and saw nothing. He was fearful and terrified. He stood motionless.

Muḥammad ﷺ looked at the sky and was surprised to see the angel *Jibrā'īl* flying in the shape of a giant man. The angel said, "O *Muḥammad*, you are the Messenger of Allāh and I am *Jibrā'īl*."

And wherever he looked, *Muhammad* ﷺ saw *Jibrā'il* flying in the distance. He stood still until the angel disappeared.

Muḥammad ﷺ rushed home in a panic and sat close to *Khadījah*. He told her all that had happened. *Khadījah*, his noble, loving and caring wife, had faith in the character of her husband and comforted him, saying, *"Rejoice, O son of my uncle, and be of good heart. Surely by Him in Whose Hand is Khadījah's soul, I have hope that you will be the prophet of this people. You have never done any wrong to anyone. You are kind to others and you help the poor. So Allāh will not let you down." Muḥammad* ﷺ asked *Khadījah* to wrap him up in blankets. He was wrapped up and fell asleep.

Khadījah then went to her cousin, *Waraqah bin Nawfal bin Asad bin 'Abdul 'Uzzā*. He was a blind old man and a Christian. He had knowledge of the scriptures of the Torah and the Gospel. *Waraqah* heard all that had happened from *Khadījah* and said, "Holy! Holy! By Him in Whose Power is *Waraqah's* soul, if what you narrate is true, O *Khadījah*, then this is the same one who keeps the secrets (angel *Jibrā'īl*) whom Allah had sent to *Moses*. Tell him to be patient and firm." *Khadījah* returned home to comfort and reassure her husband with the good news *Waraqah* had told her.

There was a pause for some days or may be a few months between the first revelation and the second revelation when *Muḥammad* ﷺ was very sad. Then he saw the angel *Jibrā'īl* again, flying in the sky seated in a floating chair. The Prophet ﷺ became frightened and rushed home. He asked *Khadījah* to cover him up. She wrapped him with blankets and he fell asleep. After a few moments, *Khadījah* noticed that the Prophet ﷺ was shivering, breathing deeply and sweating. The angel *Jibrā'īl* brought the second revelation to him which was:

"O you who lie wrapped in your mantle, arise and warn! Glorify your Lord. Purify yourself. Give up uncleanliness. Give not in order to have more in return. For the sake of your Lord, endure patiently." (74:1-7)

Seeing him in this position, *Khadījah* pleaded with *Muḥammad* ﷺ to rest a little longer. But *Muḥammad* ﷺ was now reassured and said in a firm voice, *"O Khadījah, the time of slumber and rest is past. Jibrā'īl has asked me to warn men and call them to Allāh and to His worship. But whom shall I call? And who will listen to me?"*

Khadījah encouraged and assured *Muḥammad* ﷺ about the success of his prophethood and declared her own acceptance of Islām, the first person to do so. It is very important to note and appreciate that the first human to accept Islam was *Khadījah*.

How marvellous it is! *Khadījah* accepts her husband as the Prophet of Allāh! Who can better testify to the integrity of a person than his wife? She knew *Muḥammad* ﷺ better than anyone else did, and could testify to his honesty and trustworthiness. No man can hide his weakness from his wife because she knows him so closely and intimately. The present day adult married Muslims should follow this excellent example of our beloved Prophet *Muḥammad* ﷺ. The world would be a much better place if we could achieve such trust by the Grace of Allāh.

The Islāmic Movement Begins

The revelation marked the beginning of *Muḥammad's* ﷺ role as a messenger of Allāh. It was also the starting point of the Islāmic movement carried out by him during the rest of his life. The first phase of the movement lasted for three years, from 610 CE (the year of revelation) to the end of 612 CE.

To begin with, *Muḥammad* ﷺ preached the message of Allāh only to his friends, his closest relatives and those whom he could trust. *'Alī*, his cousin, the son of *Abū Ṭālib*, was the second Muslim and the third was *Zaid* son of *Ḥārithah* (*Muḥammad's* ﷺ servant). *Abū Bakr* was the first from among *Muḥammad's* ﷺ friends to become a Muslim. It is worth noting the composition of the early Muslims.

First, *Khadījah*, Muḥammad's ﷺ wife, accepts Islām; second, *'Alī*, his cousin; third, *Zaid*, his household servant. Outside the household, *Abū Bakr,* a respected businessman and a close friend of *Muḥammad* ﷺ, accepted Islām without the slightest doubt or hesitation. All of them were near and dear to him.

'Alī Accepts Islam

This, briefly, is how *'Alī*, the cousin of the Prophet ﷺ and then a boy of only ten, accepted the truth. Allāh taught *Muḥammad* ﷺ through angel *Jibrā'il* how to make ablution *(Wuḍū')* and how to pray. *Muḥammad* ﷺ in turn taught *Khadījah* and both of them used to offer *Ṣalāh* together.

'Alī saw the Prophet ﷺ and his wife kneeling and prostrating and reciting the *Qur'ān*. *'Alī* was amazed at this unusual scene and asked the Prophet ﷺ after the prayer, "To whom did you prostrate yourselves?" The Prophet ﷺ answered, "We have prostrated ourselves to Allāh who has sent me as a Prophet and has commanded me to call human beings unto Him."

The Prophet ﷺ then invited *'Alī* to worship only Allāh and to accept the message of Allāh revealed to him.

He also recited to him some verses from the *Qur'ān*. *'Alī* felt excited and thrilled but thought for a moment and said he would consult his father, *Abū Ṭālib*, about this. He passed the night agitated and restless, thinking about the call of *Muḥammad* ﷺ. Next morning, he rushed to the Prophet ﷺ and declared his faith in Islām. The young boy said, "Allāh created me without consulting *Abū Ṭālib*, my father. Why then should I consult him in order to worship Allāh?"

The story of young *'Alī* should inspire and motivate young people to work for Islām to make living on this earth meaningful and purposeful. Rest assured, this is the way to peace and happiness. *'Alī*, the first Muslim boy, accepted this peace — Islām.

Notable Early Muslims

You should know some of the names of the people who accepted Islām and later became famous in Islāmic history.

Early Muslims included: *'Alī bin Abī Ṭālib, Zaid bin Ḥārithah, Abū Bakr bin Abī Quḥāfah, 'Uthmān bin 'Affān, Sa'd bin Abī Waqqāṣ, 'Abdur Raḥmān bin 'Awf, Ṭalḥah bin 'Ubaidillāh, Abū Dharr al-Ghifārī, az-Zubair bin al-'Awwām, Abū 'Ubaidah bin al-Jarrāḥ, al-Arqam bin Abī al-Arqam al-Makhzūmī* (also known as *al-Arqam bin 'Abdi Manāf bin Asad*), *Ṣuhaib ar-Rūmī, 'Abdullāh bin Mas'ūd, Khabbāb bin al-Aratt, 'Uthmān bin Maẓ'ūn, Ja'far bin Abī Ṭālib* and *Nu'aim bin 'Abdullāh.*

Women were not left behind. Among the great women to be Muslims were: *Khadījah bint Khuwailid, Fāṭimah bint al-Khaṭṭāb, Asmā' bint Abī Bakr, Fāṭimah bint al-Mujallil, Fukaihah bint Yasār, Asmā' bint 'Umais, Asmā' bint Salamah, Ramlah bint Abī 'Awf* and *Humainah bint Khalaf.*

End of the First Phase

During the first phase of the Islāmic movement, *Muḥammad* ﷺ preached the message of Allāh discreetly and it spread gradually among all age-groups, especially the youth, in *Makkah*. People in *Makkah* began to talk about *Muḥammad* ﷺ and his message. They did not take it seriously in the beginning. They thought the Muslims had a fantasy that would soon die away and the worship of idols would eventually triumph.

Three years passed and the message of Allah continued to spread far and wide in the valley of *Makkah*.

Islāmic Movement Becomes Public

Three years after the first revelation, Allāh commanded the Prophet ﷺ, *"Proclaim what you have been ordered and turn away from the polytheists." (15:94)* This was the command to make the call to Allāh open and public and was the beginning of the second phase of the Islāmic movement.

'Alī and the Dinner

The Prophet ﷺ prepared himself to meet the new situation with strong determination and faith. He invited his kinsmen to a dinner and after the dinner addressed them, saying:

"O sons of 'Abdul Muṭṭalib, I know of no Arab who has come to his people with a nobler message than mine. I have brought you the best of this world and the next. Allāh has ordered me to call you to Him. So, who of you will stand by me in this matter?"

The elders in the dinner were not responsive. They were about to leave when the young boy *'Alī* stood up and said, *"I am the youngest of you; I may be a boy, my feet may not be strong enough, but O Muḥammad, I shall be your helper. Whoever opposes you, I shall fight him as a mortal enemy."* The elders laughed loudly and dispersed.

Consider the courage of the boy *'Alī!* How bravely and firmly he spoke about his faith! Does it not, as young people, inspire you to follow the example of *'Alī?* To uphold the Truth and work for it is the best of everything in this world. And, of course, a very attractive and pleasing reward is awaiting you in the *Ākhirah* as well!

The Prophet ﷺ on Mount Ṣafā

Muḥammad ﷺ now prepared to call the Makkans to the message of Allāh. He climbed on top of *aṣ-Ṣafā* and called out to the people who, seeing him standing there, had gathered below. *Muḥammad* ﷺ told them, *"O men of Quraish, if I were to tell you that I see an army ready to attack on the other side of the mountain, would you believe me?"*

They answered, *"Yes, why not? We trust you and never found you telling a lie."*

Muḥammad ﷺ said, *"Know then, that I am a warner and that I warn you of severe punishment. O Banū 'Abdul Muṭṭalib! Banū 'Abd Manāf! O Banū Zuhrah! O Banū Taim! O Banū Makhzūm! O Banū Asad! Allāh has commanded me to warn you, my nearest kinsmen, that I can assure you of good on this earth and in heaven if you declare that there is no god except Allāh." Abū Lahab*, his uncle, became red with anger and exclaimed, *"May your hands perish on this day! Did you gather us for this?"*

Muḥammad ﷺ was severely shocked and looked towards his uncle for a moment. Allāh comforted His messenger and informed him of the fearful punishment awaiting *Abū Lahab*. Allāh revealed, *"May the hands of Abū Lahab perish; doomed he is. His wealth and his properties shall not save him. He shall be thrown into a flaming fire of hell." (111:1-3)*

The open invitation to Allāh's message brought hostility and opposition to the Prophet ﷺ and his followers. A new stage of the Islāmic movement began. We will see how the followers of Islām overcame this opposition with valour, vigour and steadfastness. Indeed, it is rare to find such examples of sacrifices for the noble cause of Allāh.

Hostility and Persecution

The Makkans who, for a long time, had taken no serious notice of the movement became very hostile to the open call of *Muḥammad* ﷺ. They now realised the threat to their idolatry and began to harass the followers of Islām in order to stop its increasing popularity. Hardly a day passed without some new followers joining the faith. This trend further increased the fury of the idolaters.

The *Quraish* first tried to settle the matter through *Abū Ṭālib* and asked him to withdraw his support from *Muḥammad* ﷺ. Delegations of influential people went to meet *Abū Ṭālib* twice for this purpose. He listened to them calmly and sent them back with conciliatory words. *Abū Ṭālib* asked *Muḥammad* ﷺ not to put him under so much strain, for he was the leader of the *Quraish*. The Prophet ﷺ faced a dilemma but remained firm and said to his uncle, *"O my uncle, by Allāh, if they put the sun in my right hand and the moon in my left, and ask me to give up my mission, I shall not do it until Allah has made it victorious or I perish therein!"*

Abū Ṭālib was moved by the firmness of his nephew and said, *"Go and say what you please for, by Allāh, I shall never withdraw my support from you."*

The first Muslim to suffer at the hands of the unbelievers of *Makkah* was *Sa'd bin Abī Waqqāṣ*. He was struck with a sword in a fight with the enemies as they attacked the Prophet ﷺ and his followers at prayer in a mountain pass. The Prophet ﷺ was once preaching in the area of the *Ka'bah* and he was attacked. During this encounter *Ḥārith bin Abī Hālah* tried to pacify the mob but he was attacked and killed. He was the first Muslim to give his life for Islām.

Bilāl bin Rabāḥ, an Abyssinian slave, was tortured by his master for becoming a Muslim. He was pinned down on the burning-hot sand, a heavy stone placed on his chest, and left to swelter under the blazing desert sun — for no reason other than his acceptance of Islām. *Bilāl* bravely endured this torture, proclaiming *"Allāh, the One! Allāh, the One!"* They could not turn him away from his faith. *Abū Bakr*, moved by *Bilāl's* suffering, paid his infidel master and freed him.

Others who suffered terribly at the hands of unbelievers were: *'Ammār, Abū Fukaihah, Ṣuhaib ar-Rūmī* and *Khabbāb*. The infidels did not even spare women Muslims. Among the women tortured were: *Sumaiyah, Lubainah, Nahdīyah*, and *Umm 'Ubais*.

The Prophet ﷺ himself was ridiculed, insulted and accused of being a sorcerer and of being possessed. Once he was almost strangled by an unbeliever while praying. *Abū Bakr* arrived just in time to rescue him. *Abū Lahab's* wife, *Umm Jamīl*, used to throw rubbish and thorny bushes in *Muḥammad's* ﷺ path, and all that *Muḥammad* ﷺ did was to remove them. Surprisingly, when one day he found his doorway clear of rubbish he visited her to find out whether she was ill. This shows how generous and noble he was. He was kind and considerate even to his enemies.

Muḥammad ﷺ continued his preaching with even more enthusiasm and firmness, and the hostility of the unbelievers also intensified. The Makkans did all they could to stop him and his followers but nothing worked. The Islāmic movement continued to flourish among the Makkans despite false propaganda, persecution and harassment from the idolaters.

During this period *Ḥamzah*, the young uncle of the Prophet ﷺ, joined the Islāmic movement. His acceptance of the faith added strength to Islām, for *Ḥamzah* was a brave man. His acceptance of Islām compelled the *Quraish* to abandon some of their harassment.

Abū Jahl and the Camel Seller

One day a man from *Irāsh* came to an assembly of the *Quraish*, whilst the Prophet ﷺ was sitting nearby next to the *Ka'bah*. The man called, "Who among you will help me to get what is due to me from *Abul Ḥakam bin Hishām?* I am a stranger, a wayfarer, and he will not pay his debt."

Abul Ḥakam bin Hishām was one of the most powerful people in Makkah. His hatred, hostility and violence towards the Muslims was intense. He was known as *Abū Jahl*, which means 'the father of ignorance'. Most of the people who heard the stranger were friends of *Abū Jahl*, and would not wish to displease him. Rather, they would prefer to fuel the enmity of *Abū Jahl* towards *Muḥammad* ﷺ.

They said, "Do you see that man sitting over there?" pointing to *Muḥammad* ﷺ. "Go to him. He will help you."

The stranger went to *Muḥammad* ﷺ, unaware that *Abū Jahl* was one of his fiercest enemies. The Prophet ﷺ listened as the stranger explained that he had sold camels to *Abū Jahl*, who had still not paid him despite his repeated pleading. Without hesitation the Prophet ﷺ offered to help. He acompanied him to *Abū Jahl's* house. In the distance, the *Quraish* watched, expecting a great confrontation. They asked one of their supporters to follow the Prophet to find out exactly what would happen.

Muḥammad ﷺ knocked on the door.

"Who is it?" called *Abū Jahl.*

"Muḥammad! Come out to me!"

Abū Jahl came out, pale-faced and agitated.

"Pay this man his due," Muḥammad ﷺ said firmly.

"One moment while I fetch his money," replied *Abū Jahl.* He went back inside, then returned quickly with the money and gave it to the stranger.

"Go about your business," the Prophet ﷺ told the stranger, who was very happy to be paid.

The stranger from *Irāsh* went back to the gathering of *Quraish* and said, "May Allāh reward him, for he has recovered my due." And he went happily on his way.

Then the man sent to watch the confrontation returned to report all he had seen.

"It was amazing!" he began. "Hardly had *Muḥammad* knocked on the door when out came *Abul Ḥakam (Abū Jahl)*, breathless and agitated." He continued to narrate all that he had seen.

Then *Abū Jahl* came upon the gathering. Immediately they asked, "What happened? We have never seen anything like this! What have you done?"

"Damn you!" he exclaimed angrily. "By Allāh, as soon as he knocked on my door and I heard his voice, I was filled with terror. Then when I went out to him, I thought I saw a camel towering above his head, with shoulders and teeth such as I have never seen. By Allāh, if I had refused to pay, it would surely have eaten me."

How amazing was the courage and strength of Prophet *Muḥammad's* ﷺ character! He always stood for justice and helped those in need, even in the face of his bitterest enemy. *Abū Jahl*, despite his hatred, arrogance and pride, was unable to resist the force of *Muḥammad's* ﷺ extraordinary personality, who was supported by hidden help from Allāh.

You should learn a valuable lesson here. Follow Allāh's commands and follow the example of Prophet *Muḥammad* ﷺ. Stand for justice and speak out for the weak, the oppressed and the disadvantaged. This is *Jihād fī sabī lillāh* — working for Islām using all our resources. We should not only read about the Prophet ﷺ, we should try to follow his example.

The Offer of 'Utbah bin Rabī'ah

'Utbah bin Rabī'ah, a leader of the *Quraish*, put some proposals to the Prophet ﷺ. He suggested, *"If what you want is money, we will gather for you our property, so that you may be the richest of us; if you want honour, we will make you our chief, so that no one can decide anything apart from you; if you want sovereignty, we will make you king."*

The Prophet ﷺ declined these offers and recited verses from *Sūrah* 41 (*Ḥā Mīm as-Sajdah*) of the *Qur'ān*. *'Utbah* returned to his companions with a changed face and reported to them that he heard from Muḥammad ﷺ what he had never heard before. No worldly temptation could keep the Prophet away from the Truth.

Another Cunning Proposal

The *Quraish* failed in all their attempts to discourage *Muḥammad* ﷺ and the Muslims from their faith. Harassment, ridicule, torture and false propaganda proved futile as the Muslims simply became more determined.The leaders of the *Quraish* now plotted a shrewd plot.They proposed to the Prophet ﷺ that he should adore their gods and they in return would adore his Allāh; in this way there would come about a compromise and hostility would cease.

Allāh commanded the Prophet ﷺ to tell the unbelievers in clear terms that there could be no such compromise on matters of basic principles. *Muḥammad* ﷺ was asked to declare to them, *"You have your religion, and I have mine."* (109:6) Thus, the plan of mixing the truth with falsehood was defeated.

Emigration (Hijrah) to Abyssinia (Ethiopia)

The infidels, frustrated in their attempts to make a compromise with the Prophet ﷺ, increased the levels of their persecution.The threat to life and property intensified. The Muslims who were not well-off were particularly insecure and vulnerable. *Muḥammad* ﷺ advised those Muslims who felt insecure to emigrate to Abyssinia where *Negus (an-Najāshi)*, a noble king, ruled. Eighty-three Muslims emigrated to Abyssinia in groups.The first group was of ten people.This was the first emigration *(Hijrah)* of Muslims who had to leave their country for the sake of Allāh.

Efforts to get Emigrants Back

A delegation of the *Quraish* consisting of *'Amr bin al-'Āṣ* and *'Abdullāh bin Abī Rabī'ah* went to the *Negus* to try to get the emigrant Muslims back.

They bribed the courtiers of the *Negus* and made accusations against the Muslims to succeed in their mission. They alleged that the emigrants were apostates and followers of a new religion which no one had heard of before.The *Negus* wanted to know the whole matter and called for the Muslims. He asked, "What is the new religion you follow which caused you to leave your country?"

Ja'far bin Abī Ṭālib answered on behalf of the Muslims, *"O King, we were in a state of ignorance and immorality, worshipping stones and idols, eating dead animals, committing all sorts of injustice, breaking natural ties, treating guests badly, and the strong among us exploiting the weak.*

"Then Allāh sent us a prophet, one of our own people, whose lineage, truthfulness, trustworthiness and honesty were well known to us. He called us to worship Allāh alone and to renounce the stones, the idols which we and our ancestors used to worship. He commanded us to speak the truth, to honour our promises, to be helpful to our relatives, to be good to our neighbours, to abstain from bloodshed, to avoid fornication. He commanded us not to give false witness, not to appropriate an orphan's property or falsely accuse a married woman. He ordered us not to associate anyone with Allāh.

"He commanded us to hold prayers, to fast, to pay Zakāh. We believed in him and what he brought to us from Allāh, and we follow him in what he asked us to do and forbade us not to do.

"Thereupon, our people attacked us, treated us harshly and tried to take us back to the old immorality and worship of idols. They made life intolerable for us in Makkah, and we came to your country to seek protection to live in justice and peace."

Hearing this, the *Negus* wanted to listen to part of the *Qur'ān* which came down from Allāh to the Prophet ﷺ. *Ja'far* recited to him *Sūrah Maryam* (Mary) the 19th *Sūrah* of the *Qur'ān*.

The *Negus* wept until his beard was wet, listening to the *Qur'ān*. Then he said, *"What you have just recited and that which was revealed to Mūsā (Moses) must have both issued from the same source. Go forth into my kingdom; I shall not deport you at all."*

Thus the spiteful plans of the pagans against the Muslims were frustrated once again.

'Umar Accepts Islām

'Umar bin al-Khaṭṭāb, a strong and tough person in his late twenties, became a Muslim in the sixth year of the prophethood of *Muḥammad* ﷺ. His acceptance of Islām is remarkable in the sense that he went out with a vow to kill the Prophet ﷺ. On his way to carry out his oath, he met *Nu'aim bin 'Abdullāh* who told him he should set his own house in order, referring to *'Umar's* sister *Fāṭimah* and her husband *Sa'īd bin Zaid* who had become Muslims. On hearing this, *'Umar* became enraged and immediately set out for his sister's house.

As he approached the house, he heard some recitation of the *Qur'ān*. *Khabbāb bin al-Aratt* was reading *Sūrah Ṭā Hā* (the 20th chapter) to *Fāṭimah* and *Sa'īd*. *'Umar* entered the house without knocking and demanded angrily, *"What was that nonsense I heard?"*

Fāṭimah and *Sa'īd* refused to answer. They had hidden *Khabbāb* before *'Umar* barged in. *'Umar* was furious and began hitting *Sa'īd*. *Fāṭimah* was injured as she tried to intervene to protect her husband.

Seeing his sister bleeding, *'Umar* stopped and composed himself. He demanded to see what they were reading. *Fāṭimah* told him it was from the *Qur'ān*, and that he must first cleanse himself. So *'Umar* washed himself before being given the verses to read.

'Umar was deeply moved by the beauty of the words, their captivating rhyme and rhythm, and the power and authority in their meaning. He immediately requested, *"Lead me to Muḥammad ﷺ, so that I may accept Islām."* *Khabbāb* came out from hiding and led him to *al-Arqam al-Makhzūmī's* house *(Dārul Arqam)* where the Prophet ﷺ was staying at that time. *Al-Arqam's* house, located at *aṣ-Ṣafā*, was then the centre of Islām. The Prophet ﷺ welcomed *'Umar* at the gate and asked him his intention. *'Umar* expressed his wish to be a Muslim and the Prophet ﷺ was very pleased.

'Umar was a powerful man. His entry into Islām gave a strong boost to the Muslims. Before him, *Ḥamzah*, the Prophet's uncle, became a Muslim. He was also a powerful man. The entry into Islām of these two great and brave men was a turning point in the history of the early Islāmic movement.

Boycott and Banishment

The *Quraish* were seething at the gradual increase in the strength of the Muslims. They plotted another assault and decided on a total boycott of the family of *Hāshim* and *Muṭṭalib*. They were banished to a pass named *Shi'bi Abī Ṭālib*. The boycott continued for three years and the clans of *Ḥāshim* and *Muṭṭalib* suffered badly during that time. Eventually the boycott had to be withdrawn because of differences amongst the *Quraish* themselves. The clans of *Ḥāshim* and *Muṭṭalib* demonstrated great firmness and unity during the boycott.

The document of boycott, which was kept in the *Ka'bah*, was all eaten up by white ants, except the name of Allāh at the top!

The Prophet ﷺ continued his work amid intimidation and persecution with rare patience and determination. Truth must prevail over falsehood (17:81). The call to Allāh must win over paganism. The popularity and strength of Islām was on the increase. It was going from strength to strength. That was what Allāh destined for Islam.

Year of Sorrow

Time passed. *Muḥammad* ﷺ reached the age of fifty. In the tenth year of his prophethood, apart from stiff opposition and hostility he had to face more sorrow and grief.

His uncle *Abū Ṭālib* died. It was *Abū Ṭālib* who always gave protection to his nephew. However, he died as an unbeliever. *Muḥammad* ﷺ was heartbroken. Still more sadness was to come. The Prophet ﷺ lost his most loving and caring wife, *Khadījah**, who had stood by him like a solid rock, to comfort, support and encourage him at times when no-one else did. She was the first, you should recall, to accept him as the Messenger of Allāh.

---

*Note:

During the life-time of *Khadījah*, the Prophet did not marry another woman. After her death however he married several women, mostly widows, on social and political grounds. The names of his wives (other than *Khadījah*) are *Sawdah, 'Ā'ishah, Ḥafṣah, Zainab bint al-Ḥarīth, Zainab bint Jaḥash, Umm Ḥabībah, Umm Salamah, Juwayrīyah bint al-Ḥarīth, Maimūna bint al-Ḥarīth* and *Ṣafīyah bint Ḥuyaiy*.

It was a terrible blow to *Muḥammad* ﷺ but he had to endure it. Death is an undeniable fact of life. All men and women die and so must we, one day.

The Prophet ﷺ had become used to shocks and grief ever since his childhood. Allāh tested him all through his life. The responsibility of the final prophethood needed unmatched endurance and patience. The Prophet ﷺ passed all the tests of life, however intolerable and difficult, including persecution, torture and death blows. That was how the Almighty Creator prepared *Muḥammad* ﷺ to make Islam victorious over all other systems of life. We must remember here that to live as true Muslims, we also have to go through tests and trials. The eternal bliss of *al-Jannah* (Paradise) will then be given to us by our most loving and kind Creator, in *Ākhirah*.

Ṭā'if — the Most Difficult Day

The stone-heartedness of the people of *Makkah* saddened the Prophet. He now decided to try the people of *Ṭā'if*, a city sixty miles to the east of *Makkah*, to see if they would support him.

On arriving in *Ṭā'if*, accompanied by *Zaid bin Ḥārithah*, he went to three important people of the city and invited them to Islām. All three refused and insulted him. They even incited street urchins to drive him out of the city.

The urchins pelted stones at the Prophet's legs and feet. They hooted at him and drove him out. He was weary, distressed and very sad. He took shelter in a garden where he prayed.

The owners of the garden witnessed the whole episode and felt sorry for him in his tired and bruised condition. They offered him hospitality and sent grapes for him through their Christian servant, *'Addās*, who later became a Muslim.

The Prophet ﷺ used to say that the day in *Ṭā'if* was the most difficult day in his life. But look at his greatness; he was bruised, hurt and bloodstained, yet he never pronounced one word against the people who had abused him. He rather prayed to Allāh to give them guidance. Such was the greatness and noble character of *Muḥammad* ﷺ, the mercy of Allāh to the universe. We must follow his example for our success and happiness in this world and in *Ākhirah*.

Al-Mi'rāj (The Ascent) — a timely boost to morale

After the severe shocks of the deaths of *Abū Ṭālib* and *Khadījah* رضي الله عنها, and the cruel and harsh treatment received at *Ṭā'if*, *Muḥammad* ﷺ longed for some comfort and solace. It was not long before he got it in the form of a remarkable and eventful night journey to *Jerusalem* called *al-Isrā'*. And an ascent to heaven in the same night called *al-Mi'rāj*.

The *Mi'rāj* was a remarkable event for the Prophet ﷺ. Allāh honoured him by this unique and extraordinary journey during which *Muḥammad* ﷺ saw with his own eyes the *Glory* and *Majesty* of Allāh. It was the great morale boost he sorely needed.

It further strengthened his faith that Allāh was always with him. No amount of dismay could prevent him from his task of calling people to the way of Allāh.

The Prophet ﷺ himself gave vivid details about the journey and the ascent. He said that the angel *Jibrā'īl* awoke him from his sleep and took him to *al-Masjidul Aqṣā* at *Jerusalem (Baitul Maqdis)* riding on a white animal which looked like a horse with large wings. The name of the animal was *Burāq*.

In *Jerusalem*, he met all the prophets including *Ādam, Ibrāhīm, Mūsā, Hārūn* (Aaron) and *'Īsā*. He led them in prayer. He was then taken to different heavens and he saw the *Paradise* and the *Hell*. The most important of all was his experience of the *Glory* and *Majesty* of Allāh. It is simply not possible to describe this unique experience in human language. He had many more experiences. It is beyond the grasp of ordinary people like us to understand every aspect of the journey. But it was not impossible for the last messenger of Allāh to grasp the significance of these things. He had to have such experiences to fulfil his duty as Allāh's final messenger.

Five times daily prayers were laid down for Muslims at the time of *al-Mi'rāj*. The whole miraculous journey lasted for a short part of the night. Amazing and incredible! But very real and undoubtedly true.

Next morning, when *Muḥammad* ﷺ described his experience, the *Makkans* laughed at him and started saying that he must have gone crazy. The Muslims believed him but some of the new entrants to the faith became a bit doubtful and the unbelievers, as usual, refused to accept the truth. *Muḥammad* ﷺ gave graphic details of the journey and a caravan which he had seen on his way to *Jerusalem* confirmed details he gave when it arrived in *Makkah*.

Remember here that *Muḥammad* ﷺ was nicknamed by his own people *al-Amīn* (the Trustworthy) and *aṣ-Ṣādiq* (the Truthful). Later, these same people behaved quite strangely. *Muḥammad* ﷺ, after receiving his prophethood, had done everything according to Allāh's wish. Understanding and accepting the truth is not as easy as it may appear. Guidance in life comes from Allāh alone. He guides whom He wills and does not guide whom He wishes.

Abū Bakr, upon hearing about *al-Mi'rāj*, believed without hesitation all the Prophet ﷺ had narrated. For this reason the Prophet ﷺ called him *aṣ-Ṣiddīq* (the testifier to the truth).

First Covenant of al-'Aqabah

During his open, public preaching, *Muḥammad* ﷺ met a group of people from *Madīnah* (then called *Yathrib*) at the time of *Ḥajj* and he invited them to accept Islām. They responded positively to his call and became Muslims. There were six of them. They returned to *Madīnah* as believers and invited others of their tribes to join the new faith of Islām.

Next year twelve people from *Madīnah* came during *Ḥajj* and the Prophet ﷺ entered into an agreement with them at a place called *al-'Aqabah* in 621 CE. This agreement is known as *the Covenant of al-'Aqabah.* In this pledge, they agreed to obey none but Allāh, neither to steal nor commit adultery, neither to kill their children nor commit any evil and not to disobey Allāh. They were told by *Muḥammad* ﷺ that if they lived under this covenant, Allāh would be pleased with them and reward them with *Paradise* in the life after death *(Ākhirah).*

Second Covenant of al-'Aqabah

A second covenant with the Muslims of *Madīnah* was concluded in 622 CE in the same place, *al-'Aqabah.* In all, seventy three men and two women took part in this pledge. This covenant was an extension of the first. It was agreed that the Muslims of *Madīnah* would protect and help the Prophet ﷺ against all odds, as they would protect their own women and children. All the dangers which would arise out of this covenant were explained by *al-'Abbās*, the Prophet's uncle, to the Madinan Muslims in clear terms. However the Madinan Muslims still said, *"We take him (the Prophet) despite all threats to property, wealth and life. Tell us, O Prophet of Allāh, what will be our reward if we remain true to this oath?"*

The Prophet answered, *"Paradise."*

They stretched out their hands to him and he to them, and in this way made it a duty of the Madinan Muslims to defend the Prophet ﷺ in the event of external attacks from Makkah.

Hijrah (Emigration) to Madīnah

The conclusion of the second covenant of *al-'Aqabah* was another turning-point in the history of the Islāmic movement. The Muslims now had a place in which to take shelter. They had an ally for support in time of war and danger.

The unbelievers eventually came to know about the covenant after it was completed. It had been done in secrecy so that the infidels could not have an opportunity to foil it. When they found out, they reacted in anger and resorted to torturing some of the people from *Madīnah.*

The Prophet ﷺ now changed the strategy of his work. For thirteen years he had tried his best to preach the message of Allāh to the people of *Makkah* but the Makkan soil was not fertile for this. *Madīnah* provided him with fresh, receptive ground in which to sow the seed of Islām and he planned to use this opportunity.

He commanded the Muslims of *Makkah* to start emigrating to *Madīnah* and strengthen the bond with the Muslims there. The Muslims of *Madīnah* are known as the *Anṣār* (Helpers) and those of *Makkah* as the *Muhājirūn* (emigrants) in Islāmic history. Following the command of the Prophet ﷺ, the Makkan Muslims started moving to *Madīnah* individually and in small groups. The unbelievers tried relentlessly to stop this and became even more malicious and ferocious.

Think of the emigration! The Makkan Muslims left their homes for the sake of Allāh and to seek His pleasure! At the moment of need, this was what was required

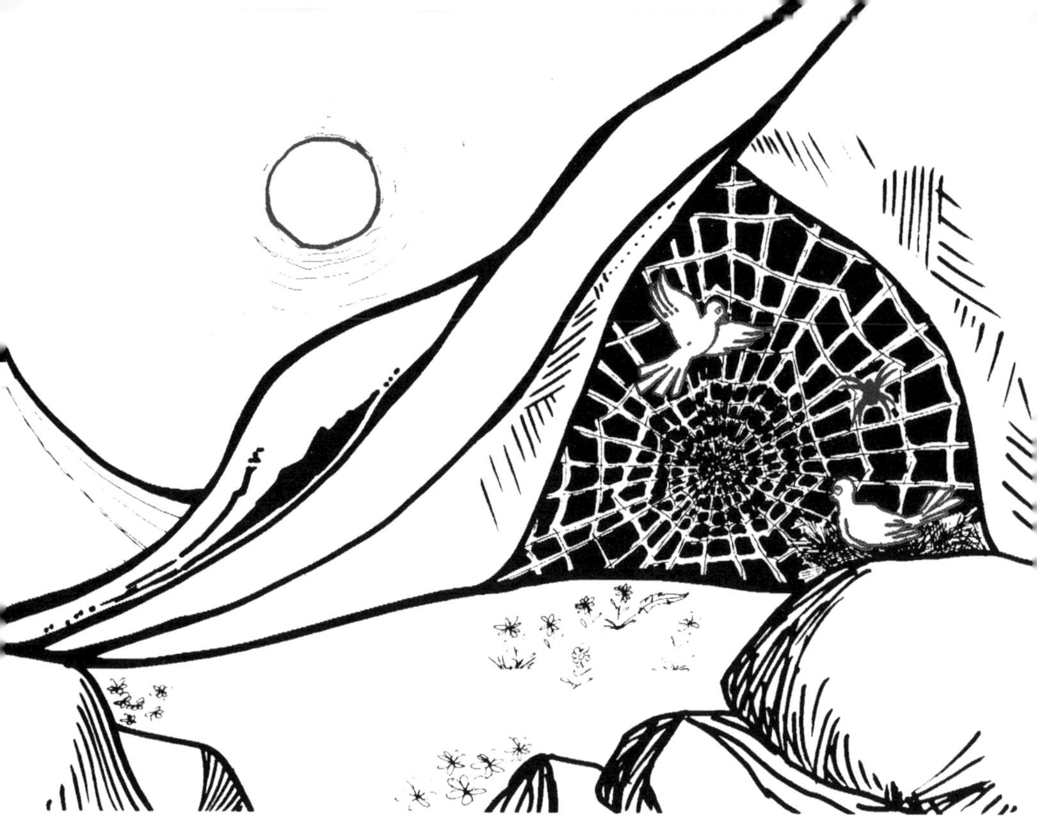

Thawr Cave

of them. As Muslims, we too must be ready to do the same for the sake of our faith. Life on this earth will have meaning and purpose only when we can attain this attitude. We will then be able to do our duty as Allāh's true slaves.

The Hijrah of the Prophet ﷺ

After most of his companions had left for *Madīnah*, *Muḥammad* ﷺ waited for permission from Allāh to emigrate himself. *Abū Bakr*, his closest friend, wanted to leave for *Madīnah*.

Prophet *Muḥammad* ﷺ would answer to the request of *Abū Bakr*, *"Don't be in a hurry; it may be that Allāh will give you a companion."* *Abū Bakr* hoped that it would be *Muḥammad* ﷺ himself. When Allāh granted *Muḥammad* ﷺ permission to migrate, *Abū Bakr* accompanied the Prophet ﷺ. He was very lucky indeed.

The unbelievers now plotted to kill *Muḥammad* ﷺ. Permission for him to migrate to *Madīnah* had also come so *Muḥammad* ﷺ secretly left *Makkah* one night in 622 CE with *Abū Bakr.* A specially-formed group of unbelievers lay in wait around the Prophet's house to kill him as he came out. *'Alī* was left behind to sleep in the Prophet's bed and the Prophet ﷺ quietly left, without the unbelievers noticing him. Such was the plan of Allāh. When Allāh wants to do something he only says *"Be!"*

and *"it is there"* (36:82). In the morning, the unbelievers found *'Alī* in the Prophet's bed and were dumbfounded. They looked very foolish!

The Prophet ﷺ and his companion *Abū Bakr* had left just before dawn and proceeded to a cave called *Thawr*, to the south of *Makkah*. They stayed in the cave for three days and *Abū Bakr's* servant brought them food in the evening. They left *Thawr* on the third day and started out for *Madīnah*.

The unbelievers, fooled by the way the Prophet ﷺ had escaped despite their vigilance, now organised a thorough search on the road to *Madīnah* and offered a prize of 100 camels for the capture of *Muḥammad* ﷺ. *Surāqah bin Mālik* almost succeeded, but when his horse stumbled three times in his pursuit of *Muḥammad* ﷺ, he gave up his sinister aim, taking the falls as bad omens. He later accepted Islām.

After a tiresome, exhausting and very difficult journey, the Prophet ﷺ, accompanied by *Abū Bakr*, reached *Qubā'*, a place near *Madīnah*. They stayed there for two weeks and the Prophet ﷺ founded a mosque in *Qubā'* where *'Alī* had joined them.

The Prophet ﷺ entered *Madīnah* and allowed his camel to kneel where it liked. It knelt first in a place which was owned by two orphans, and got up only to kneel finally in front of *Abū Ayyūb al-Anṣārī's* house which became the first residence of the Prophet ﷺ in *Madīnah*.

The People of *Madīnah*, who had anxiously awaited the arrival of *Muḥammad* ﷺ, became very happy and excited when they found him among them. They gave him a hero's welcome.

The *Hijrah* of the Prophet ﷺ started a new chapter in the history of the Islāmic movement. There are two contrasting aspects to this historic migration: the heart-breaking feeling of leaving the beloved birthplace; and the feeling of security together with the hope that Islām would spread more freely than before.

The *Islāmic calender* starts from the day of the *Hijrah* of Prophet *Muḥammad* ﷺ from *Makkah* to *Madīnah*. It occurred in 622 CE in the 13th year of the prophethood of *Muḥammad* ﷺ.

The *Hijrah* was the beginning of a new role for the Prophet ﷺ as a statesman and a ruler. With this ended his fifty three years of life in *Makkah*, of which he had spent thirteen eventful years as the Prophet of Allāh.

The Prophet ﷺ at Madīnah

Muḥammad's ﷺ arrival in *Madīnah* was a memorable and important event for the people of the city. They felt elated and jubilant because they had Allāh's messenger among them.

Madīnah, situated to the north of *Makkah* (447km by road, 360km by air), was known at that time as *Yathrib.* From the time of the Prophet's arrival, it came to be known as *Madīnatun Nabiyy* — the Prophet's city. Later it became known simply as *Madīnah.*

The Makkan migrants added a new dimension to the life of *Madīnah*. The city now

Al-Masjidun Nabawī (The Prophet's Mosque) in Madīnah

had three communities: the *Anṣār* (the Helpers) of the tribes of *Aws* and *Khazraj*, the *Jews* from the tribes of *Qainuqā'*, *Naḍīr* and *Quraiẓah* and the *Muhājirūn* (migrants from *Makkah*). The *Muhājirūn* had to be accommodated by the local community of the *Anṣār*.

Some of the companions of the Prophet ﷺ had reached *Madīnah* before Muḥammad ﷺ himself and were living with the *Anṣār* as their guests. With the arrival of the Prophet ﷺ, the situation became more settled. The *Muhājirūn* arrived with almost no material wealth.

The Prophet's first task was to form a solid bond of faith and brotherhood between the *Anṣār* and the *Muhājirūn*.

He called a meeting of both communities and asked each of the *Anṣār* to take one of the *Muhājirūn* as his brother-in-faith. He also suggested they should share their property and other belongings with their migrant brothers. The *Anṣār* did as they were asked by the Prophet ﷺ. This was a rare event unmatched in human history; such was the powerful influence of Islām on the *Anṣār*. The worldly belongings and wealth were less important to them than the reward in *Ākhirah*.

The *Anṣār* practically shared their property with the *Muhājirūn* equally, on the basis of a shared faith. It sounds too good to be true, but it is the fact of Islamic history.

Muḥammad ﷺ became the leader of the city. With the cementing of the bond of brotherhood, he had virtually inaugurated the Islāmic society. *Madīnah* was now the capital of the Islāmic community, the first Islāmic state.

The Islāmic State of *Madīnah* knew no distinction between the ruler and his subjects. Every citizen enjoyed equal rights. Islām does not recognise any preference of one over another except on the basis of piety *(taqwā)*. *"The noblest among you to Allāh is the one who is the most pious,"* says the *Qur'ān* (49:13). In the Islāmic state of *Madīnah* there was no discrimination on the basis of colour, class or descent.

The Madīnan Treaty between the Muslims and the Jews

After laying the foundations of the Islāmic state, Allāh's messenger took steps to secure its internal peace. A treaty was drawn up between the Muslims (the *Muhājirūn* and the *Anṣār*) and the Jews of *Madīnah* (then still known as *Yathrib*) on the instructions of Prophet *Muḥammad* ﷺ. It joined the various communities living in Madīnah as a single community, offering mutual support and protection, based on justice and kindness. The Prophet ﷺ ensured this unique treaty was written down. An English translation of the treaty is given here:

In the name of Allāh, the most Merciful, the most Kind.

This is a document from Muḥammad, the Prophet ﷺ for the believers and the Muslims from the Quraish and Yathrib, and whoever follows them, joins them and fights alongside them; they are a single community (Ummah), apart from all other people. The Muhājirūn of the Quraish are in charge of their own affairs, paying collectively among themselves the blood money (compensation paid to the relatives of a murdered person) they incur. They pay for the release of those taken prisoner from among them, with the familiar kindness and justice of the believers.

The Banū 'Awf according to their present custom shall pay the blood money as they have been paying before (i.e. before Islām). Every clan shall pay for the release of its prisoners with the familiar kindness and justice of the believers.

The treaty goes on here to repeat these last words with each of the *Anṣār* clans and every house including: *Banū Sā'idah, Banū al-Ḥārith, Banū Jusham, Banū an-Najjār, Banū 'Amru bin 'Awf, Banū an-Nabīt* and *Banū al-Aws*. It then continues:

The believers shall not leave any one of them destitute without reasonably helping him in the payment of blood money or ransom. No believer shall take as an ally the freedman of another believer without the permission of his previous master.

All pious believers (those with taqwā) stand together against anyone amongst themselves who transgresses or is guilty of oppression or indulges in an act of sin or aggression or corruption. They shall stand together against him even though he may be the son of any one of them.

No believer shall kill another believer in retaliation for the killing of an unbeliever, nor shall he support an unbeliever against a believer. Just as Allāh's Protection is One, so all believers shall stand behind the commitment of protection given by even the weakest of them. Believers are one another's friends to the exclusion of outsiders. Any Jew who joins us shall have our support and equal rights with us, suffering no oppression and fearing no alliance against him. The peace of the believers is one: no believer shall make a peace agreement to the exclusion of another believer in fighting for Allāh's cause unless this agreement applies to all of them equally and fairly. In every military expedition, each group shall follow another. The believers must retaliate if the blood of any one of them is shed in the way of Allāh. The pious believers follow the best and straightest guidance.

No mushrik (one who make partners with Allāh) shall extend protection to any property or any person belonging to the Quraish, nor shall he stand between them and any believer. Whoever is convicted of killing a believer deliberately and without good reason shall be subject to retaliation, unless the victim's next of kin forgoes his right. All the believers shall unite against the killer but it shall not be lawful for them to do anything other than bring him to justice.

No believer who accepts this agreement and believes in Allāh and Last Day shall protect or give shelter to any criminal. Anyone who gives such support or shelter to a criminal incurs Allah's curse and His anger on the Day of Judgement. No compensation shall be accepted from him. On whatever you may differ, the matter must be referred for judgement to Allāh and to Muḥammad ﷺ.

The Jews shall share expenses with the believers as long as they are fighting alongside them. The Jews of Banū 'Awf are one Ummah with the believers. The Jews have their own religion and the Muslims have their own religion; both enjoy the security of their allies, except the unjust and criminal among them who hurt but themselves and their families. The Jews of the clans of Banū an-Najjār, Banū al-Ḥārith, Banū Sā'idah, Banū Jusham, Banū al-Aws and Banū Tha'labah enjoy the same rights as the Jews of Banū 'Awf. Jafnah is a branch of Banū Tha'labah, who enjoy the same rights. Banū ash-Shuṭaibah have the same rights as the Jews of Banū 'Awf. Fulfilment of these conditions should be a barrier which prevents their violation. Whatever applies to the clans of Banū Tha'labah also applies to their allies. The families and households of the Jews are in the same position as themselves. None of them shall go to war without the permission of Muḥammad ﷺ. Nothing shall be allowed to prevent retaliation for an injury. Whoever murders anyone actually murders himself and brings his household to ruin, with the exception of one who is a victim of injustice. Allāh is Guarantor for those who observe their undertaking.

The Jews shall bear their own expenses and the Muslims shall bear their own expenses.

*Each shall assist the other against anyone who fights any party to this agreement. Their relationship shall be one of mutual advice and consultation. Fulfilment of the terms of this agreement should prevent its violation. No one is responsible for a sinful action of his ally. The wronged must be helped. The Jews are required to share the expenses with the believers as long as the war continues. The city of Yathrib shall be a sanctuary to the parties of this agreement. Their neighbours shall be treated as themselves as long as they do no harm or commit a sin. No woman shall be offered protection without the consent of her family. Anything that takes place between the parties to this agreement, or any dispute that may develop between them, shall be referred for judgement to Allāh and to Muḥammad the Messenger of Allāh ﷺ. Allāh is the Guarantor of piety and goodness that is contained in this agreement. The Quraish and their helpers shall not be given protection. The parties to this agreement shall support each other against anyone who attacks Yathrib. If they are called upon to cease hostilities and to enter into any peace agreement, then they will do so. If they are invited to something like that, then the believers are required to support it, except with those who fight to suppress the religion. Everyone shall have his share from the side to which he belongs. The Jews of Banū al-Aws, their own people and their allies, have the same rights and obligations as the parties to this agreement, and this shall be sincerely honoured by the parties to this agreement. Fulfilment of the terms and conditions of this agreement shall prevent their violation. There is no responsibility except for one's own deeds. Allāh is the Guarantor of the truth and the goodwill of this agreement. This agreement does not give protection from punishment to the unjust and the criminal. He who goes to fight as well as who stays at home shall be safe unless he is guilty of injustice or sin. Allāh is the Protector of those who fulfil their pledges and the pious, and so is Muḥammad the Messenger of Allāh ﷺ.**

This treaty, which Prophet *Muḥammad* ﷺ concluded in the seventh century CE, shows the importance Islām places on freedom of faith and expression, and the sanctity of human life and property. It also demonstrates the upholding of justice, equality and fairness. This unique document also forbade exploitation, injustice, crime and violation of treaty terms. This agreement, drawn up fourteen centuries ago, undoubtedly demonstrates the extraordinary statesmanship and the wisdom of the last and final messenger of Allāh ﷺ.

The building of the mosque in Madīnah

The Prophet ﷺ now decided to build a mosque in *Madīnah*. Soon, work began at a place which was purchased from the orphan brothers who owned it, *Suhail* and *Sahl*, the sons of *Rafi' bin Abī 'Amr al-Balawī*. This was the place where the Prophet's camel had first knelt before it finally knelt in front of the house of *Abū Ayyūb al-Anṣārī*. The Prophet's residence was built next to the mosque.

---

* The translaton is based on the Arabic version of *As-Sirātun Nabawiyyah* - Ibn Hishām Vol I pp 106 - 108, Dārul Jil, Beirut 1975.

Muḥammad ﷺ himself took part in the construction as an ordinary labourer. In fact it was difficult to identify him from other workers on the site. *Muḥammad* ﷺ never hesitated to do any ordinary work. He used to mend his own clothes, repair his own shoes, do the shopping and milk the goats. In this respect he left for us a shining example.

Adhān (Call to Prayer)

You have already learnt that *Ṣalāh* five times a day was laid down for Muslims at the time of the *Mi'rāj* (the Ascent). In *Madīnah*, Muslims were now a cohesive and united community and the Prophet ﷺ felt it necessary to call the believers to offer *Ṣalāh* in congregation. Usually during this time, the Muslims would collect themselves together for *Ṣalāh* when the time came. Many suggestions were put forward about how to announce the *Ṣalāh* time. When *'Abdullāh bin Zaid bin Tha'labah* told Prophet *Muḥammad* ﷺ of a dream which he had seen, the Prophet ﷺ confirmed that the dream was a true vision willed by Allāh. The Prophet ﷺ then asked *Bilāl*, the Abyssinian Muslim who had a sonorous voice, to use those words which *'Abdullāh* heard in his dream to call the Muslims to *Ṣalāh*. The words were:

Allāh is the Greatest! (four times)
I bear witness that there is no god except Allāh (twice)
I bear witness that Muḥammad is the messenger of Allāh (twice)
Rush to prayer! (twice)
Rush to success! (twice)
Allāh is the Greatest! (twice)
There is no god except Allāh.

When *'Umar bin al-Khaṭṭāb* heard the words used by *Bilāl*, he rushed to Prophet *Muḥammad* ﷺ and told him that he too had seen the same dream.

This is the *Adhān* (the call to prayer) and *Bilāl bin Rabāḥ* thus became the first *Mu'adhdhin* of Islām. The introduction of *Adhān,* with its beautiful and magnetic appeal, made possible the pronouncement of the Greatness of Allāh five times a day in *Madīnah*. This system of *Adhān* is still in use in all Muslim countries. The rhyme and rhythm of the words used are wonderful and inspiring. The Arabic words for the *Adhān* are given on pages 44–45.

More Islāmic Duties Laid Down

Madīnah, the first Islāmic state, began to thrive under the unique and dynamic leadership of *Muḥammad* ﷺ. The Islāmic society of *Madīnah* needed more guidance and training from the messenger of Allāh for its development, welfare and prosperity. This society, which was passing through its infant stage, made a tremendous and lasting contribution to the history of mankind.

The programme of training introduced during the second and third years of the *Hijrah* included *Ṣawm* (fasting in the month of *Ramaḍān*), *Zakāh* (welfare contribution) and the prohibition of drinking wine and transactions involving interest *(Ribā)*. Also during this period, laws regarding orphans, inheritance, marriage and the rights of married women were revealed.

In the second year of the *Hijrah* (during the month of *Sha'bān*) the direction of prayer *(Qiblah)* was changed by revelation from *Baitul Maqdis* in *Jerusalem* to *al-Ka'bah* in *Makkah* (2:144).

Hard Task

The Islāmic society was growing and the task of making it strong, solid and dynamic also continued. During this time *Muḥammad* ﷺ was virtually fighting on four fronts:

i) to maintain cohesion and discipline among the rank and file of the Islāmic society;
ii) to guard against the intrigues and conspiracies of the Hypocrites (Munāfiqūn);
iii) to remain alert to the dangers from the Quraish of Makkah, and
iv) to remain vigilant about the sinister motives of the Jews of Madīnah.

History shows how wonderfully Allāh's messenger faced all these dangers and led the Islāmic state towards more and more success and to the eventual victory over all other systems of his time.

The duty of the final messenger of Allāh was to make Allāh's *Dīn* (Allāh's system) victorious and supreme over all other man-made systems and laws (9:33, 48:28, 61:9).

The Battle of Badr (624 CE)

Muḥammad ﷺ was a brilliantly wise and an exceptionally practical man. Almighty Allāh made him so. He took steps to counter the dangers from both inside and outside the city of *Madīnah*. He left no stone unturned to make the small community of Muslims a solidly united force, to combat any threat to its existence.

He had very little human and material resources. The economy of *Madīnah* was under strain from absorbing the migrants from *Makkah*, but the messenger of Allāh was full of hope and confidence. He was sure that Allāh's help would be coming at the right moment. What the Muslims needed more was the strength of faith, rather than the material resources. The strength of faith *(Īmān)* supported by actions *(A'māl)* was far more important.

The unbelievers of *Makkah* were raging with anger at the comparative safety of the Muslims in *Madīnah*. All their previous attempts to finish off *Muḥammad* ﷺ had failed. Their trade route to *ash-Shām* was now within easy reach of the Muslims. They became restless and were simmering with anger within themselves, unable to find a way to tackle *Muḥammad* ﷺ. They were desperately looking for some excuse to attack the new Islāmic society and get rid of it once and for all.

Such was the situation when news came of an unusual caravan of about a thousand camels laden with goods and arms travelling to *Makkah* from *ash-Shām*. The leader of the caravan was *Abū Sufyān* — a chief of the *Quraish* of *Makkah*. *Abū Sufyān* feared there might be an attack from the Muslims and lost no time in sending exactly such a message to *Makkah*. Soon an army of a thousand was ready to march on to *Madīnah* to attack the Muslims.

News of the Makkan army reached the Prophet ﷺ and he decided to face them outside *Madīnah* with the help of Allāh. The aggression of the unbelievers must not go unchallenged. A small army of three hundred and thirteen people, including young teenagers, ill-equipped with arms and ammunition, started from *Madīnah* under the Prophet's command and camped at a place called *Badr,* 128 km south-west of *Madīnah*. The Muslim army had only a few horses and a small quantity of armour but they were full of faith in Allāh's help, courage, valour and determination. They knew they were on the right side.

Meanwhile, *Abū Sufyān's* caravan changed its route and was out of any danger. However the Makkan army would not leave until they had finished off the Muslims. An encounter between the two armies took place on the 17th day of *Ramaḍān* 2 AH.

The Muslims responded to the Makkan attack with unmatched bravery and determination. They repelled the Makkan army and the unbelievers were decisively defeated. They left seventy dead and another seventy were taken as prisoners of war by the Muslims.

The Battle of Badr proved beyond doubt that real strength lies in faith in Allāh and not in arms and ammunition. The battle decided the future course of history for the Muslims.

On that day, in spite of their meagre resources, the soldiers of the truth were triumphant and the military might of falsehood was humiliated, defeated and tarnished. *"Truth prevails, falsehood vanishes,"* declares the *Qur'ān* (17:81). Indeed, the victory at *Badr* was possbile only with Almighty Allāh's help and mercy (8:17). Of course, the Muslims, under the leadership of Prophet *Muḥammad* ﷺ, fought valiantly with total reliance on Allāh.

In the battle of *Badr*, each Muslim soldier had to face three infidels, because the size of the Makkan army was three times that of the Muslim army. Still the Muslims won. Defeat for the Muslims in this battle would have proved fatal. The Makkans left this battle with a grudge, defeated and humiliated. Another encounter could not be far off.

The Battle of Uḥud (625 CE)

The Makkans could not forget the shattering blow inflicted on them by the Muslims at *Badr*. They were very thirsty for revenge. The year that followed was their year of preparation.

The Muslims were consolidating the gains they had made at *Badr* and strengthening their community ties. The Prophet ﷺ sent messengers and delegations to various parts of Arabia during this time.

Al-'Abbās, one of the uncles of the Prophet ﷺ, still lived in *Makkah* though he accepted Islām. His feelings for his nephew and the Muslims were very strong. He was watching all the preparations the unbelievers were making and sent an envoy to *Muḥammad* ﷺ in *Madīnah* with the details of the Makkans' preparations for war.

The Prophet ﷺ received news that an army three thousand strong, including two hundred horsemen, was marching towards *Madīnah*. *Muḥammad* ﷺ called for the elders and consulted them on the matter. The elders of *Madīnah*, among them *Anṣār* and *Muhājirūn*, favoured defence from inside *Madīnah* but the younger men, vibrant with their youthful energy and vigour, wanted combat outside *Madīnah*. They saw it as an opportunity to be a *Shahīd* (martyr) for Allāh's *Dīn*. Those elder companions of the Prophet ﷺ who could not participate in *Badr* also favoured combat outside. *'Abdullāh bin Ubayy bin Salūl*, leader of the *Khazraj* tribe, did not want combat outside the city.

After *Jumu'ah* prayer one Friday, the Prophet ﷺ started out for Mount *Uḥud* with an army of one thousand. When the Muslim army reached *ash-Shawṭ*, between *Madīnah* and *Uḥud*, *'Abdullāh bin Ubayy* withdrew with a third of the men. So the Prophet ﷺ had to fight with just seven hundred men. *'Abdullāh bin Ubayy* thus became the leader of the *Munāfiqūn* (hypocrites). The *Quraish* of *Makkah* had already camped there. The Prophet ﷺ reached *Uḥud* and after the dawn prayer put the Muslim army into position. He took particular care to place fifty archers under the command of *'Abdullāh bin Jubair* to protect a strategic mountain pass and ordered them not to leave their position under any circumstances.

The two armies faced each other in the morning. Fierce fighting broke out and soon the Muslim army got the upper hand and the Makkan army was forced to retreat. The Muslims captured the supplies and baggage of the Makkans.

Before the battle was really over, most of the archers stationed in the mountain pass left their post and joined in the collection of booty, despite the repeated pleas of *'Abdullāh bin Jubair*. This indiscipline provided *Khālid bin al-Walīd*, one of the Makkan commanders, with a rare opportunity to make a counter attack from the rear. *'Abdullāh bin Jubair* and six other archers who had not left their position put up a desperate fight until, finally, all of them were martyred.

Khālid's men took the Muslim army by surprise and soon the Muslims' celebration ended in grief. They found themselves surrounded and in the fighting that followed, *Ḥamzah*, the Prophet's uncle and a great warrior, was martyred by *Waḥshī*. Many other Muslims became *Shahīd* and the Prophet ﷺ himself was injured.

A rumour that *Muḥammad* ﷺ was dead caused confusion amongst the Muslims, draining their morale and leading some of them to flee. The Prophet ﷺ was taken by some of his followers to a position on the hill, and he called to the Muslims at the top of his voice and ordered them to regroup. Before long the scattered and battered Muslims regrouped, seeing that the Prophet ﷺ was alive.

In the battle, the enemy violated all norms of civilised behaviour. They mutilated the dead bodies of Muslims and *Hind*, the wife of *Abū Sufyān*, was so terrible that she took out the liver of *Ḥamzah* and chewed it raw.

By the end of the day the regrouped Muslim army was ready for a counter attack, but the Makkan army had already left, satisfied that they had taken revenge for *Badr*.

On his return to *Madīnah*, the Prophet ﷺ sent out a contingent of Muslims to pursue the Makkans, to ensure that they did not come back. When *Abū Sufyān* heard of it, he quickened his pace to *Makkah*.

The overall result was almost a draw — neither side could claim victory. But the battle had some very costly lessons for the Muslims. The disobedience and indiscipline of the archers at the mountain pass, spurred on by their love for the spoils of war (booty), caused the Muslims to suffer badly in a battle which they had almost won. How costly the love of worldly things was! Love for this world should not distract us from our true goal of salvation and reward in the *Ākhirah*.

Discipline and obedience to the commander are very important in a battlefield. Had the fifty archers under *'Abdullāh bin Jubair* not disobeyed him, the outcome of the battle of *Uḥud* would have been different.

The Battle of Aḥzāb or Khandaq (627 CE)

Muḥammad ﷺ had a very busy life. Hardly a day passed without some incident taking place somewhere in the new state. Skirmishes, plots, conspiracies and violations of treaties were rife. So was the molesting and mockery of the Muslims and the Prophet ﷺ. All this happened by the collusion of the Jews and Makkan infidels. They joined together against the Muslims.

The Jewish tribe of *Banū Naḍīr* violated treaty obligations and plotted to kill the Prophet ﷺ so action had to be taken against them. They were given the option: either fight or be deported. At first they refused to leave *Madīnah* but later they were expelled for their treachery. They moved to *Khaibar* and turned the place into an enemy den against the Muslims. They incited the Makkans to make a new offensive against the Muslims and try decisively to finish them off.

Badr had been a fatal blow to the dreams of the Makkans; at *Uḥud*, their mission remained unfulfilled. But it gave them encouragement to launch another attack, because the impression they had of the Muslims at *Badr* had changed at *Uḥud*. Incitement by *Banū Naḍīr* added fuel to their evil objectives.

Emissaries were sent on secret trips between the Makkans and the Nadirites. Finally an agreement was reached about the new assault on *Madīnah*. Forces were gathered to make the assault, drawing on people from *Makkah*, *Ghaṭafān*, *Ṭā'if*, *Fazara* and other towns.

News of these sinister moves reached the Prophet ﷺ, and he consulted his companions about the preparations to counter the latest enemy offensive. The decision was made to face the enemy from within the city and *Salmān al-Fārisī*, a Persian Muslim, advised digging trenches around the city to hold the enemy hordes outside the boundary of the city of *Madīnah*. This novel idea was put into effect.

Deep, wide trenches were dug around *Madīnah* and it took twenty days to complete the digging. *Muḥammad* ﷺ himself took part in the digging. After the trenches had been completed, the Prophet ﷺ placed the Muslims in position to defend the city from inside.

An allied force ten thousand strong marched against *Madīnah* in the fifth year of the *Hijrah*. The number was so large, it appeared as if the enemy forces were advancing from all directions — the north, the south, above and below. They alighted on the outskirts of the city beating drums and chanting their war songs. When they found themselves separated from the Muslims by the very deep and wide trenches they were surprised.

The enemy could not understand this new war technique. They were greatly astounded. They had no other alternative but to wait but how long could they do this?

A boring wait of about four weeks made them very weary, tired and restless. Nothing happened during this long seige except a few exchanges of arrows. Some desperate attempts to cross the trench were made, but the vigilant and valiant Muslims repelled them.

The stocks of the enemy's food and other supplies were depleting and they felt worried, anxious and undecided about what to do.

A treacherous plot was now hatched to instigate a surprise attack on the Muslims at night by the Jews of the *Banū Quraiẓah* who were still in *Madīnah* at the time. The Prophet ﷺ heard of the plot and took measures to foil it. He sent a message to the Jews in *Madīnah* asking them to think over the consequences of their treachery should the allied enemy forces be defeated! After the battle of *Aḥzāb*, the Jews of *Banū Quraiẓah* were beseiged for about two to three weeks following which all male adults were killed on a judgement by *Sa'd*, chief of the *Aws* tribe, an ally of the *Quraiẓah.*

Allāh, the Almighty, is always with the lovers of Truth. His help is crucial for success. The Muslims beseiged in *Madīnah* badly needed such help. Indeed, they did get that help at the time chosen by Almighty Allah.

The weather changed suddenly. Strong winds, thunder and heavy rain storms made the enemy flee in disarray. Soldiers were trampled under the feet of the horses and camels in the rush. The hordes eventually fled in a wild frenzy. What a scene it must have been! And what a timely intervention by Allāh! He is the Most Powerful and the Most Wise. *He does what He chooses (85:16).*

The enemies were greatly dispirited, while the Muslims were equally relieved and elated. The Muslims expressed their gratitude to Allāh, the Merciful, for His timely help and mercy.

Ḥudaibiyah Agreement (628 CE)

In the sixth year of the *Hijrah*, the Prophet ﷺ announced his intention to pay a visit to *al-Ka'bah* in *Makkah* for a short pilgrimage *('Umrah)*. He set out with 1400 of his followers who were under strict orders not to carry any weapons, except their traveller's swords.

The *Quraish* of *Makkah* knew full well that the only purpose of the Prophet's visit was for pilgrimage, but how could they let the Muslims enter *Makkah* when they had not been able to enter *Madīnah*? The Muslims, they decided, must be stopped.

Plans were put in hand. The top generals — *Khālid* and *'Ikrimah* — were alerted to be ready with their armies to stop the Prophet ﷺ and his followers from entering *Makkah*.

The Muslims continued their journey to *Makkah* until they had reached a place called *Ḥudaibiyah*. Steps were taken to find out what sort of mood the *Quraish* were in; it was clear they were in no mood to let the Muslims into Makkah, they were in the mood for a battle.

The *Quraish* on their part gathered information about the strength and armoury of the Muslims and realised they had come for no other purpose than the pilgrimage to *al-Ka'bah*. Envoys were sent from each side. The Prophet ﷺ made his intentions crystal clear to the *Quraish* through his envoy but the *Quraish* misbehaved with the Muslim envoy and threatened the Muslims. The patience of the Muslims was put to a severe test. They could teach the *Quraish* a good lesson even with their traveller's swords, but Allāh's Prophet ﷺ ordered them to show extreme restraint.

The *Quraish* were determined not to allow the Muslims into Makkah for the pilgrimage that year. They made it an issue of prestige and pride. It was humiliating for the Muslims, but what could they do? Allāh's messenger was their leader and all his steps were guided by Allāh, so they had to be followed.

Eventually, after intense negotiations, an agreement between the *Quraish* and the Prophet ﷺ was signed. This agreement is the *Ḥudaibiyah* agreement.

The terms of the agreement were:

a. *The Muslims would not visit Makkah that year, but would come a year later and remain there for three days only.*

b. *There would be one-sided extradition — the Makkans taking refuge with the Prophet ﷺ would be handed over on demand to the Quraish, but Muslims taking refuge in Makkah would not be handed over to the Prophet ﷺ.*

c. *There would be peace for ten years and during this period Muslims could go to Makkah and Ṭa'if and the Quraish could go to ash-Shām through the Muslim areas.*

d. *Each party would remain neutral in the event of a war between the other and a third party.*

e. *Any tribe wishing to sign an agreement with either the Muslims or the Quraish would be able to do so.*

The terms of the agreement were apparently against the Muslims, but they eventually turned out to be favourable for them. Later events proved beyond doubt that the agreement gave rare opportunities to Muslims to gain decisive victory.

The Muslims were disheartened but they were soon given the news of victory by Allāh. It was revealed: *"Surely we have granted you a clear victory."* (48:1)

You might wonder in what way was this one-sided treaty a victory? The treaty eased the long years of tension and made possible communication between the two parties. The Makkans could now come to *Madīnah* and stay with the Muslims; this provided an opportunity for the Muslims to influence the stone-heartedness of the Makkans. In fact, during the years that followed the *Ḥudaibiyah* treaty, the number of new Muslims increased dramatically. *Khālid bin al-Walīd*, who later became the most famous general in Islāmic history, and *'Amr bin al-'Aṣ*, the conqueror of Egypt, became Muslims during this time.

The treaty proved beyond doubt that the Prophet ﷺ and the Muslims stood for peace. It also paved the way for the escape of the detained Muslims in *Makkah*, as the extradition clause was later dropped on the initiative of the Makkans.

The *Ḥudaibiyah* agreement also opened the way to the conquest of *Makkah* in *630 CE* — the eighth year of *Hijrah*.

During the years that followed the *Ḥudaibiyah* treaty, the Prophet ﷺ sent emissaries to the *Roman Emperor*, the *Persian Emperor*, the *ruler of Egypt*, the *King of Abyssinia*, the *chiefs of ash-Shām* and other leaders, inviting them to accept Islām.

Letter to Heraclius — the Emperor of Byzantine

The Prophet ﷺ asked his companions: *"Who is prepared to carry my letter to the ruler of Byzantine and be rewarded with Jannah (Paradise)?"* A man asked: "Even if he rejects it?" The Prophet ﷺ replied that the reward would still be his even if *Heraclius* rejected the message. *Diḥyah bin Khalīfah,* a pleasant and handsome man of the *Kalb* tribe, accepted the Prophet's ﷺ offer, and set forth to carry the Prophet's ﷺ message to *Heraclius*, the *Byzantine* emperor (Eastern Roman Empire).

Heraclius had just conquered the territory lost to the Persians, who had taken away the *Holy Cross* (crucifix) from *Jerusalem*. He vowed to restore the crucifix and place it in the Church of *Jerusalem*. He was given a hero's welcome when he came to *Jerusalem* to replace the crucifix .A grand celebration was organised for the occasion. It was at this time that *Diḥyah* arrived there to deliver the Prophet's ﷺ message, which read as follows:

In the name of Allāh, the Most Merciful, the Most Kind.

From Muḥammad, the servant of Allāh and His Messenger, to Heraclius, the ruler of the Byzantines. Peace be on those who follow right guidance. I call on you to believe in Islām. Accept Islām and you will be safe and Allāh will give you a double reward. If you refuse, you shall bear the responsibility for the Arians (the followers of Arius, who denied the Trinity and believed in the oneness of God). And (I recite to you Allāh's statement). 'O People of the Book (Jews and Christians)! Come to a word that is just between us and you, that we worshop none but Allāh and that we associate no partners with Him, and that none of us shall take others as lords beside Allāh. Then, if they turn away, say, "Bear witness that we are Muslims."' (Sūrah 3, verse 64)

Heraclius treated the Prophet's ﷺ representative (envoy) with dignity but he wanted to find out for himself about the Prophet's ﷺ claim. So he ordered his aides to find any person from *Arabia* that he could ask questions about the Prophet ﷺ. *Abū Sufyān bin Ḥarb,* the *Quraish* leader who considered the Prophet ﷺ his enemy, happened to be in *Gaza* with some of his companions on a business trip. They were taken to *Heraclius* who asked them through a translator: "Who among you is the closest relative of *Muḥammad* who claims to be a Prophet?" *Abū Sufyān* said that he was the closest relative. *Heraclius* asked *Abū Sufyān* to come forward and answer his questions. He also asked *Abū Sufyān*'s companions to point out if *Abū Sufyān* would tell any lie.

Heraclius then asked *Abū Sufyān* a series of questions:

Heraclius: *What is his family status amongst you?*

Abū Sufyān: *He belongs to a good (noble) family amongst us.*

Heracluis: *Was any of his forefathers a king?*

Abū Sufyān: No.

Heraclius: *Has anyone among you made a similar claim before him?*

Abū Sufyān: No.

Heraclius: *Do the rich or the poor follow him?*

Abū Sufyān: *It is the poor who follow him.*

Heraclius: *Are his followers increasing or decreasing?*

Abū Sufyān: *They are increasing.*

Heraclius: *Does any of them become displeased or turn away from his religion after having embraced it?*

Abū Sufyān: No.

Heraclius: *Have you ever known him to lie before he started to make his claim?*

Abū Sufyān: No.

Heraclius: *Does he ever betray or break his promises?*

Abū Sufyān: *No. We, however, have a peace agreement with him for the time being, and we do not know what he will do during this period.*

Heraclius: *Have you ever had a war with him?*

Abū Sufyān: *Yes.*

Heraclius: *What was the outcome of your battles?*

Abū Sufyān: *Sometimes he was victorious and sometimes we.*

Heraclius: *What does he order you to do?*

Abū Sufyān: *He tells us to worship Allāh alone, and not to worship anything along with Him. He tells us not to follow our forefathers. He commands us to pray and to be truthful and chaste and kind to our relations.*

Heraclius: *I asked you about his family and your reply was that he belonged to a very noble family. In fact all the Messengers come from noble families amongst their respective peoples. Then I asked you whether anyone of his ancestors was a king. Your reply was in the negative, and if it had been in the affirmative, I would have thought that this man wanted to take back his ancestral kingdom. I questioned you whether anybody else amongst you claimed such a thing, your reply was in the negative. If the answer had been in the affirmative, I would have thought that this man was following the previous man's statement. I then asked you whether the rich people followed him or the poor. You replied that it was the poor who followed him. And in fact all the Messengers have been followed by this very class of people. Then I asked you whether his followers were increasing or decreasing. You replied that they were increasing, and in fact this is the way of true faith, till it is complete in all respects. I further asked you whether there was anybody who, after embracing his religion, became displeased and discarded his religion. Your reply was in the negative, and in fact this is (the sign of) true faith, when its delight enters the hearts and mixes with them completely. I further asked whether he was ever accused of telling lies before he said what he said, and your reply was in the negative. So I wondered how a person who does not tell a lie about others could ever tell a lie about Allāh. I asked you whether he had ever betrayed. You replied in the negative and likewise the Messengers never betray. Then I asked you what he ordered you to do. You replied that he ordered you to worship Allāh alone and not to worship any thing along with Him and forbade you to worship idols and ordered you to pray, to speak the truth and to be chaste. If what you have said is true, he will very soon occupy this place underneath my feet and I knew it (from the Scriptures) that he was going to appear but I did not know that he would be from you, and if I could reach him definitely, I would go immediately to meet him and if I were with him, I would certainly wash his feet.*

Heraclius thus was close to accepting Islam, but he did not do so for fear of the loss of his Throne. He therefore sent back a diplomatic reply, pretending that he personally accepted Islām but was not in a position to announce this publicly. He sent gifts to the Prophet ﷺ through *Diḥyah* and the Prophet ﷺ gave them away to the poor Muslims in *Madīnah*.

Letter to the Negus (an-Najāshi) the ruler of Abyssinia

The Prophet ﷺ sent *'Amr bin Ummaiyah aḍ-Ḍamri* to the *Negus (an-Najāshi)* about *Ja'far bin Abī Ṭālib* and his companions and sent a letter with him. This letter was sent before the conquest of *Makkah*. The translation of the letter is given here:

In the name of Allāh, the most Merciful, the most Kind.

From Muḥammad, Allāh's messenger, to the Negus, the King of Abyssinia. Peace be with you. I praise Allāh, the One, the King, the Praised one, the Peace and the One Who watches over everything. I bear witness that Jesus, son of Mary, was Allāh's spirit and His word given to Mary, the Virgin, the chaste. She thus conceived Jesus, whom Allāh created of His own spirit, as He created Ādam with His own hand. I call upon you to believe in Allāh alone, and not to make partners with Him, and to His obedience, and to follow me and to believe in that which has been.revealed to me. I am Allāh's messenger and I call upon you and upon your subjects and soldiers to believe in Allāh, the Almighty. I have thus conveyed my message and given good counsel. It is better for you to accept my good counsel. Peace be upon all those who follow true guidance."

'Amr bin Ummaiyah aḍ-Ḍamrī also spoke to the *Negus*, saying:

"*You are kind to us as one of us, and we trust you as if we belong to your people. You have met all our good expectations and we feared nothing from you whatsoever. However, we find in your own words what supports our case. The Bible is our ultimate witness and fair arbiter (judge). There can be no clearer evidence or stronger argument. If you do not submit to its word, then your attitude towards the Prophet ﷺ is like the attitude of the Jews towards Jesus, son of Mary. The Prophet ﷺ has sent envoys to all people, but he has far greater hopes in you than in them. He has trusted you with what he has not been able to trust them with, for your history of good deeds. Besides, a fine reward awaits you.*"

The *Negus* sent a reply to the Prophet's ﷺ letter:

In the name of Allāh, the most Merciful, the most Kind.

From the Negus, al-Asham bin Abjar, to Muḥammad, Allāh's Messenger. Peace of Allāh be upon you, O Prophet of Allāh, and mercy and blessings from Allāh, beside Whom there is no God, Who has guided me to Islām. I have received your letter in which you mention about Jesus. By the Lord of Heavens and the Earth, Jesus, son of Mary is nothing more than what you have stated. We know that with which you were sent to us and I have extended hospitality to your cousin and his companions. I declare that you are Allāh's Messenger who tells the truth. I pledge my allegiance to you and to your cousin and I have surrendered myself through him to the Lord of all the Universe."

Thus, the *Negus* became a Muslim, and his was the most favourable response received by the Prophet ﷺ.

The rulers of Persia, Egypt and the chiefs of *ash-Shām* either ridiculed the Prophet's ﷺ envoys or delayed the acceptance of his message on this or that pretext.

By sending envoys to almost all known areas of his time, the Prophet ﷺ performed his duty of conveying the message of Islām to all the human race of every creed and colour. Thus he accomplished his responsibility of being "a mercy to all mankind."

The Conquest of Makkah (630 CE)

In the seventh year of the *Hijrah*, an expedition was made against the Jews of *Banū Naḍīr* who had been expelled to *Khaibar*. *Khaibar* became the centre of anti-Islāmic activities and the Prophet ﷺ decided to take action against the trouble-makers there. After a long seige and protracted battles in a number of different places, the fortress of the Jews was conquered.

The strength of the Muslims was ever on the increase and new followers were joining. The *Ḥudaibiyah* treaty gave freedom to the tribes to make agreements with either the *Quraish* or the Muslims. The tribe of *Banū Khuzā'ah* sided with the Muslims, while *Banū Bakr* went on the side of the *Quraish*.

Two years after the agreement, *Banū Bakr* attacked *Banū Khuzā'ah* while they were asleep. *Banū Khuzā'ah* took refuge in *al-Ka'bah*, but were butchered in the sacred area of *al-Ka'bah*. The news of this violation of the treaty reached the Prophet ﷺ, and he sent an ultimatum to the *Quraish* asking them to accept any of the following options:

1. *to pay compensation for the victims of the Banū Khuzā'ah;*
2. *to withdraw their support for Banū Bakr;*
3. *to declare that the Ḥudaibiyah agreement no longer holds valid.*

The Quraish did not agree to the first two options and declared the *Ḥudaibiyah* treaty to be null and void. The Prophet ﷺ then had no alternative but to take action against the *Quraish*. He set forth for *Makkah* with an army of ten thousand and took care to see that the news of his advance remained a secret. It was the tenth of the month of *Ramaḍān*, in the eighth year of the *Hijrah*.

The *Quraish* had no power to resist the mighty Muslim advance. All the famous warriors were now on the Muslim side. How could the *Quraish* fight? They were totally demoralised by the might of the Muslim army.

Abū Sufyān, the arch-enemy of the Prophet ﷺ, saw that there was no route to escape. He asked *al-'Abbās*, the Prophet's uncle, to take him to the Prophet ﷺ. *Muḥammad* ﷺ granted an unconditional pardon to *Abū Sufyān*. Such a generous person was the final messenger of Allāh to his arch-enemy. *Abū Sufyān* embraced Islām on this occasion.

The Muslim army entered *Makkah* without any unfavourable incident. Inside, Makkans locked themselves within their homes and only a few who were unable to accept the new situation put up vain resistance.

The Prophet ﷺ declared a general amnesty for the entire community of *Makkah*. He forgave them for their past crimes. It was a unique scene! The *Quraish* could not believe it! But even if they were unable to understand, it was the beauty and splendour of Islām which *Muḥammad* ﷺ, Allāh's messenger, was trying to make them understand and follow. Now they saw it with their own eyes. It was *Muḥammad* ﷺ whom they compelled to migrate, called a sorceror, a madman and an apostate; it was the same *Muḥammad* ﷺ who granted a pardon to them at the crucial time of their utter helplessness.

Now *Makkah* was safe, peaceful and free of vengeance and enmity. Everyone enjoyed peace and happiness in their hearts.

The conquest of *Makkah* without any bloodshed is one of the most memorable events in Islāmic history. The amnesty granted by the Prophet ﷺ was unique and unmatched. The greatness of Islām and its Prophet ﷺ is proved splendidly in the conquest of *Makkah*. Where can you find an example of such forgiveness and mercy? It is only in Islām, which ensures real peace, happiness and contentment of heart.

The Prophet stayed in *Makkah* until the 9th day of *Shawwāl* in the eighth year of the *Hijrah*.

The Farewell Address

The Prophet ﷺ completed his mission and the duty given to him by Allāh. He had endured every sort of trial and tribulation for the sake of his Master and Creator. For twenty long years he left no stone unturned and did everything he could to make the rule of Allāh supreme on earth. He carried out this difficult duty on the soil of Arabia, a country which was most reluctant to accept the rule of the One God, Allāh.

The system to guide the whole human race for all time was now complete. The Prophet ﷺ could feel that his days were coming to an end.

After the performance of his last *Ḥajj*, he delivered his farewell speech at *'Arafāt* before about *120,000* of his followers. This speech was one of the most memorable and important for its contents in the history of Prophet *Muḥammad's* ﷺ life.

The Prophet ﷺ delivered the speech sitting on his camel and his devoted followers listened intently to every word of it. Praising and thanking Allāh, *Muḥammad* ﷺ, the last and final messenger of Allāh said:

"O people, listen to my words carefully, for I know not whether I would meet you again on such an occasion.

O people, just as you regard this month, this day, this city as sacred, so regard the life and property of every Muslim as a sacred trust. Remember that you will indeed appear before Allāh and answer for your actions.

Return the things kept with you as a trust (Amānah) to their rightful owners. All dues of interest shall stand cancelled and you will have only your capital back; Allāh has forbidden interest, and I cancel the dues of interest payable to my uncle al-'Abbas bin 'Abdul Muṭṭalib.

O people, your wives have a certain right over you and you have certain rights over them. Treat them well and be kind to them, for they are your partners and commited helpers.

Beware of Satan, he is desperate to divert you from the worship of Allāh, so beware of him in matters of your religion.

O people, listen carefully! All the believers are brothers. You are not allowed to take the things belonging to another Muslim unless he gives it to you willingly.

O people, none is higher than the other unless he is higher in obedience to Allāh. No Arab is any superior to a non-Arab except in piety.

O people, reflect on my words. I leave behind me two things, the Qur'an and my example (Sunnah), and if you follow these, you will not fail.

Listen to me carefully! Worship Allāh and offer Ṣalāh, observe Ṣawm in the month of Ramaḍān and pay Zakāh.

O people, be mindful of those who work under you. Feed and clothe them as you feed and clothe yourselves.

O people, no prophet or messenger will come after me and no new faith will emerge.

All those who listen to me shall pass on my words to others, and those to others again."

He then faced the heavens and asked, *"Have I conveyed the message of Allāh to you, O people?"* The audience answered in one voice, *"Yes, you have; Allāh is the witness."*

As the Prophet ﷺ finished the following revelation came to him:

"Today I have perfected your religion for you, completed my favour upon you and have chosen for you Islām as the way of life." (5:3)

May the Almighty Allāh bless us with His Mercy and His ever-flowing Kindness to follow His *Dīn* only for His sake and only to seek His Pleasure. May He grant us the ability to think of our death and shape our life emulating the excellent example of the last and final messenger of Allāh, *Muḥammad* ﷺ — the mercy to all creation. *Āmīn.*

The Sad News

Back in *Madīnah*, the Prophet ﷺ was taken ill. His health deteriorated and the illness became serious. He was unable to lead *Ṣalāh*. So, he asked *Abū Bakr*, his closest friend, to lead the *Ṣalāh* in his place.

During his last days of illness, he had terrible headaches and a very bad fever. The illness eventually took the life of the Prophet ﷺ, the most illustrious personality in the history of mankind.

It was heart-breaking news for the Muslims. At first, they could not believe it; *'Umar*, one of the well-known companions of the Prophet ﷺ, became so furious on hearing the news that he threatened to kill anyone who said *Muḥammad* ﷺ was dead. It was the depth of his love and attachment to the Prophet ﷺ that made him behave this way.

The Prophet ﷺ was a man (18:110). He was mortal. He died. However painful and upsetting the news was for the Muslims, they had to believe it. *Abū Bakr*, pale and saddened with grief, went in and kissed the Prophet's ﷺ forehead. He came out weeping to the waiting crowd outside the mosque. He heard what *'Umar* had said. He addressed the crowd with tears in his eyes but with a firm voice:

"Surely he who worshipped Muḥammad should know that Muḥammad is dead, but he who worshipped Allāh should know that Allāh is alive and never dies."

He then recited the verse of the *Qur'ān*, *"Muḥammad is but a messenger and messengers have passed away before him. Will it be that when he dies or is slain you will turn back on your heels? He who turns back does no harm to Allāh and Allāh will reward the thankful." (3:144)*

These words of *Abū Bakr* brought the Muslims back to face the hard reality, and gave them the confidence and hope they needed. Allāh was there to help them and the *Qur'ān* and the *Sunnah* of the Prophet ﷺ were there to guide them.

Muḥammad ﷺ, Allāh's last messenger on earth and supreme example for mankind, breathed his last on *12 Rabī'ul Awwāl, 11 AH* (8th June, 632 CE), at the age of sixty-three.

"Innā lillāh wa innā ilaihi rāji'ūn."

"Truly to Allāh we belong and to Him we shall return." (2:156)

Mission Accomplished

The victory at *Makkah* was followed by an expedition led by *Khālid* to demolish the Temple of *al-'Uzzā*, the battle of *Ḥunain*, the seige of *Ṭā'if* and the battle of *Tabūk*. During the last two years of the Prophet's life, laws regarding *Zakāh*, *Jizyah* (a tax on non-Muslims, who were exempt from paying *Zakāh* and performing *Jihād*, to provide for their security), *Ḥajj* and interest dealings were revealed.

Muḥammad ﷺ had a mission, a goal to achieve. It was to make the Law of Allāh hold supreme in all human affairs. His duty was to call people to worship Allāh alone and none other. His task was to form a society based on the worship of Allāh, obedience to *Tawḥīd*, belief in *Risālah* and a firm conviction in the *Ākhirah*.

Muḥammad ﷺ, the Prophet of Allāh, accomplished his assigned mission very successfully. He started preaching in the centre of idolatry, suffered torture, faced strong opposition, tolerated harassment and finally had to leave his own home and birth place for the sake of the truth and the pleasure of Allāh, the Creator.

He fought evil and untruth and never compromised on matters of basic principles. He was offered all kinds of worldly allurements and temptations, but he was not drawn into such traps.

He practised meticulously what he preached. His character and demeanour had a magnetic quality about them. His conduct and behaviour impressed even his bitterest enemy. He had a superb personality. His life is the perfect example of total obedience to Allāh's commands.

He was loved by his companions more than anybody else. His was the life of an unrivalled leader, teacher, general, statesman, husband, father, friend and brother; and, above all, a true and most obedient servant of Allāh.

When he had to fight, he fought for the Truth and never violated the principles of war. He showed the highest degree of patience in the face of the strongest provocation and incitement. He loved his companions so deeply that they did not hesitate to give their lives at his call.

Muḥammad's ﷺ life is the shining example for us to follow. He left for us teachings for all areas and affairs of our life. His life is the complete embodiment of Islām, based on the *Qur'ān*, the complete book of guidance from Allāh.

Muḥammad ﷺ was sent as a Prophet to show mankind the best way to worship Allāh. During his twenty-three years as Allāh's messenger he fulfilled this duty perfectly and meticulously.

Prophet Muḥammad's ﷺ Life at a Glance

Life at Makkah

Birth	**571 CE** (see footnote on page 85). Father *'Abdullāh* died before the Prophet's ﷺ birth.
6 years of age	Death of mother *Āminah*.
8	Grandfather *'Abdul Muṭṭalib* died.
12	First business trip to *ash-Shām* (Syria).
15	*Ḥarbul Fijār*.
16	Member of *Ḥilful Fuḍūl*.
24	Second business trip to *ash-Shām*.
25	**Marriage with *Khadījah*.**
35	Settlement of *al-Ḥajarul Aswad* dispute.
40	**Prophethood in 610 CE.**
1st year of prophethood	*Fajr* and *'Aṣr* prayers 2 *rak'ahs* each.
1st–3rd year	Secret preaching of Islām at *al-Arqam's* house.
3rd year	Open call to Islām from Mount *Ṣafā*.
3rd–5th year	Hostility of Makkan infidels.
5th year	Migration of Muslims to Abyssinia (Ethiopia).
6th year	*Ḥamzah* and *'Umar* accept Islām.
7th–9th year	Boycott and confinement by Makkan infidels at *Shi'bi Abī Ṭālib*.
10th year	**Year of Sorrow** — uncle *Abū Ṭālib* and wife *Khadījah* died.
10th year	Visit to *Ṭā'if*.
10th year	**Mi'rāj** *(27 Rajab)* — five times daily *Ṣalāh* made obligatory.
11th year	First covenant of *al-'Aqabah*, 621 CE.
12th year	Second covenant of *al-'Aqabah*, 622 CE.
13th year	***Hijrah* to *Yathrib* (*Madīnah*)** 622 CE *(27 Ṣafar)*.

Life at Madīnah

1st year of Hijrah	Arrival at *Qubā', 8 Rabī'ul Awwāl*.
	Arrival at *Madīnah* on a Friday in 622 CE.
	Treaty with the Jews.
	Construction of *al-Masjidun Nabawī*.
	Establishment of the first Islāmic State.

2nd Hijrah	**Jihād ordained** *(12 Ṣafar).*
	Adhān and *Zakāh* introduced.
	Change of *Qiblah* revealed *(15 Sha'bān).*
	Ramaḍān prescribed as month of fasting.
	'Īdul Fiṭr (1 Shawwāl).
	Battle of *Badr* *(17 Ramaḍān).*
	Marriage of *'Alī* and *Fāṭimah*, after *Badr.*
	Siege of *Banū Qainuqā'.*
3rd Hijrah	1st restriction on drinking wine revealed.
	Battle of *Uḥud* *(5 Shawwāl).*
	First order about *Ribā* (interest) revealed.
	Revelation of laws about orphans, inheritance, marriage and the rights of wives.
4th Hijrah	Order of *Ḥijāb* for women revealed.
	Revelation of prohibition on drinking wine.
5th Hijrah	Battles of *Dawmatul Jandal* and *Banū al-Muṣṭaliq.*
	Laws about adultery and slander revealed.
	Battle of *Aḥzāb*.
	Punishment of *Banū Quraiẓah.*
6th Hijrah	***Ḥudaibiyah* agreement.**
	Khālid bin al-Walīd and *'Amr bin al-'Aṣ* accept Islām.
7th Hijrah	Letters to rulers of different countries.
	Siege of *Khaibar*.
	Performance of postponed *'Umrah.*
	Laws about marriage and divorce revealed.
8th Hijrah	Battle of *Mu'tah.*
	Conquest of Makkah *(20 Ramaḍān).*
	Battle of *Ḥunain* (month of *Shawwāl*).
	Siege of *Ṭā'if.*
	Final order prohibiting *Ribā* (interest) revealed.
9th Hijrah	Battle of *Tabūk.*
	Order of *Jizyah* (a tax on non-Muslims) revealed.
	Ḥajj prescribed.
10th Hijrah	**Farewell address** *(9 Dhul Ḥijjah).*
11th Hijrah	**Death of *Muḥammad*** ﷺ, the Final Messenger of Allāh, on *12 Rabī'ul Awwal* (632 CE).

What did you learn? (3a)

Key Stage 3 (11–14)

1. Where and when was *Muḥammad* ﷺ born?
2. Who were his father and mother?
3. What does the name *Muḥammad* mean?
4. Describe the rebuilding of *al-Ka'bah.*
5. What other names were given to *Muḥammad* ﷺ because of his good character?
6. Name his first wife. How old were they when they got married?
7. Name *Muḥammad's* ﷺ children.

Key Stage 4 (15–16)

1. Describe *Muḥammad's* ﷺ meeting with *Baḥīrā?*
2. How might the important events of *Muḥammad's* ﷺ childhood experiences have taught him compassion?
3. What was the *Ḥilful Fuḍūl?*
4. What do you think impressed *Khadījah* about *Muḥammad* ﷺ?
5. What were the titles given to *Muḥammad* ﷺ by the Makkans before he became a prophet? What was ironic about their attitude after he became a prophet?

Key Stage 5 (17–18)

1. What do you think were the main qualities in the Prophet's ﷺ character that made him a suitable person to receive prophethood.
2. Discuss the role of young *Muḥammad* ﷺ in social welfare activities. What lessons can you learn from this?
3. Choose some of the key events in *Muḥammad's* ﷺ early life before prophethood, and explain their implications for his later life.

What did you learn? (3b)

Key Stage 3 (11–14)

1. When and how did *Muḥammad* ﷺ become a prophet of Allāh?
2. How is the story of *'Alī* and the Dinner such a good example for young Muslims?
3. Who was *an-Najāshī?* How did the Muslims convince him to give them his protection?
4. Describe the story about *'Umar's* acceptance of Islām. Why was it such an important event in the history of the early Muslims?
5. Write down the names of five early male Muslims and five female Muslims.
6. Why did Prophet *Muḥammad* ﷺ have to leave *Makkah?*
7. Describe the *Hijrah* of the Prophet ﷺ.

Key Stage 4 (15–16)

1. When and where did *Muḥammad* ﷺ receive the revelation from Allāh?
2. Describe in your own words how ten year old *'Alī* accepted Islām.
3. Write a newspaper article describing the story of the Prophet ﷺ on Mount *Ṣafā.*
4. What were the chief results (bad and good) of the Prophet ﷺ starting to preach in public?
5. Discuss the ways in which the *Quraish* tried to make the Prophet ﷺ give up his mission. Why do you think they did not work?
6. What were *al-Isrā'* and *al-Mi'rāj?*
7. Why did the prophet ﷺ leave *Makkah?* What is this important event called?
8. Describe the Prophet's ﷺ emigration to *Madīnah.* Why was this a turning point in the spread of Islām?

Key Stage 5 (17–18)

1. Describe the circumstances that led to the *Hijrah* of Prophet Muḥammad ﷺ from *Makkah* to *Madīnah.*
2. Discuss the reasons behind the hostility of the Makkans to the message of Prophet *Muḥammad* ﷺ.
3. Write an account of *al-Mi'rāj* and explain its significance.

What did you learn? (3c)

Key Stage 3 (11–14)

1. What is the meaning of:
   a. *Muhājirūn* b. *Anṣār*
2. What was the first *Qiblah* (direction of prayer), and what was it changed to?
3. Which uncle of the Prophet ﷺ was martyred during the battle of *Uḥud?*
4. Who was *Salmān al-Fārisī*, and how did he help the Muslims prepare for the battle of *Aḥzāb?*
5. Write about what happened during *al-Mi'rāj*.
6. Imagine you witnessed the conquest of *Makkah* by the Muslims. Describe what you would have seen.
7. When did Prophet *Muḥammad* ﷺ die?

Key Stage 4 (15–16)

1. Why did *Madīnah* become so important to Muslims everywhere?
2. Why was *Adhān* introduced? Write the sentences which are said loudly at the time of *Adhān* in English.
3. How did the Prophet ﷺ ensure solidarity between the *Muhājirūn* and *Anṣār* in *Madīnah?*
4. Write in your own words about the *Ḥudaibiyah* agreement.
5. Give some examples from the Prophet's ﷺ life in *Madīnah* that show Islām's rejection of any form of racism.

Key Stage 5 (17–18)

1. Write an account of the battle of *Badr* and comment on the outcome of this battle.
2. What vital lessons should we learn from the battle of *Uḥud?*
3. What were the main features of the *Ḥudaibiyah* agreement? In what way was it helpful for the Muslims in the long run?
4. Describe the conquest of *Makkah* and comment on the general amnesty declared by the Prophet ﷺ at the time of this conquest.

What did you learn? (3d)

Key Stage 3 (11–14)

1. What did Prophet *Muḥammad* ﷺ leave behind for us?
2. Write about what makes Prophet *Muḥammad's* ﷺ character special. How can we learn from his good character?

Key Stage 4 (15–16)

1. Choose five of the important events in the Prophet *Muḥammad's* ﷺ life, and explain why they were important.
2. Describe in detail the character of the Prophet ﷺ. Use examples of incidents from his life to explain your answer.
3. What did *Muḥammad* ﷺ leave behind for our guidance?
4. Describe any one of the famous battles during the Prophethood of *Muḥammad* ﷺ, and explain its importance.
5. Who were these people, and what part did they play in the Prophet's ﷺ life:
   a. *Abū Ṭālib* b. *Khadījah* c. *Abū Bakr* d. *'Alī*

Key Stage 5 (17–18)

1. *"Indeed in the Messenger of Allāh, you have for you, the best example." (33:21)* Explain in your own words the meaning of this verse of the *Qur'ān*.
2. Highlight the important changes made by the Prophet ﷺ to the social structures of Makkan and Madīnan society.
3. Describe the principles established by *Muḥammad* ﷺ for warfare, treaties and the treatment of prisoners, and explain their importance for conduct in the 21st century.

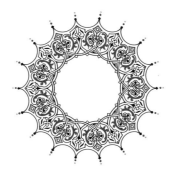

Al-Khulafā'ur Rāshidūn (Rightly guided Caliphs) 4

Abū Bakr ﵁

Now that the beloved Prophet ﷺ was no more, who would lead the Muslim community? That question was in the minds of all those present at *al-Masjidun Nabawī*. It was a crucial matter — a community cannot continue without a leader. Without leadership, a community becomes disorganised and indisciplined, and eventually loses its potential and prospects.

Indeed, so great was its importance that the issue of leadership had to be decided before Allāh's messenger ﷺ could be buried.

There was much discussion amongst the *Ṣaḥābah* (companions of the Prophet ﷺ). After consultation, *Abū Bakr* was unanimously chosen as the leader of the Muslim community. He was the first *Khalīfah* (Caliph or successor to the Prophet ﷺ) of the Muslims. Who else could lead the Muslim community at this crucial time except *Abū Bakr?* He was the closest friend of the Prophet ﷺ and had acted as the Prophet's deputy, leading the prayers when the Prophet ﷺ was ill.

After the election of the *Khalīfah*, the Prophet ﷺ was buried on the night of 13 *Rabī'ul Awwal* 11 AH.

Abū Bakr's real name was *'Abdullāh*. He had been given the title of *aṣ-Ṣiddīq* (testifier to the truth). His father, *'Uthmān*, was known as *Abū Quḥāfah* and his mother, *Salmā*, was known as *Ummul Khair*. He was two and a half years younger than *Muḥammad* ﷺ.

After his election as the *Khalīfah*, *Abū Bakr* addressed the Muslims with these words:

"O people, I have been chosen by you as your leader, although I am no better than any one of you. If I do any good, give me your support. If I do any wrong, set me right.

Listen, truth is honesty and untruth is dishonesty.

The weak among you are the powerful in my eyes, as long as I do not get them their due. The powerful among you are weak in my eyes, as long as I do not take away from them what is due to others.

Listen carefully, if people give up striving for the cause of Allāh, He will send down disgrace upon them. If a people become evil-doers, Allāh will send down calamities upon them.

Obey me as long as I obey Allāh and His messenger. If I disobey Allāh and His messenger, you are free to disobey me."

Abū Bakr was asking people to obey him only if he obeyed Allāh and His messenger. Such was the first *Khalīfah* of the Muslims! Indeed, the world would be a better place to live in if we had leaders like *Abū Bakr*.

He was the first among the Prophet's friends to accept Islām and he accompanied the Prophet ﷺ during the *Hijrah* to *Madīnah*.

Abū Bakr was a trader. He was kind and willing to help others. He freed a number of slaves, including *Bilāl bin Rabāḥ*, *'Āmir bin Fuhairah*, *Umm 'Ubais*, *Zinnīrah*, *Nahdiyah* and her daughter. He participated in all the battles which the Prophet ﷺ had to fight against unbelievers.

Abū Bakr loved his faith more than anything else. At *Badr*, his son *'Abdur Raḥmān* was fighting on the side of the unbelievers. After accepting Islām, *'Abdur Raḥmān* once said to his father, *"O father, at Badr you were twice under my sword, but my love for you held my hand back."* To this, *Abū Bakr* replied, *"Son, if I had you only once under my sword, you would have been no more."* So uncompromising was *Abū Bakr's* faith!

At the time of the battle of *Tabūk*, he donated all his belongings to the war fund and when the Prophet ﷺ asked, *"What have you left for your family?"* he replied, "Allāh and His messenger." A rare example of sacrifice indeed!

Before his death, the Prophet ﷺ appointed *Usāmah bin Zaid* to lead an expedition to *ash-Shām* against the Roman (then called Byzantine) army on the northern border of Arabia. The Romans killed the envoy of the Prophet ﷺ and refused to accept any negotiated settlement. *Usāmah* could not go on because of the death of the Prophet ﷺ. *Abū Bakr* sent *Usāmah* to complete the expedition initiated by the Prophet ﷺ, even though he had to attend to internal problems facing the Islāmic state that had arisen after the death of the Prophet ﷺ.

Indeed, the news of the Prophet's ﷺ death made some new Muslims think that the Islāmic state would crumble, so they refused to pay the *Zakāh*. These new Muslims were not used to their new faith and its requirements. *Abū Bakr* declared, *"By Allāh! Even if a single baby goat is due from a man, he must give it. If he refuses I will declare war against him."*

A number of imposters appeared, causing a great deal of trouble and confusion. Already, during the Prophet's ﷺ lifetime, *al-Aswad bin 'Anzah al-'Ansī* had claimed prophethood, and was taken care of by the Muslims in Yemen. Other imposters and false prophets were: *Musailimah bin Ḥabīb*, *Ṭulaiḥah bin Khuwailid* and a woman named *Sajāḥ bint al-Ḥārith*. *Mālik bin Nuwairah* happily sided with the claim of *Sajāḥ*. *Abū Bakr* was quick to take strong action against these imposters. *Khālid bin al-Walīd* was sent to deal with *Ṭulaiḥah* who fled to *ash-Shām* and later became a Muslim. *Mālik bin Nuwairah* was also killed.

'Ikrimah bin Abī Jahl and *Shuraḥbīl bin Ḥasanah* were sent to take action against the notorious *Musailimah*, but they were defeated. So *Abū Bakr* dispatched *Khālid* to tackle *Musailimah,* who by now had married *Sajāḥ*. In the fighting that followed, *Musailimah* was killed by *Waḥshī*. *Waḥshī* had become a Muslim after the conquest of *Makkah*. He felt deep remorse about killing the Prophet's uncle, *Ḥamzah*, at *Uḥud*. Killing *Musailimah,* he thought, would help make up for his earlier mistake.

Abū Bakr's swift and bold steps saved the Islāmic state from the serious threat of chaos and confusion. He could now attend to other urgent problems.

During his *Khilāfah* (Caliphate), *Abū Bakr* had to take action against the Persian empire. The emperor of *Persia*, *Khosraw Parwīz II* (Arabic: *Kisrā*; English: *Chosroes II*), tore up the letter the Prophet ﷺ sent to him through *'Abdullāh bin Ḥudhāfah* and demanded that the Prophet ﷺ be arrested. However, *Khosraw II* was murdered by his son, *Shīrūyah (Qubādh II* or *Kavadh II)* and the whole empire fell into chaos and disorder. *Hurmuz*, the Persian governor in *'Irāq*, was very hostile and was cruel to the Muslims living in his area.

Abū Bakr sent *al-Muthannā* to take action against the Persians in *'Irāq*. His forces were insufficient and *Khālid* was then sent with reinforcements. The Muslim army captured large areas of the Persian empire in several battles.

Khalīfah Abū Bakr then turned his attention to the Romans, who were causing trouble on the Islāmic state's north-western borders. The Prophet ﷺ himself led an expedition against the Romans and this is known as the Battle of *Mu'tah*.

Abū Bakr dispatched four separate armies under *Abū 'Ubaidah bin al-Jarrāḥ, 'Amr bin al-'Āṣ, Yazīd bin Abī Sufyān* and *Shuraḥbīl bin Ḥasanah* to deal with Roman power.

The four generals merged themselves into a unit to face the Romans most effectively. The Romans had amassed 150,000 soldiers but the total Muslim army was only 24,000. Reinforcements were requested and *Abū Bakr* asked *Khālid* to hand over the command of the Iraqi front to *al-Muthannā* and rush to the Syrian front to help fight the colossal Roman army.

Abū Bakr fell ill during this time and he died on 21 *Jumāda'ul Ākhirah* 13 AH (22 August 634 CE). His rule had lasted two years and three months.

The armies met in *Yarmūk* after *Abū Bakr's* death during the *Khilāfah* of *'Umar* and the Romans were defeated.

One of the many contributions of *Abū Bakr* was the compilation of the *Qur'ān* into one volume.

Abū Bakr lived a simple, pious and upright life. He was a true servant of Allāh and a meticulous follower of the Prophet ﷺ.

Abū Bakr's advice to the Muslim Army

1. *Always fear Allāh; He knows what is in men's hearts.*
2. *Be kind to those who are under you and treat them well.*
3. *Give brief directions; directions that are too long are likely to be forgotten.*
4. *Improve your own conduct before asking others to improve theirs.*
5. *Honour the enemy's envoy.*
6. *Maintain the secrecy of your plans.*
7. *Always speak the truth, so that you get the right advice.*
8. *Consult your men when you are free to do so; this will develop participation.*
9. *Take suitable measures to keep a watch on the enemy.*
10. *Be sincere to all with whom you deal.*
11. *Give up cowardice and dishonesty.*
12. *Give up bad company.*

Before his death, *Abū Bakr* consulted the senior companions of the Prophet ﷺ and selected *'Umar* as the second *Khalīfah* of the Muslims.

'Umar was the son of *al-Khaṭṭāb* and he is famous in Islāmic history as *al-Fārūq* (one who distinguishes between right and wrong). His acceptance of Islām is notable and was mentioned earlier in the Prophet's ﷺ biography.

'Umar was a brave and straightforward person. He was tough in his attitude and uncompromising in basic principles. He was a great and talented ruler. During his Caliphate, the frontiers of the Islāmic state expanded greatly.

'Umar was a strong administrator. He noticed the tremendous popularity of *Khālid*, the Commander-in-Chief of the Muslim forces, and feared the people might think too highly of him. So he removed *Khālid* and appointed *Abū 'Ubaidah bin al-Jarrāḥ* as the Commander-in-Chief. The other reason for this bold decision was to make it clear that no one was indispensable and victory in war was actually due to Allāh's help. According to *Shiblī Nu'mānī*, the deposition of *Khālid* took place in 17 AH after the conquest of Syria *(ash-Shām)*. Some historians, however, maintain that this was the first command given by *Khalīfah 'Umar.*

Khālid, who had been given the title of the 'Sword of Allāh' *(Saifullāh)* by the Prophet ﷺ, gracefully accepted the *Khalīfah's* order. He worked as an ordinary soldier under *Abū 'Ubaidah.* Thus he was an example of the Islāmic teaching of obedience to leadership.

Khālid had left *al-Muthannā* in command of the Muslim forces on the 'Irāqi front when he rushed to *Yarmūk. Muthannā* was finding it difficult to counter the enemy and went personally to *Madīnah* to ask *Abū Bakr* for reinforcement. *Abū Bakr* was by then on his deathbed.

Al-Muthannā's absence from *'Irāq* made things worse. The Persians regrouped and, under the command of *Rustam*, recaptured the Muslim-occupied areas. *Rustam* sent out two columns of his army, one to *Ḥirah* and the other to *Kaskar.*

'Umar sent *Abū 'Ubaid ath-Thaqafī* to deal with the situation and he defeated both the Persian columns. *Rustam* despatched a still larger force, including elephants, under the command of General *Bahman.* The two armies fought and the Muslims were defeated in the Battle of the Bridge *(al-Jisr).*

Khalīfah 'Umar raised another large army and *al-Muthannā* regrouped the defeated troops. They put up a valiant fight and the Persians were defeated this time.

However, the Persian court raised a larger army still, and forced *al-Muthannā* to withdraw. The report of the new situation was sent to *'Umar* and reinforcements were sent under *Sa'd bin Abī Waqqāṣ.*

The Persian army and the Muslim army met at *Qādisiyyah.* After a prolonged battle on several fronts, the outnumbered Muslim army defeated 120,000 Persian troops and recaptured *Ḥirah* and other areas in 14 AH (636 CE).

Muslims laid siege to *Damascus* during the *Khilāfah* of *Abū Bakr.* They continued after *Abū Bakr's* death and the siege lasted 70 days during the rule of *'Umar.* After this long siege, *Khālid* took the Romans by surprise and entered the city. The Governor surrendered and a peace treaty was signed.

Meanwhile, *'Amr bin al-'Āṣ* was laying siege to Jerusalem. Later, *Khālid, Abū 'Ubaidah bin al-Jarrāḥ* and others joined him there. The Christians had little hope and decided to give in. They put forward a proposal to the Muslims that they would hand over the city if *Khalīfah 'Umar* himself came to Jerusalem.

The proposal was relayed to *Madīnah* and the *Khalīfah* agreed to go to Jerusalem. He started out for the city with one attendant, riding a camel. They rode the camel in turns. Sometimes the *Khalīfah* would walk and the attendant would ride and other times the *Khalīfah* would ride and the attendant would walk. This is an example of equality of rights. The ruler and ruled have equal rights. The ruler of an Islāmic state must acknowledge the rights of the citizens over his own rights.

The *Khalīfah* of the Muslims entered Jerusalem dressed in ordinary clothes and flanked by the Muslim generals. The Christians could hardly believe that the Muslim leader had arrived; such was the simplicity of *'Umar.* He used to live like a very humble ordinary man, but he was a strong leader and the most able ruler of his time. He had no pride, no pomp and no grandeur. This is the teaching of Islām. This is what present-day Muslim rulers have forgotten and what Muslims need to restore.

A treaty to guarantee the safety and security of the Christians in Jerusalem was signed.

During the *Khilāfah* of *'Umar,* vast areas of the Roman and Persian empires and the whole of Egypt were brought under Islāmic rule.

'Umar was a gifted orator. He was very concerned for the welfare of the citizens under his rule and left a memorable legacy for Muslims after him.

The second *Khalīfah 'Umar* died after being stabbed by a Persian non-Muslim, *Fīroz*, nicknamed *Abū Lu'lu'*. *Fīroz* complained to *'Umar* about his master *al-Mughīrah bin Shu'bah* who imposed a tax on him. *'Umar* heard the details of the complaint and told *Fīroz* that the tax was reasonable. This made *Fīroz* angry and the next day during the dawn prayer he struck the *Khalīfah* with a dagger six times, wounding him fatally. *'Umar al-Fārūq* died three days later in 23 AH (644 CE).

Before his death, *'Umar* appointed a six-man committee to elect his successor from among themselves. The six members of the committee were: *'Uthmān bin 'Affān, 'Abdur Raḥmān bin 'Awf, 'Alī bin Abī Ṭālib, az-Zubair bin al-'Awwām, Sa'd bin Abī Waqqāṣ*, and *Ṭalḥah bin 'Ubaidullāh.*

'Umar al-Fārūq ruled the Islāmic state for ten years, six months and four days.

'Umar's advice

1. *Do not be misled by someone's reputation.*
2. *Do not judge a person only by his performance of Ṣalāh and Ṣawm; rather look into his truthfulness and wisdom.*

3. *One who keeps his secrets controls his affairs.*
4. *Fear the person whom you hate.*
5. *Prudent is he who can assess his actions.*
6. *Do not defer your work for tomorrow.*
7. *He who has no idea of evil can easily fall into its trap.*
8. *Judge a man's intelligence by the questions he asks.*
9. *Less concern for material well-being enables one to lead a free life.*
10. *It is easier not to indulge in sins than to repent.*
11. *Contentment and gratitude are two great virtues; you should not care which one you get.*
12. *Be grateful to him who points out your defects.*

'Uthmān ﷺ

The six-member committee appointed by *'Umar al-Fārūq*, after long deliberations and consultation, elected *'Uthmān*, the son of *'Affān*, as the third *Khalīfah* of Islām.

'Uthmān was born six years after the Prophet ﷺ and he belonged to the *Umaiyah* clan of the *Quraish*. He was a cloth merchant and was very rich. His title was *al-Ghanī* (the rich).

He had accepted Islām on *Abū Bakr's* invitation and migrated to *Abyssinia* with his wife *Ruqaiyah* (the prophet's daughter). He acted as the Prophet's ﷺ envoy during the *Ḥudaibiyah* negotiations. After the death of *Ruqaiyah* he married *Umm Kulthum*, another daughter of the Prophet ﷺ. This is why he is called *Dhun Nūrain* — The One with Two Lights.

His state policy can be understood from his letter to the officers of the Islāmic army. He wrote:

"You are the protectors of Islām from the onslaughts of the enemies. 'Umar had issued some regulations which are known to me. In fact, they were drafted in consultation with me.

Beware! I do not want to hear reports of any transgression by you. If you do so, you will be replaced by someone better. You should always be mindful of your conduct. I will watch over whatever Allāh has entrusted to my care."

He once spoke to the tax collectors with these words:

"Allāh has created everything with fairness and justice. He accepts only what is right and just. Give what is right and take what is right. Trust produces trust. Follow it strictly and do not be one of those who fail to discharge it. Faithfulness begets faithfulness. Do not oppress the orphans and those with whom you have made a covenant. Allāh will punish those who will do so."

Sa'd bin Abī Waqqāṣ was the Governor of *Kūfah* in *'Irāq*. *'Uthmān* dismissed him for non-payment of a state loan. He was succeeded by *al-Mughīrah*.

During the Caliphate of *'Uthmān*, the rebellion in *Ādharbaijān* and *Ārmenia* was quelled. *Mu'āwiyah*, Governor of *ash-Shām*, with the help of *Ibn Abī Sarḥ*, the Governor of Egypt, made a naval attack on Cyprus and brought it under Islāmic rule. Vast areas of North Africa including *Tripoli* were brought under Islāmic rule during the *Khilāfah* of *'Uthmān*.

The Romans, although defeated several times by the Muslim army in the past, made another attempt during the *Khilāfah* of *'Uthmān* to recapture the territories they had lost.

Constantine, then Emperor of *Rūm* (Byzantium), made great preparations and attacked *Alexandria* with a naval fleet five to six thousand strong. But the *Romans* were decisively defeated by the new Muslim naval force under the command of *Ibn Abī Sarḥ* and *Mu'āwiyah.*

During the last six years of his *Khilāfah, 'Uthmān* faced internal dissension and trouble. This trouble took the shape of a civil war which eventually led to his murder by an unruly and angry mob.

'Uthmān's Khilāfah lasted for twelve years. He was murdered by rioters on Friday, *17 Dhul Ḥijjah 35 AH* (656 CE).

'Uthmān was a very kind-hearted man. His simplicity and kindness did not allow him to take strong action against the trouble-makers and rioters. Above all, because of his polite and soft nature, the administration was not as good as it had been during *'Umar's* time.

'Uthmān was a generous man. He used to spend a lot of money for Islām and to free slaves. He was a pious man who feared and loved Allāh above everything else. The compilation of *al-Qur'ān* into a book *(muṣḥaf)* was the crowning achievement of *'Uthmān's Khilāfah.*

'Alī رضي الله عنه

"I am the youngest of you. I may be a boy, my feet may not be strong enough but, O Messenger of Allāh, I shall be your helper. Whoever opposes you, I shall fight him as a mortal enemy."

These were the words of *'Alī*, the cousin of the Prophet ﷺ and then only a boy of ten. He spoke these words before the elders of the *Quraish* during the dinner hosted by the Prophet ﷺ to invite them to Islām.

'Alī was the person who risked his life for the Prophet ﷺ and slept in the Prophet's ﷺ bed when the unbelievers laid a siege to the Prophet's ﷺ house to kill him on the night of his migration.

The same *'Alī* was elected the fourth *Khalīfah* of Islām after *'Uthmān*. He was the son of *Abū Ṭālib*, the Prophet's uncle.

'Alī was married to the Prophet's ﷺ daughter, *Fāṭimah.* They had three sons: *al-Ḥasan, al-Ḥusain* and *al-Muḥassin;* and two daughters: *Zainab* and *Umm Kulthūm. Al-Muḥassin* died in his infancy. The Prophet ﷺ loved *al-Ḥasan* and *al-Ḥusain* very dearly.

He took part in the battles of *Badr, Aḥzāb* and *Khaibar.* At *Khaibar* it was *'Alī* who subdued the Jews by his furious assault.

'Alī held many important positions during the life of the Prophet ﷺ and the three Caliphs *(Khulafā')* before him.

He was elected *Khalīfah* at a very delicate time, when the Muslim *Ummah* (community) was torn by internal strife after the sad incident of the murder of *'Uthmān*, the third *Khalīfah*, had taken place.

'Alī first concentrated on consolidating his administration and pledged then to take action against *'Uthmān's* murderers. The supporters of *'Uthmān* would not listen to the *Khalīfah* until he took action against *'Uthmān's* murderers.

The murder of *'Uthmān* had tremendous consequences for Islāmic history. It divided the once cohesive, united and determined Muslim *Ummah* into factions who fought bloody battles among themselves. The damage to Muslim unity was irreparable.

The once powerful Islāmic army which fought the wrongdoers and rescued those suffering from the exploitation and tyranny of the mighty Persian and Roman empires had now become seriously involved in internal strife.

The talented ruler, *'Alī*, had to spend much of his time pacifying the warring factions of the Muslims. He tried his best to reconcile the opposing groups and restore peace but without much success. The *Ummah* was divided and catastrophic consequences followed.

During this turmoil, *'Alī*, the fourth *Khalīfah* of Islām, was fatally wounded during *Ṣalātul Fajr* by one *Ibn Muljam*. *'Alī* died on Friday, *20 Ramaḍān 40 AH* (661 CE).

'Alī's rule lasted for four years, nine months and the whole of that time was a period of unrest.

'Alī lived a very simple and austere life. He was a very courageous person and had a keen sense of justice.

'Alī loved learning. He was given the title of *Bābul 'Ilm* – 'Gate of Learning' – by the Prophet ﷺ. He was also called *al-Murtaḍā* (the one with whom Allāh is pleased) and *Asadullāh* (Lion of Allāh).

Some important sayings of 'Alī

1. *One who knows himself, knows his Creator.*
2. *If you love Allāh, tear out your heart's love of the world.*
3. *The fear of Allāh makes one secure.*
4. *How can you rejoice about this life that grows shorter each hour?*
5. *A world-wide reputation can be undone by an hour's degradation.*
6. *Three defects make life miserable:*
   i. Vindictiveness; ii. Jealousy; iii. A bad character.
7. *One who is proud of worldly possessions in this fleeting existence is ignorant.*
8. *Joy is followed by tears.*
9. *Each breath of a man is a step nearer to death.*
10. *The best man is he who is most helpful to his fellow men.*
11. *One who thinks himself the best is the worst.*
12. *The hated person is one who returns evil for good.*

13. *Virtue is the key to success.*
14. *Learned men live even after death; ignorant men are dead although alive.*
15. *There is no treasure like knowledge gained.*
16. *Knowledge is wisdom and the educated man is the wise man.*
17. *Experience is knowledge gained.*
18. *He who never corrects himself will never correct another.*
19. *Listen, and you will teach yourself: remain silent, and you risk nothing.*
20. *One who reflects on Allāh's gifts, succeeds.*
21. *Ignorance harms a man more than a cancer in the body.*
22. *One of the signs of a stupid man is the frequent change of opinion.*
23. *Never speak when it is not the time for speech.*
24. *Beware of backbiting: it sows the seeds of bitterness, and separates you from Allāh and man.*
25. *The best truth is the keeping of promises.*
26. *Better be dumb than lie.*
27. *Do not flatter, it is no sign of faith.*
28. *A hypocrite's tongue is clean, but there is sickness in his heart.*
29. *Better to be alone than with bad company.*
30. *Whoever sows good reaps his reward.*

Conclusion

Abū Bakr aṣ-Ṣiddīq, 'Umar al-Fārūq, 'Uthmān al-Ghanī and *'Alī al-Murtaḍā* were the consecutive successors of the Prophet ﷺ. These four *Khulafā'* are called *al-Khulafā'ur Rāshidūn* or the rightly-guided *Khulafā'*.

Together, these four *Khulafā'* ruled the Islāmic State for about thirty years. They are called 'rightly-guided' because they ruled the people of their time exactly in accordance with the teachings of the *Qur'ān* and the *Sunnah* of the Prophet ﷺ.

Despite the unpleasant happenings, this period of Islāmic rule is the golden period of justice unrivalled in human history. Islāmic principles were put into practice in full during this time.

A detailed and serious study of the lives of al-Khulafā'ur Rāshidūn would open before us a treasure of knowledge and experience about the Islāmic system of life which could solve the present and future problems of mankind. We need to follow the Islāmic teachings most faithfully in order to get the promised good out of it. Mere lip service to the greatness and beauty of Islām will not establish the Islāmic system. Even though the projection of Islām using all modern means of communication is commendable, it is only the practice of Islām which will eventually make a real impact.

Let us resolve to understand, practise and preach Islām. Only then shall we ourselves find peace and happiness and the whole of humanity be freed from unhappiness and injustice.

What did you learn? (4a)

Key Stage 3 (11–14)

1. What do the words *Khalīfah* and *Khilāfah* mean?
2. What is the title of *Abū Bakr?*
3. What did he say in his first speech as Caliph?
4. Name *Abū Bakr's* son who fought against him at the time of *Badr.*
5. What is the title of *Khalīfah 'Umar?*
6. Name one commander of the Muslim army at the time of *'Umar.*
7. When and how did *'Umar* die?
8. Why do you think the Prophet ﷺ chose *Abū Bakr* as his special friend?
9. What do you think we can find out about the character of *Abū Bakr* by studying his twelve points of advice?

Key Stage 4 (15–16)

1. What is the meaning of *al-Khulafā'ur Rāshidūn?*
2. Who were the false prophets against whom *Khalīfah Abū Bakr* fought?
3. What did *Abū Bakr* say to his son after the battle of *Badr?* What can we learn from this?
4. Who were the members of the committee formed by *Khalīfah 'Umar* to elect his successor?
5. Write a newspaper article describing *Khalīfah 'Umar's* visit to Jerusalem?
6. Discuss some incidents from *Abū Bakr's* life that can inspire us all.
7. What important lessons can be learnt from *Khalīfah 'Umar's* twelve points of advice?
8. Describe *'Umar's* character using specific incidents to explain your answer.

Key Stage 5 (17–18)

1. Discuss the importance of leadership in the Islāmic community. Why does Islām prefer elected rulers to a hereditary monarchy?
2. Why was the speech that *Khalīfah Abū Bakr* delivered after his election unusual in relation to leaders of the world today?
3. Why was *Khālid bin al-Walīd* replaced as Commander-in-Chief of the Muslim army?
4. In Islām, the leader is really the servant of the community. What are the dangers and temptations that might corrupt a ruler?

What did you learn? (4b)

Key Stage 3 (11–14)

1. What were the titles given to *'Alī* by Allāh and the Prophet ﷺ?
2. Choose ten points from *Khalīfah 'Alī's* 30 points of advice and explain why you think they are important.
3. Select one example from each *Khalīfah* to show their noble characters.

Key Stage 4 (15–16)

1. What did *Khalīfah 'Uthmān* write to the officers of the Islāmic Army?
2. What title was given to *Khalīfah 'Uthmān?*
3. Name the daughters of the Prophet ﷺ who married *Khalīfah 'Uthmān* and *Khalīfah 'Alī*.
4. What was *Mu'āwiyah's* post when *'Uthmān* was the *Khalīfah?*
5. Which countries came under Muslim rule whilst *'Uthmān* was the *Khalīfah?*
6. Who was the father of *Khalīfah 'Alī?*
7. Name the children of *Fāṭimah* and *'Alī*.
8. When and how did *Khalīfah 'Alī* die?

Key Stage 5 (17–18)

1. Examine the roots of the civil troubles whilst *'Uthmān* was the *Khalīfah*, and discuss his response.
2. What observations could you make about the *Khilāfah* of *'Alī?* Why do *Shi'ites* claim him as the first *Khalīfah?*
3. Discuss the concepts of democracy, hereditary control, tyranny and nationalism, as seen in the light of Islām.

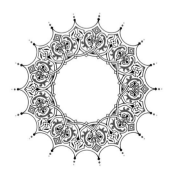

Three Great Muslim Women 5

Khadījah رضي الله عنها

"**W**hen none believed me, Khadījah did. She made me a partner in her wealth." Those are the words of Prophet *Muḥammad* ﷺ about his first wife — *Khadījatul Kubrā* (*Khadījah* the Great).

Khadījah, the daughter of *Khuwailid*, was born 15 years before the year of the elephant, in 555 CE. Her mother was *Fāṭimah bint Zaidah.*

She was a noble, fine-natured wealthy lady of *Makkah*. She married the Prophet ﷺ when she was 40 and he was 25. They had six children: two boys, *al-Qāsim* and *'Abdullāh* (also known as *Ṭāhir* and *Ṭaiyīb*), and four girls, *Zainab*, *Ruqaiyah*, *Umm Kulthūm* and *Fāṭimah.*

Khadījah lived with the Prophet ﷺ for 25 years and was his only wife during that time.

When the revelation came from Allāh and *Muḥammad* ﷺ was made the Prophet, it was *Khadījah* who immediately accepted the faith and became the first Muslim. She was 55 years old at that time. Her acceptance of Islām greatly helped its spread among the Makkans. She stood by the Prophet ﷺ all the time. In moments of trial and tribulation the Prophet ﷺ was consoled and comforted by her. She did all she could to help the Prophet ﷺ carry on his mission *(da'wah).*

Khadījah's wealth was used for the cause of Islām. The Prophet ﷺ remained busy in preaching Islām and his devoted and loving wife looked after the children and family affairs.

The Prophet ﷺ and *Khadījah* had many sorrows. They had to bear the death of their sons *al-Qāsim* and *'Abdullāh* in their infancy and in the fifth year of the prophethood their daughter *Ruqaiyah* migrated to *Abyssinia* with her husband, *'Uthmān bin 'Affān.*

Ruqaiyah left her parents at the age of 12 and returned after four years; that time was a long and painful separation for her mother, *Khadījah.*

During the prophethood, the *Quraish* did all they could to stop the Prophet ﷺ preaching Islām. None of their resistance worked. The Prophet ﷺ continued his mission, relying on Allāh. *Khadījah* was his source of encouragement and comfort. She also had to bear enormous strain and suffering during the boycott at *Shi'bi Abī Ṭālib* for three years.

The great Muslim lady *Khadījah*, the first Muslim, died on *10 Ramaḍān* in the tenth year of the prophethood, 620 CE, at the age of 65. Her death was a great loss to Prophet *Muḥammad* ﷺ. He said, *"I cannot bear the scene. I believe that Allāh has kept much good in it."* He loved *Khadījah* so dearly that after her death he used to remember her often.

The angel *Jibrā'īl* used to bring *salām* (greetings) for her from Allāh.

Fāṭimatuz Zahrā' became so sad at her mother's death that she stuck to her father and continued crying, "*Where is my mummy? Where is my mummy*?" The Prophet ﷺ consoled her and told her of the good news of *Khadījah's* acceptance by Allāh in Paradise.

Young Muslim girls should know how devoted *Khadījah* was to her husband and how much she did for him for the cause of Allāh. Any Muslim of today would feel proud to have such a wife. The world could be changed by great Muslim ladies like *Khadījah*.

Fāṭimah رضي الله عنها

Fāṭimah was the youngest of the four daughters of the Prophet ﷺ. She is known as *Saiyidatun Nisā'* (Leader of the Women), and one of her titles is *az-Zahrā'* (radiantly beautiful), which is why she is also called *Fāṭimatuz Zahrā'*. She was born five years before the prophethood of *Muḥammad* ﷺ, and migrated to *Madīnah* after the Prophet ﷺ, with her sisters and step-mother *Sawdah*.

After the death of her mother, *Khadījah*, she served her father with total devotion and love. The Prophet ﷺ loved her very much and kept her with him in deep affection. She was loved by all the wives of the Prophet ﷺ. She looked like *Khadījah* and this reminded people of her great mother.

Fāṭimah was married to *'Alī* after the battle of *Badr* in a simple marriage ceremony. The guests were served dates and drinks made from honey. She was about 18 years old, though some say she was only 15 at the time.

Her married life was happy and peaceful. *'Alī*, her husband, respected her and the Prophet ﷺ always advised *Fāṭimah* to obey and serve her husband in every respect. She kept her house clean and tidy, giving it a simple and pure look. There was always an atmosphere of peace and quiet.

Fāṭimah and her husband had five children: three sons, *al-Ḥasan*, *al-Ḥusain* and *al-Muḥassin;* and two daughters, *Zainab* and *Umm Kulthūm*. *Al-Muḥassin* died while still a baby.

According to *Aḥādīth* (plural of *Ḥadīth*), *Fāṭimah* was regarded as a great and respected lady by the women of her day because of her delightful personality, kindness, politeness and dignity.

The Prophet ﷺ said, *"Among the women of the whole world, four are great: Khadījah, Fāṭimah, Maryam (Mary) and Āsiyah (wife of Fir'awn [Pharaoh])."*

Fāṭimah resembled her father very closely in habits, traits and in conversation. When she came to any meetings of the Prophet ﷺ, he used to get up for her and make room for her to sit by his side.

Fāṭimah took part in the battle of *Uḥud* and nursed the wounded Muslim soldiers. She bandaged the wound sustained by the Prophet ﷺ during the battle. She also took part in the conquest of *Makkah*.

The Prophet ﷺ was always seen off by *Fāṭimah* when he was going out from *Madīnah* and was met by her when he returned home.

Fāṭimah died a few months after the death of the Prophet ﷺ, on *3 Ramaḍān* in 11 AH at the age of 30. Before her death she willed that her body be carried for burial prayers in such a way that no one could recognise whether it was the body of a male or female.

Since she died so soon after the death of the Prophet ﷺ, she could narrate no more than eighteen or nineteen *Aḥādīth*.

Fāṭimah was an ideal Muslim daughter, wife and mother. Her life should be an example for Muslim girls of all ages.

'Ā'ishah رضي الله عنها

This great Muslim lady was married to the Prophet ﷺ after the death of his first wife, *Khadījah*. She was born in 613 or 614 CE, the fourth year of the Prophet's ﷺ mission, and was married to the Prophet ﷺ when she was nine, although she only went to live with him when she was 12 (some say at 15).

Her father was *Abū Bakr*, the closest friend of the Prophet ﷺ and the first *Khalīfah* of Islām. Her mother was *Umm Rūmān*.

'Ā'ishah was a great Muslim lady. She was very talented and had a wonderful memory. She had a great love of learning and became noted for her intelligence, learning and sharp sense of judgement.

She grew up in an Islāmic environment. Her father was a great Muslim and the Prophet ﷺ himself was a frequent visitor to their house. She became a Muslim as soon as she reached the age of reason and understanding.

During her childhood, *'Ā'ishah* memorised quite a number of *Sūrahs* of the *Qur'ān*. Her father was a man of learning and she inherited his love of knowledge.

'Ā'ishah and her elder half-sister, *Asmā'*, helped in packing for the famous *Hijrah* of the Prophet ﷺ.

'Ā'ishah was fortunate to be trained under the care of the greatest teacher of mankind, Prophet *Muḥammad* ﷺ. This training made her one of the most notable Muslim ladies in Islāmic history. She was totally devoted to the Prophet ﷺ, her husband, and he loved her very dearly.

She loved and enjoyed serving her husband. She used to do the household work, including grinding flour and baking bread. She would make the beds and do the family's washing. She always kept water ready for the Prophet's ﷺ ablutions before prayer.

The Prophet ﷺ did not love her only for her physical beauty but also for her intelligence, sound judgement and personality. She liked what the Prophet ﷺ liked and disliked what he disliked.

If *'Ā'ishah* loved anyone more than her husband *Muḥammad* ﷺ, it was Almighty Allāh. This was the teaching of the Prophet ﷺ.

The Prophet ﷺ used to live a very simple life. There were occasions when the family had nothing to eat and times when guests were served with whatever they had while they went hungry themselves. They believed the comfort of the life after death was more important to them than the comforts of this world. This also is the teaching of Islām.

'Ā'ishah used to accompany the Prophet ﷺ in prayers. They would remain standing for long hours in prayer, weeping and asking Allāh's forgiveness.

The Prophet ﷺ fell ill in 11 AH and *'Ā'ishah* nursed him with all the love and care of a devoted wife. He died in her lap.

'Ā'ishah was also present at her father's death bed. *Abū Bakr* asked her how many pieces of cloth were used to bury the Prophet ﷺ and she told him three. He asked his daughter to wrap him also in three sheets for burial.

'Ā'ishah saved the place beside her father's grave for her own burial but, after the injury which was to prove fatal, *'Umar* the second *Khalīfah* of Islām, sent his son *'Abdullāh* to *'Ā'ishah* to ask her permission for him to be buried beside *Abū Bakr*. She agreed to *'Umar's* wish, saying, *"Today I prefer 'Umar to myself,"* which shows how great she was.

'Ā'ishah always stood for the truth. She taught Islām to many people, She was an authority on many matters of Islāmic Law, especially those concerning women. She narrated 2,210 *Aḥādīth*. She died at the age of 67 on *17 Ramaḍān,* 58 AH.

Her life shows to what heights a Muslim woman can rise. Before Islām, women had a low status in society; Islām gave them a very important position.

Islām wants to see a woman develop her talents and contribute to society as a mother and a wife and to remain loyal and chaste. Muslim women can rise to prominence within Islām. Allāh the Creator has fixed their rights and duties according to their nature and biological make-up.

'Ā'ishah's life is an example for young Muslim girls, who should try to follow her devotion and love for her husband and her special aptitude for knowledge and learning.

What did you learn? (5)

Key Stage 3 (11–14)

1. Give two facts about *Khadījah* before she married the Prophet ﷺ.
2. How long did she live with the Prophet ﷺ?
3. When did she die?
4. What did the angel *Jibrā'īl* used to do for *Khadījah?*
5. Who is called *Saiyidatun Nisā'* and why?
6. Name the four great women of the world according to the Prophet ﷺ?
7. In which battle did *Fāṭimah* take part?
8. Who was *'Ā'ishah's* father?
9. Choose one of the great Muslim women and describe something from her life which you really admire.

Key Stage 4 (15–16)

1. Discuss the contribution of the great Muslim lady *Khadījah* towards the cause of Islām.
2. What were the special qualities of *Fāṭimah*, the youngest daughter of the Prophet ﷺ?
3. Write a short narrative on the life of *'Ā'ishah*, up to the death of the Prophet ﷺ.

Key Stage 5 (17–18)

1. Allāh granted enormous rights and responsibilities to Muslim women. Discuss the various attitudes of Muslim men towards these rights and responsibilities.
2. Contrast the status of women in the pre-Islāmic period with that in an Islāmic society. How does that transformation compare to present-day developments in the status of women?

Stories of Some Prophets 6

"There is a lesson for the men of understanding in their stories." (12:111)

Ādam عليه السلام

Long, long ago, Allāh announced to the *Angels* and *Jinn* that He would create human beings to worship Him and live on the earth: *"I am going to place my Khalīfah (deputy or agent) on earth."* (2:30)

The angels asked, *"Will You place therein someone who will make mischief and shed blood, while we praise You and glorify You?"* (2:30) Allāh replied, *"Surely I know what you do not know."* (2:30) The angels were silent.

Allāh informed the angels, *"I am about to create a mortal being (Bashar) from clay. When I have fashioned him and given him life, you must prostrate before him."* (38:71–72)

Allāh created *Ādam* from clay and gave him the best of forms. He then commanded the angels and *Jinn* to prostrate before *Ādam*.

The angels obeyed; they never disobey Allāh. But *Iblīs*, who was one of the *Jinn* (18:50), refused to prostrate. Allāh asked, *"What prevented you from prostrating before that which I have created?" Iblīs* replied, *"I am better than him. You have created me from fire but him You created from clay."* (7:12; 15:32–33) His pride led him to disobey Allāh.

Allāh then said, *"Get out of here. You are an outcast. My curse is on you till the Day of Judgement."* (15:34–35)

Iblīs vowed to misguide *Ādam* and his children (7:14–18). But, as you know, Allāh has given man knowledge and guidance to distinguish between right and wrong to avoid being misguided.

Allāh taught *Ādam* some names and asked the angels to say those names (2:31). The angels said, *"Glory to You, we do not know more than You have taught us. Surely You are All-Knowing and the Most Wise."* (2:31) Allāh then asked *Ādam* to say those names, and he did so (2:33).

Turning to the angels, Allāh said, *"Did I not tell you that I know everything that is in the earth and the heavens and I also know whatever you disclose and whatever you hide?"* (2:33)

Allāh then asked *Ādam* to live in *al-Jannah* (Paradise). He had everything to enjoy. But he was alone. So Allāh created *Ḥawwā'* (Eve) as his wife. Now, *Ādam* was happy and living in *al-Jannah*.

Allāh said to *Ādam*, *"Live with your wife in al-Jannah. Eat freely whatever you like in here. But do not go near that tree."* (2:35) This was intended to test them and teach them self-control. Allāh also wanted to see whether they used the knowledge given to them to save themselves from the tricks of *Iblīs*.

Iblīs was trying hard to misguide *Ādam* and *Ḥawwā'*. At last, he succeeded and tempted them to go to that tree. As soon as they had eaten from the forbidden tree,

Ādam and *Ḥawwā'* realised they were naked. Until then, they did not know what nakedness was. They had no cause to be ashamed of it. But now they felt ashamed. They tried to cover themselves with leaves and tried to hide. But there was nowhere they could hide from Allāh, the All-knowing (7:20–22; 20:116–122).

Ādam and *Ḥawwā'* asked Allāh's forgiveness and it was granted. They prayed:

"Our Lord, we have wronged ourselves, and if You do not forgive us and grant us mercy, surely we shall be losers." (7:23)

Allāh then commanded *Ādam* and *Ḥawwā'* to go down to earth and live there. He was very kind and taught them the way to seek forgiveness (2:38–39).

He also told them that He would send guidance for them, so that they would not deviate from the *Right Path*.

Allāh revealed guidance to *Ādam* and he was made the *first prophet on earth*. There are important lessons for us to learn in this story.

Nūḥ (Noah) عليه السلام

Many hundreds of years passed after *Ādam*, and the earth was filled with his children. As time passed, the children of *Ādam* forgot Allāh and started to worship statues made of stones. They became bad and would lie and steal and some became mean and greedy.

Allāh, the most Merciful, sent *Nūḥ* to those people to bring them back to His worship. *Nūḥ* invited the people to come back to *Tawḥīd*. He asked them to give up idol worship and all the other vices which were ruining them. He warned them about the Day of Judgement (7:59–64).

Nūḥ tried his best for many years to guide his people to worship Allāh but they would not listen. They laughed at him, mocked him, despised him and called him crazy and a liar (26:105; 45:9).

Nūḥ lived for 950 years (29:14) but during this long period of time only a few people responded to his call. Even his son and wife did not believe in him.

Nūḥ was tired and shocked to see the stone-heartedness of his people. He became so displeased with the stiffness of their opposition to the truth that he ultimately prayed to Allāh, *"O Lord, leave not upon the land any one from the unbelievers."* (71:26) He cried unto his Lord saying, *"I am vanquished, so give help."* (54:10) He also prayed to Allāh to rescue him and his followers (26:118).

Almighty Allāh accepted *Nūḥ's* prayers and asked him to build an ark. *Nūḥ* started to build the ark. It was not an easy task but Prophet *Nūḥ* persevered (11:37). When the people saw *Nūḥ* building the ark they laughed at him and thought that he must have gone mad. They could not see the reason for building so huge an ark hundreds of miles away from the sea (11:38).

"What is the ark for?" they asked. Soon they were to find out. It was Allāh's plan to cleanse the whole land of unbelievers except the ones who believed and helped *Nūḥ*.

Nūḥ told the mockers that a flood would soon overcome them and they would have no place to take shelter. The people laughed even more. But Allāh's plans soon materialised and the disbelievers saw it happen before their own eyes.

After many days of hard work, the ark was complete and Allāh asked *Nūḥ* to take a pair (one male, one female) of all animals into the ark. He and his followers boarded afterwards (11:40–41).

Suddenly the skies became dark. It began to thunder and rain. Water poured from above and gushed up from the ground. It rained and rained until the whole land was flooded. Every living thing drowned except those that were in the ark, which was floating on the water (54:11–15).

The flood water lasted five months and it destroyed all the disbelievers. Even *Nūḥ's* own son (an unbeliever) was not saved. *Nūḥ* had asked permission from Allāh to take his son in the ark but this was refused. He was told that an unbelieving son was no part of his family. *Nūḥ* felt remorse for asking Allāh to rescue his son. He begged Allāh to forgive him. *Nūḥ* and his followers were safe in the ark (11:45–47).

At last, the skies began to clear and the ark halted at *Mount Jūdiyy* (in Turkey). *Nūḥ* and his followers disembarked (11:44). Thus Allāh saved *Nūḥ* and his followers (29:15).

Allāh bestowed prosperity and abundance on *Nūḥ's* children. They spread all over the earth (11:48).

Such is the dreadful punishment meted out to the disbelievers. Allāh says in the *Qur'ān*, *"We drowned those who denied our signs. Lo! they were (such) blind folk." (7:64)* We should take a lesson from this story that disobedience to Allah leads to total destruction!

Ibrāhīm (Abraham) عليه السلام

Ibrāhīm, known as *Khalīlullāh* (friend of Allāh, 4:125), lived in the country south of present day *'Irāq*. His father, *Āzar,* used to make idols and sell them. The people of the area used to worship these idols, which they had made themselves, in a temple.

Ibrāhīm was an intelligent young man. It was strange for him to see people bowing down before stone idols which could neither move nor talk. They could not even drive away the flies which sat on their eyes and noses. *Ibrāhīm* wondered why people were so foolish to worship such powerless statues.

Ibrāhīm's enquiring mind was in search of Allāh. He thought and thought. It occurred to him that the shining moon might be his Lord.

But when the moon vanished he said to himself, *"No, a vanishing thing cannot be my Lord."* He looked at the sun and said, *"It is the biggest and it is my Lord."* But when the sun also went down, *Ibrāhīm* said to himself, *"No, this cannot be my Lord."* He came to the conclusion that only the Ever-lasting, Ever-present and All-knowing Almighty can be his Lord. The stars, the moon and the sun cannot be the Lord (6:76–79).

Ibrāhīm once asked his father, *"O my father, why do you worship idols which can neither speak nor hear?" Āzar* became angry and warned *Ibrāhīm* not to ask such questions. *Ibrāhīm* wished he could show his people the stupidity of worshipping idols.

He thought of an idea which would give the people a practical lesson. Once, when people were busy celebrating a festival, *Ibrāhīm* went to the temple where the idols were kept.

He asked the idols, *"How do you do? Here is food and drink. Why don't you help yourselves?"* The stone idols were silent, of course.

Ibrāhīm now took an axe and began to break all the idols except the biggest which he spared for a purpose. When he had finished, he left the axe hanging round the neck of the biggest idol (21:58).

On their return from the festival, people came to the temple to worship the idols and were astonished to see the pitiful condition of their gods. They were shocked, grieved and furious. *"Who has done this mischief?"* they asked themselves.

They thought of *Ibrāhīm*, the only one who talked disrespectfully about the idols.

They confronted *Ibrāhīm*, asking *"Who broke the idols?" Ibrāhīm* calmly replied, *"Ask the biggest one."* The people knew that the idols could not talk. They said, "O

Ibrāhīm, don't you know that the idols can't talk?" Ibrāhīm retorted, *"Why do you worship them, then? They can't talk, move or understand anything. Why do you ask them for favour?"* The people had no answer. They were sure that it was *Ibrāhīm* who broke the idols. They could not let the matter rest easily. They called a meeting and decided to burn *Ibrāhīm* alive. They had to defend their gods (21:59–68).

However, *Ibrāhīm* was favoured by Allāh, so nothing could harm him as he had done the right thing.

A big fire was prepared and *Ibrāhīm* was thrown into it. But a miracle happened! The fire did not burn him. Allāh protected him. People were amazed to see it and they could not believe their eyes. But it was so. *Ibrāhīm* was safe and his persecutors felt sad and helpless (21:69–70).

In this way, *Ibrāhīm* was given the light of the truth by Allāh. *Ibrāhīm* was a messenger and servant of Allāh (16:120–122; 19:41). He loved Allāh more than anything else. He was ready to sacrifice his son *Ismā'īl* on Allāh's command. Allāh accepted *Ibrāhīm's* readiness and sent a ram to be sacrificed instead (37:101–107).

We observe the festival of *'Idul Aḍḥā* to commemorate this.

It was Prophet *Ibrāhīm* who rebuilt *al-Ka'bah* in *Makkah* with his son *Ismā'īl* (22:26–27; 2:125–129; 14:35–37).

Mūsā (Moses) عليه السلام

Mūsā, the son of *'Imrān*, was born in Egypt 450 years after *Yūsuf* (Joseph). In Egypt at that time the kings were known as *Fir'awn* (Pharaoh).

The followers of Prophet *Ya'qūb* (Jacob), father of Prophet *Yūsuf*, are called *Banū Isrā'īl* (Israelites). *Banū Isrā'īl* had lived in Egypt since the days of Prophet *Yūsuf*. Prophet *Ya'qūb* was known as *Isrā'īl*.

Fir'awn, the ruler of Egypt, looked upon the *Banū Isrā'īl* as 'foreigners' and treated them harshly. He feared that one day the *Banū Isrā'īl* would grow in number and be powerful. So *Fir'awn* issued orders to kill every male child born in the family of *Isrā'īl* (28:4–6).

Mūsā was born during this critical time. His mother managed to conceal him for three months and when she could not manage any longer, she was inspired by Allāh to put *Mūsā* into a waterproof basket and throw it into the river (20:38–39). *Maryam*, *Mūsā's* sister, was asked to watch the floating box from a distance to avoid suspicion (28:11).

The box reached the other shore and one of the members of *Fir'awn's* family picked it up and was excited to find a lovely baby boy inside. *Mūsā* was then taken to *Fir'awn's* wife and she was very glad to have the baby and adopted him (28:8–9). *Mūsā's* sister went to *Fir'awn's* palace and suggested a nanny to look after the baby, a woman who would be suitable to suckle him. This woman was none other than *Mūsā's* mother (28:12).

So *Mūsā* came back to his mother's lap. This is how Allāh protects whoever He wills.

Mūsā grew up in *Fir'awn's* house and during this time he came across an Egyptian who was beating an Isrāelite. *Mūsā* gave the Egyptian a blow and killed him accidentally (28:15).

He left *Fir'awn's* house and went to *Madyan* (Midian) (28:22–28). He stayed there for ten years before moving on to *Ṭuwā*, a valley at the foot of *Mount Sinai*. Here, *Mūsā* received divine guidance and was selected as a messenger of Allāh (28:30).

Allāh bestowed on *Mūsā* two signs: a 'stick' which, when thrown down, would turn into a living serpent, and the ability to make his hand shine after it was drawn out from under his arm (20:17–22).

Allāh commanded *Mūsā* to go to *Fir'awn* and invite him to *Tawḥīd* (20:42–44). He begged Allāh to make his brother *Hārūn* his helper and Allāh granted his prayer (20:24–36).

Mūsā and *Hārūn* went to *Fir'awn*. They exhorted him to obey Allāh and grant the Israelites their freedom. *Fir'awn* refused to do either (20:47–54; 26:16–17).

Instead, he made fun of *Mūsā*. *Mūsā* showed his signs to impress upon *Fir'awn* that his message was true. He threw his stick to the ground and it changed into a serpent. *Mūsā* picked it up and it turned back into a stick. *Fir'awn* and his followers were amazed to see this, but he thought that *Mūsā* was a magician and challenged him to face his own magicians who could show ever more stunning magic (26:23–37).

On the appointed day, the magicians of *Fir'awn* were badly defeated. The false snakes they produced by their sticks were all swallowed up by the serpent of *Mūsā's* stick. *Fir'awn* and his magicians could hardly believe their eyes. His magicians bowed to the truth and professed their faith in Allāh (26:38–47).

Fir'awn became angry and began to torture the *Banū Isrā'īl* even more.

It was during this time that Allāh commanded *Mūsā* to leave Egypt with his followers (20:77). *Mūsā* asked his followers to get ready and they slipped out at night to avoid *Fir'awn's* attention and reached the shore of the sea. They were chased by *Fir'awn* and his soldiers. They almost caught the Israelites, in front of whom was the mighty sea. At this moment, Allāh ordered *Mūsā* to throw his stick in the water and, as he did so, the sea was divided into two and a road was ready in the middle, allowing the Israelites to cross (26:52–65).

Fir'awn followed in hot pursuit. *Mūsā* and his people safely reached the other shore. *Fir'awn* and his soldiers were still in the middle of the sea when suddenly the water on both sides began to pour over them.

Fir'awn and his soldiers were drowned (26:66). This is how Allāh punishes transgressors and helps His servants.

'Īsā (Jesus) عليه السلام

The *Banū Isrā'īl* were given many favours by Almighty Allāh but they were very ungrateful. They violated Allāh's orders, ridiculed the prophets and even killed some of them. They started to worship idols and made a mockery of Allāh's message.

Allāh, the Merciful, again sent a prophet to bring them to the right path. This prophet was *'Īsā*, son of *Maryam* (Mary)(2:87). Allāh bestowed on him the *Injīl* (Gospel) and *'Īsā* confirmed what was in the *Tawrāh* (Torah)(5:46, 61:6).

Prophet *'Īsā* had a miraculous birth. He was born of the virgin *Maryam* (Mary) without a father, by Allāh's command (19:17–21). Allāh can do anything He likes. Everything is possible for Him. When He wants to get something done, He only says, 'Be' and there it is (2:117).

We know that *Ādam* was created by Allāh without a father and a mother. So, it was no wonder that Allāh could create *'Īsā* without a father.

'Īsā, born of virgin *Maryam*, could talk even as a baby. He was made a prophet when he was 30, and he did his duty as a prophet for three years (19:29–34).

Allāh endowed him with some miraculous powers. He could make birds out of clay, heal leprosy within minutes, restore the eyes of the blind and also make the dead come alive. He could do all these miracles by the mercy of Allāh. The *Qur'ān* mentions the miraculous powers and the birth of *'Īsā* in *Sūrah Āli 'Imrān:*

"(And remember) when the angels said: O, Mary! Allāh gives you the glad tidings of a word from Him, whose name is the Messiah, Jesus, son of Mary, illustrious in the World and the Hereafter and one of those brought near (unto Allāh).

He will speak to mankind in his cradle and in his manhood, and he is of the righteous.

She (Mary) said: My Lord! How can I have a child when no mortal has touched me? He said, So (it will be). Allāh creates what He wishes. If He decrees a thing, He says to it only: Be, and it is.

And He will teach him the Scripture and wisdom, and the Torah and the Gospel.

And will make him a messenger to the Children of Isrā'īl, (saying): I come to you with a sign from my Lord. See! I fashion for you out of clay the likeness of a bird, by Allāh's leave. I heal him who was born blind and the leper, and I raise the dead, by Allāh's leave. And I announce to you what you eat and what you store up in your houses. Here truly is a portent for you, if you are to be believers.

And I come to you confirming what was before me of the Torah, and to make lawful some of what was forbidden to you. I come to you as a sign from your Lord, so keep your duty to Allāh and obey me.

Allāh is my Lord and your Lord, so worship Him. That is a straight path." (3:45–51)

He asked the people to obey Allāh alone but some of his followers made fantasies about him and they considered him a part of Allāh, even a son of Allāh (5:116–117).

Muslims believe in *'Īsā* as a prophet and a servant of Allāh (43:59). They do not believe that he is the son of Allāh. Allāh does not have a son or daughter. He is not like any of the creatures He has created. There is none like Him. Allāh is One and Indivisible. There is no idea of a Trinity in Islām (4:171). Trinity is clear partnership *(Shirk)*. Muslims believe it is a big sin to say anyone is the son of Allāh (5:17; 19:35).

According to the *Qur'ān*, Prophet *'Īsā* was not crucified; rather, he was taken up by Allāh, the Almighty and the Most Wise (4:157–158). Everything is possible for Allāh. It was He who saved *Ibrāhīm* from the fire and *Mūsā* from *Fir'awn*. He is the only Creator of the whole universe and all that is in it.

What did you learn? (6a)

Key Stage 3 (11–14)

1. Who or what lived on earth before human beings?
2. Who was *Ādam* and why did Allāh create him?
3. Who was *Ḥawwā'* and why did Allāh create her?
4. Where did *Ādam* and *Ḥawwā'* live at first?
5. Who refused to prostrate before *Ādam* and why?
6. What mistakes did *Ādam* and *Ḥawwā'* make when they were in Heaven?
7. Write out the prayer *Ādam* and *Ḥawwā'* made to Allāh after they were trapped by the devil.
8. Why did prophet *Nūḥ* have to build an ark?
9. What happened to the people who would not listen to Prophet *Nūḥ?*

Key Stage 4 (15–16)

1. What does the *Qur'ān* state about the creation of *Ādam?*
2. Why do you think *Iblīs* refused to bow to *Ādam?*
3. Describe what happened to *Ādam* and *Ḥawwā'* after they were sent to live in *al-Jannah?*
4. Briefly narrate the story of *Nūḥ's* ark. What hard lesson did *Nūḥ* learn through the fate of his son?

Key Stage 5 (17–18)

1. What important lessons do we learn from the story of *Ādam* and *Ḥawwā'* as regards the origin of evil, the forgiveness of Allāh, and the equality of women with men?
2. *"Many people die in catastrophes of nature but they are all judged as individuals."* Discuss this statement.
3. Contrast the Islāmic understanding of creation with the theories developed by physicists and evolutionists to explain our existence.

What did you learn? (6b)

Key Stage 3 (11–14)

1. Who was *Khalīlullāh* and what does this name mean?
2. Who was Prophet *Ibrāhīm's* father?
3. What did Prophet *Ibrāhīm* say to his father about the worship of idols?
4. What did Prophet *Ibrāhīm* do on the day of the festival?
5. Did the fire burn Prophet *Ibrāhīm?* What does this show about Allāh's power?
6. Make a list of the miracles that happened during Prophet *Mūsā's* life.

Key Stage 4 (15–16)

1. What was the significance of the incident of Prophet *Ibrāhīm* not being burnt by the fire of the idol worshippers?
2. Why do Muslims think idol worship is foolish and unreasonable?
3. *"Prophet Ibrāhīm's life was one of true sacrifice."* Explain this statement using examples from his life.
4. Describe incidents from Prophet *Mūsā's* life to show how his *Īmān* was tested. Give examples of how Muslims are being tested nowadays.

Key Stage 5 (17–18)

1. *"Fir'awn epitomizes tyrannical rulers of today and clearly displays where arrogance can lead."* Discuss this statement.
2. The prophets *Ibrāhīm* and *Mūsā* were 'saved' by Allāh. Why do you think Allāh does not save all noble martyrs? Discuss the importance of faith in Allāh's justice and the *Ākhirah*.
3. How is the story of Prophet *Ibrāhīm's* life connected with the rituals of *Ḥajj?*

What did you learn? (6c)

Key Stage 3 (11–14)

1. Who was *'Īsā?*
2. Who was Prophet *'Īsā's* mother? Briefly write about his birth.
3. What book did Allāh reveal to Prophet *'Īsā?*
4. Was Prophet *Īsā* crucified? Explain your answer.
5. What was special about Prophet *'Īsā?*

Key Stage 4 (15–16)

1. *"Prophet 'Īsā's life includes many miraculous things, but he was still a human being."* Justify this statement.
2. What was the teaching of Prophet *'Īsā?* Did he ask his followers to worship him?

Key Stage 5 (17–18)

1. Explain the doctrine of *Tawḥīd* and the doctrine of the Trinity. Can you reconcile the two? Give your reasons.
2. *"Risālah was the channel of communication between man and Allāh."* Discuss.
3. Although Islām is totally opposed to *shirk*, can you outline the teaching in the *Qur'ān* that commends some Christians?

Sharī'ah (Islāmic Law) 7

S*harī'ah* is the code of law for the Islāmic way of life. The word *Sharī'ah* means a clear straight path or example. It is the best system of law from Allāh for humanity to follow.

Sharī'ah, or Islāmic law, is the code of conduct for Muslims and is based on two main sources: the *Qur'ān* and the *Sunnah* of the Prophet ﷺ. It aims at the success and welfare of mankind both in this life and the life after death.

Sharī'ah prescribes a complete set of laws for the guidance of mankind so that Good *(Ma'rūf)* is established and Evil *(Munkar)* is removed from society. It provides a clear and straight path which leads to progress and fulfilment in life and the attainment of Allāh's pleasure.

The *Qur'ān* is the main basis of *Sharī'ah*. It states the principles while the *Sunnah* of the Prophet ﷺ provides the blueprint of how to apply them. For example, the *Qur'ān* says: establish *Ṣalāh*, observe *Ṣawm*, pay *Zakāh*, take decisions by consultation, do not earn or spend in wrong ways — but it does not describe how to do these things. It is the *Sunnah* of the Prophet ﷺ which shows us how to act on Allāh's commands.

The *Qur'ān* is the main book of guidance and the Prophet ﷺ taught us how to follow it. The Prophet ﷺ not only told us how to follow the guidance, he also practised it himself. Prophet *Muḥammad's* ﷺ life was the living *Qur'ān*.

Sharī'ah has rules for every aspect of life. It is complete and perfect, and its application guarantees success, welfare and peace here on this earth and in the *Ākhirah*.

Man-made laws differ from *Sharī'ah* in a number of significant ways.

Man-made Law	Sharī'ah or Allāh's Law
1. Men make laws when they feel the need; these laws start from a few and then grow in number over the years.	Islāmic Law is complete and perfect, and covers all aspects of human life. Men of learning explain and clarify *Sharī'ah* for the benefit of ordinary people.
2. Laws made by men are not permanent; they are changed to suit people's wishes and desires. For example, in a particular country at a particular time, drinking alcohol may be banned; but this can change when public pressure grows. The American Government once banned all alcoholic drinks, but removed the ban after a time because it could not be enforced.	*Sharī'ah* is permanent for all people all the time. It does not change with time and conditions. For example, drinking wine and gambling are not allowed under Islāmic law. No one can change this; it is law that is valid for all time and for all places.

3. Man does not have knowledge of the future. Hence, man-made laws cannot stand the test of time.	Allāh is All-knowing and All-powerful; He is the most Wise; His laws are the best and are complete.
4. Man is a created being. His laws are the creation of the created.	Allāh is the Creator and His laws are for Man, His creation.
5. Man-made laws may be suitable for a particular nation or country. They cannot be universal.	Allāh's laws are for all nations, all countries and for all time. They are universal.
6. Men make laws to suit their own needs. If members of parliament want to decrease the rate of tax on the rich, they can do so even if the majority of the people suffered and there was high unemployment in the country.	Allāh is above all needs. He is not dependent on anything, so His laws are for the good of all people and not for a few, selfish people.

Sharī'ah has two other sources: *Ijmā'* (consensus) and *Qiyās* (analogy or reasoning on the basis of similar circumstances). These sources must still be based on the *Qur'ān* and the *Sunnah*.

Ijmā', or consensus, applies to a situation where no clear conclusion can be made from the *Qur'ān* and the *Sunnah*. In this situation the representatives of the people who are knowledgeable and well-versed in the *Qur'ān* and the *Sunnah* will sit together and work out an agreed formula to solve the particular problem. *Ijmā'* developed during the period of *al-Khulafā'ur Rāshidūn*.

Qiyās means a reference or analogy of a comparison of one thing with a similar one. It is applied in circumstances where guidance from the *Qur'ān* and the *Sunnah* is not directly available. A solution to a problem is reached by a process of deduction from a comparison with a similar situation in the past.

Sunnah

The word *Sunnah* means a system, a path or an example. In Islām it refers to the practice of the Prophet ﷺ, his life example. It is embodied in the *Aḥādīth* (plural of *Ḥadīth*) which are the Prophet's ﷺ sayings, actions and the actions done with his approval. *Aḥādīth* have been very carefully collected and compiled since the death of the Prophet ﷺ. Six collections of *Ḥadīth* are regarded as the most authentic. They are:

1. *Saḥīḥ al-Bukhārī* — (Collected and compiled by *Muḥammad bin Ismā'īl* known as *Imām Bukhārī*, born 194 AH, died 256 AH/870 CE).
2. *Saḥīḥ Muslim* — (*Muslim bin al-Ḥajjāj*, known as *Imām Muslim*, born 202 AH, died 261 AH/875 CE).
3. *Sunan Abū Dāwūd* — (*Sulaimān bin Ash'ath*, known as *Abū Dāwūd*, born 202 AH, died 275 AH/888/CE).

4. *Sunan Ibn Mājah* (*Abū 'Abdullāh Muḥammad bin Yazīd al-Qazwinī*, known as *Ibn Mājah*, born 209 AH, died 273 AH/886 CE).

5. *Jāmi' at-Tirmidhī* (*Abū 'Īsā Muḥammad bin 'Īsā at-Tirmidhī*, date of birth not recorded, died 279 AH/892 CE).

6. *Sunan an-Nasā'ī* (*Abū 'Abdur Raḥmān Aḥmad bin Shu'aib an-Nasā'ī*, born 215 AH, died 303 AH/915 CE).

In addition to this, the *Muwaṭṭa'* of *Imām Mālik* (born 93 AH, died 179 AH), *Musnad* of *Aḥmad bin Ḥanbal* (born 164 AH, died 241 AH/855 CE) and *Mishkāt al-Maṣābīḥ* of *Abū Muḥammad al-Ḥusain bin Mas'ūd* (died 516 AH) are also well known. There are many more collections and commentaries.

Fiqh

Fiqh is the science of Islāmic law or jurisprudence. It refers to the explanation, collection and compilation of Islāmic laws based on the *Qur'ān* and the *Sunnah* of the Prophet ﷺ. The word *Fiqh* means knowledge and understanding.

The scholars of Islāmic Law have made *Sharī'ah* easier to understand and practise by the science of *Fiqh*. A person who has a detailed knowledge and understanding of *Fiqh* is called a *Faqīh*. A person qualified to give a ruling on issues in *Sharī'ah* is called a *Muftī*. The ruling he gives is called a *fatwā* (pl. *fatāwā*).

Some great Muslims devoted themselves to the task of developing the science of understanding Islāmic law and its practice. The four best known compilers and interpreters of Islāmic law or *Sharī'ah* are:

1. *Abū Ḥanīfah Nu'mān bin Thābit*, known as *Imām Abū Ḥanīfah* (born 80 AH, died 150 AH/767 CE).
2. *Mālik bin Ānas*, known as *Imām Mālik* (93–179 AH/795 CE).
3. *Muḥammad bin Idrīs ash-Shāfi'ī*, known as *Imām Shāfi'ī* (150–240 AH/820 CE).
4. *Aḥmad bin Ḥanbal*, known as *Imām Ibn Ḥanbal* (164–241 AH/855 CE).

Islāmic law divides human activities into: (1) *Farḍ* or *Wājib* (duty or obligatory) — performance of these actions is rewarded and their omission is punished. (2) *Mandūb* (recommended) — actions the performance of which is rewarded but omission of which is not punished. (3) *Mubāḥ* (silent) — actions permitted by silence. (4) *Makrūh* (disliked or reprehensible) — actions disapproved of but not punishable. (5) *Ḥarām* (forbidden) — actions punishable by law.

Islāmic Law or *Sharī'ah* embodies the ideal Islāmic life. Islām is the complete way of life and *Sharī'ah* is the means to arrive at the ideal life recommended by Islām. *Sharī'ah* enables us to bring our life in line with the will of Allāh. It is the means of achieving our goal of life.

What did you learn? (7)

Key Stage 4 (15–16)

1. What is *Sharī'ah* and why do we need it?
2. What are the sources of *Sharī'ah?*
3. What is *Sunnah* and where can we find examples of it?
4. What are the six authentic books of *Sunnah?*
5. What does the word *Fiqh* mean and what does it cover?
6. What are the names of the four most famous compilers of Islāmic Law?
7. Discuss the importance of *Sharī'ah* in comparison with man-made laws.
8. Divide human activities into five groups according to Islāmic Law.

Key Stage 5 (17–18)

1. Discuss the need for *Sharī'ah* in the modern world. Include the shortcomings of man-made laws.
2. What are *Sunnah* and *Fiqh?* Discuss how they help Muslims to answer problems facing them in the present day.
3. Many societies are afraid of *Sharī'ah*. Are these fears justified? How might *Sharī'ah* be abused? Is Western society too 'soft' on criminals?

Social Life in Islām 8

Family Life in Islām

Family is the basis of Islāmic society. Its origin goes back to the beginning of the creation of man and woman — *Ādam* and *Ḥawwā'* (Eve). So, it is an institution founded by Allāh's will. Allāh says in the *Qur'ān:*

"O mankind, be mindful of your duty to your Lord who created you from a single soul and from it created its mate and from the two created many men and women." (4:1)

Marriage is the basis of the Islāmic family. A good and sound society can only grow if a man and a woman are bound in a solid relationship through the sacred contract of marriage.

Marriage develops love, care and cooperation between the husband and wife. It gives peace of mind and provides a secure and solid basis for the growth and progress of the whole human race. Without marriage, the human race would come to a standstill. Marriage was the practice of most of the prophets including *Muḥammad* ﷺ.

Marriage (Nikāḥ)

Marriage is a sacred social contract between a bridegroom and a bride. A great deal of thought is necessary therefore before a man and a woman decide to marry.

Piety should come before all other considerations. Prophet *Muḥammad* ﷺ said, *"Do not marry only for the sake of beauty, maybe the beauty becomes the cause of moral decline. Do not marry even for the sake of wealth; maybe the wealth becomes the reason of disobedience; marry rather on the grounds of religious devotion."* (*Ibn Mājah*) *"A woman is married for four things: her wealth, her family status, her beauty and her religion. So you should marry the religious woman (otherwise) you will be a loser."* (*al-Bukhārī*)

A Muslim man is expected to marry a Muslim woman although in some cases chaste Jewish and Christian women can be married. However, a Muslim woman is not allowed to marry a non-Muslim man. In Islām, marriage is a religious and social institution and not simply a sexual relationship.

Muslim marriages are traditionally arranged by parents but the final say lies with the man and the woman. Islām does not allow free mixing of grown-up boys and girls, nor does it allow sex outside marriage. The Islāmic way of life does not approve of the boyfriend/girlfriend system, or mixed parties of grown-ups and the like.

Arranged Marriages, Forced Marriages

Islām recognises a marriage arranged by parents or relatives where the bride and groom have freely and willingly given their consent; indeed, consent of both parties to a marriage is a must. Without this a marriage is not valid.

This was made very clear by the Prophet ﷺ. *Khansā bint Khidhān al-Ansarīyā*

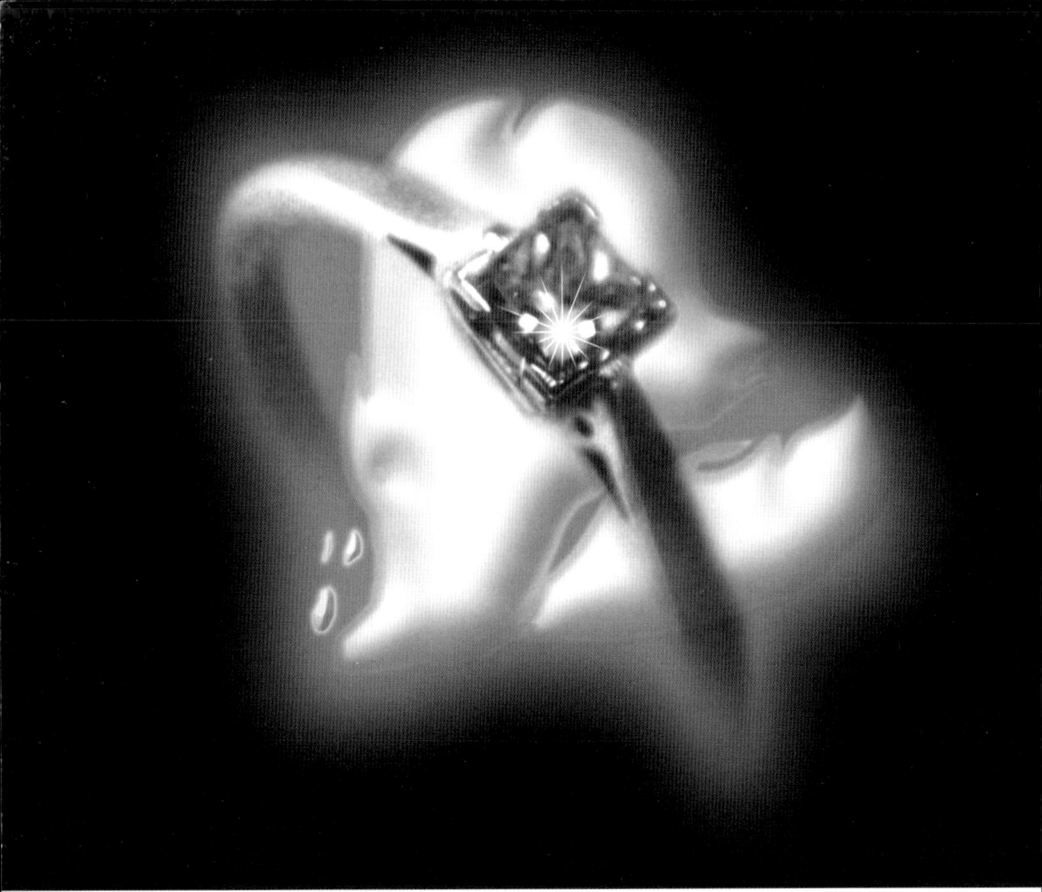

narrated that her father gave her in marriage when she was a matron (childless woman, divorcee or a widow) and she disliked that marriage. So, she went to Allāh's Messenger ﷺ, and he declared the marriage null and void *(al-Bukhārī)*.

Abū Hurairah narrated that the Prophet ﷺ said, "A matron should not be given in marriage except after consulting her (i.e. getting her consent), and a virgin should not be given in marriage without her permission (consent)." *(al-Bukhārī)*

There is no room for forced marriages in Islām. To force anyone into a marriage is not lawful in Islām. Freely-given consent is a basic requirement in Islāmic marriage. No one should force either a male or a female into a marriage; even the parents who always want the best for their children should not force them into marriage to which they have not consented. Lack of the correct knowledge about Islam and insistence on local customs and culture may be the reason for doing un-Islāmic things. Muslims should follow the teachings of the *Qur'ān* and the *Sunnah* of the Prophet ﷺ. There is nothing wrong in following local customs and culture if they do not violate Islāmic teachings.

Divorce

Islāmic society is based on submission and obedience to the will of Allāh. Husband and wife, bound by marriage, are Allāh's servants and representatives *(Khalīfah)*. Marriage must not conflict with the purpose of life (seeking Allāh's pleasure), rather it should lead towards its achievement.

Divorce is allowed but is regarded as the least desirable of all lawful acts. Prophet *Muḥammad* ﷺ said, "Of all things which have been permitted, divorce is the most hated by Allāh." *(Abū Dāwūd, Ibn Mājah)* Islām encourages adjustment, reconciliation and happiness but when living together is impossible, Islāmic law does not prohibit divorce *(Ṭalāq)*.

Status of Women in Islām

Women are an important and integral part of Islāmic society. Unlike a number of other religions, Islām holds a woman in high esteem. Her importance as a mother and a wife has been clearly stated by Prophet *Muhammad* ﷺ.

A man came to the Prophet ﷺ and said, *"Messenger of Allāh, I desire to go on a military expedition and I have come to consult you."* The Prophet ﷺ asked him if he had a mother, and when he replied that he had, he said, *"Stay with her, for Paradise is at her feet." (an-Nasā'ī)*

Once a person asked the Prophet ﷺ, *"Who deserves the best care from me?" The Prophet ﷺ replied, "Your mother (he repeated this three times), then your father and then your nearest relatives." (al-Bukhārī)*

In his farewell speech at *'Arafāt* in the tenth year of the *Hijrah*, the Prophet ﷺ said, *"O people, your wives have certain rights over you and you have certain rights over them. Treat them well and be kind to them, for they are your partners and committed helpers."*

The Prophet ﷺ also said, *"The best among you is the one who is the best towards his wife." (at-Tirmidhī)*

These sayings clearly prove the important position given to women in Islām yet there are people, especially in the West, who have misgivings about the status of women in Islām. To these people, the Muslim woman is seen almost as *'a prisoner within the four walls of the house'*, a *'non-person'*, and *'someone who has no rights and living always under the domination of a man'*. These notions are totally wrong and are based on ignorance rather than correct knowledge of Islām.

One of the rites of *Ḥajj* is a fast walk between *Ṣafā* and *Marwah*, which is observed to remember the event of *Hājar* (Hagar), mother of Prophet *Ismā'īl*, who ran between these two hills to find water. This is another proof of the importance and respect given to women by Islām.

In order to judge the incorrect ideas held by western people, it would be useful to survey the attitudes to women in different societies in the past.

During the Roman civilization, for example, a woman was regarded as a slave. The Greeks considered her a commodity to be bought and sold. Early Christianity regarded women as temptresses, responsible for the fall of Adam from Heaven[1].

In India, the Hindus until recently considered their women worse than death, pests, serpents or even Hell. A wife's life ended with the death of her husband. In the past, a widow had to jump into the flames of her husband's funeral pyre[2].

In pre-Islāmic Arabia, a woman was treated as a cause for grief and unhappiness and baby girls were sometimes buried alive after birth. This is mentioned in the *Qur'ān* when Allāh says: *"And when the female (infant) buried alive (as the pagan Arabs used to do) is questioned. For what sin was she killed?"* (81:8–9)

In France, in 587 CE, a conference was held to study the status of women and to determine whether a woman could truly be considered a human being or not! Henry VIII in England forbade the reading of the Bible by women and throughout the middle ages the Catholic Church treated women as second-class citizens. In the universities of Cambridge and Oxford, male and female students were not given the same rights until 1964. Before 1850, women were not counted as citizens in England and English women had no personal rights until 1882[3].

If we keep this status in mind and look into the position of the women in Islām, we must conclude that Islām liberated women from the dark age of obscurity, insecurity and being non-entities fourteen hundred years ago!

Islām is a religion of common sense. It conforms with human nature. It recognises the realities of life. This does not mean it has recognised equality of man and woman in every respect. Rather, it has defined their duties according to their different biological make-up (2:228). Allāh has not made man and woman identical, so it would be against nature to try to have total equality between a man and a woman.

That would destroy the social balance. Society would not prosper but would instead have insoluble problems such as broken marriages, children born outside marriage and the break-up of family life. These problems are already rife in Western society. Schoolgirl pregnancies, an increase in abortions, divorce and many other problems have resulted from a permissive outlook and the so-called freedom of women championed by feminists.

Rights of Women in Islām

Allāh has created every living being in pairs, male and female (51:49), including mankind. Allāh has honoured the children of *Ādam* — both male and female (17:70). Men and women who believe are friends of one another (9:71). Allāh will reward both men and women in the life after death (3:195).

Notes:

1 *Encyclopaedia Britannica*, vol. 19, p. 909 (1977 edition)

2 *Islām: beliefs, legislation and morals*, Dr Aḥmad Shalaby, p. 308, (1970 Cairo)

3. *Ibid* – pp. 312, 314

In Islām a woman has a distinct and separate identity. She is not just an appendage of her husband. Islām has given her the right to own property. She is the owner of her earnings. No one (father, husband or brother) has a right over them. She can use her earnings and property as she wishes, within the bounds of *Ḥalāl* (lawful) and *Ḥarām* (unlawful).

Islām has given women a right to inheritance. She has a claim on the property of her dead father, husband or childless brother (4:7, 32, 176).

A woman has the right to choose her husband. No one can impose a decision on her against her will. She has the right to seek separation *(Khul')* from her husband if their marriage becomes impossible to sustain.

If any man falsely questions a woman's chastity, that man is declared unfit for giving evidence (24:4). This shows how a woman's honour is safeguarded from false accusations.

The *Qur'ān* asks the Muslims to treat women kindly (4:19). It makes Muslim husbands responsible for their wife's maintenance. Women, in return, are expected to remain loyal and chaste (4:34).

A woman has a right to develop her talents and to work within the limits of Islām. Islām allows a non-Muslim married woman to retain her religion and her husband cannot interfere in this freedom. This applies to Christian and Jewish women with Muslim husbands. However, a Muslim husband's Islāmic lifestyle is expected to persuade his non-Muslim wife to accept Islām.

Duties of a Woman in Islām

Islām is a fair and balanced system of life. While it specifies the rights of women it also lays down duties. A Muslim woman is expected to observe the following:

1. Belief in *Tawḥīd* and the practice of Islām should be her foremost duty. A Muslim woman must perform her *Ṣalāh*, observe *Sawm*, pay *Zakāh* on her own wealth (if it is applicable) and go to *Ḥajj* if she can afford it. She is exempted from *Ṣalāh* and can defer *Ṣawm* during her monthly period, but she must make up the days lost afterwards. Friday prayer *(Ṣalātul Jumu'ah)* is optional for women.
2. She is required to maintain her chastity at all times. She must not have any extramarital relationship. The same is the case with men.
3. It is her duty to bring up children according to the rules of Islām. She has to look after the family and has almost absolute control over domestic affairs, although the family is run by mutual consultation and cooperation. She is the queen of the family and is the manager of household affairs.
4. She should dress modestly and should put on *Ḥijāb* (covering cloak) while going out and meeting adult males beyond her close relatives (33:59, 24:30–31). She should not dress as a man.

5. She is her husband's helpmate. A faithful wife is like a garment, a source of peace, love, happiness and contentment for her husband (30:21, 2:187).
6. If she is asked to go against the commands of Allāh, she must defy even her husband, father or brother (9:23).
7. She is expected to look after her husband's property and belongings in his absence.

Islām considers a husband and a wife as complementary to one another. Neither dominates the other. Each has his or her own individual rights and duties — together they form a peaceful and happy family which is at the core of a sound, stable and peaceful society.

Man and woman are not exactly equal in Islām. They have different physical and biological features. Islām recognises the leadership of a man over a woman (4:34, 2:228) but that does not mean domination.

An average man is usually stronger, heavier and taller than an average woman. Women can become pregnant and bear children but men cannot. Women tend to be sensitive, emotional and tender while men are comparatively less emotional. Allāh has given different qualities to a man and a woman, and in marriage they are expected to love, support and help one another to build a happy family.

Throughout history, men and women have never been treated the same. Islām has given women the right position and has not attempted to violate divine laws. Other religions and man-made systems have failed to define the exact and appropriate role of women. In the West, women have been reduced almost to a plaything of enjoyment and fancy. Women have tended to degrade themselves probably unwittingly in modern times for the sake of real or imaginary equality. They have become objects of exploitation by men and the slogans of liberty and equality have virtually reduced them to playful commodities. Even a cursory look at advertisments in the media shows how women continue to be exploited for commercial purposes. The display of scantily-clothed and even naked women to exploit male desires has become the hallmark of Western materialism. They have neither gained liberty nor achieved full equality; rather they have lost their natural place in the home.

The natural balance, fairness and mutuality have been disturbed. The outcome has been horrendous for social peace and stability. The natural peace at home cannot be restored unless the exploitation of women stops.

Polygamy and Islām

Islām is a practical religion. It can answer all human problems. Islām allows restricted polygamy — marriage to more than one woman (polygyny), with a maximum of four. The normal Muslim practice is monogamy — one man married to one wife; polygamy is not the norm.

The *Qur'ān* has imposed strict conditions for marrying several wives: *"And if you fear that you will not deal justly with the orphans, marry of the women who seems good to you, two or three or four; and if you fear that you cannot deal justly (with them), then one only or (slaves) that your right hands possess. Thus it is more likely to prevent you from doing injustice"* (4:3) This verse says that in order to marry more than one woman, a man must be able to be fair and just to each of them. If he is not able to be so, he should marry only one woman.

Another verse of the *Qur'ān* says: *"You will not be able to deal fairly between wives, however much you wish. So do not incline too much to one of them so that you leave another in suspense, if you come to a friendly understanding and fear Allāh, Allāh is ever Forgiving and most Merciful."* (4:129) This further emphasizes fair treatment. But in special circumstances Islām allows polygamy. These situations are:

1. When a wife is barren and cannot bear children but the husband wants children. It is better to have a second wife than to divorce the barren one. However, a barren wife has the option to seek separation from her husband if she wishes, on the grounds of the second marriage of her husband.
2. If the first wife is chronically ill and she is unable to carry out her marital and household chores, the husband may marry another woman and thus help restore family stability.
3. Polygamy may be the solution to the problems of a society which has more women than men. This happens especially after a war. The verse in the *Qur'ān* allowing more than one wife was revealed after the battle of *Uḥud* in which many Muslim men were martyred.

The proportion of women to men increased considerably in the countries which took part in the First and Second World Wars. A solution to such a situation is marriage to more than one woman by those men who are able to and can be fair to each wife. This is better than leaving a large number of unmarried women.

Islām strictly forbids any sexual relationship outside marriage. There is no such thing as a mistress in Islāmic society. Islām has given dignity to women by marriage and has protected them from exploitation of greedy and selfish men. Having more than one wife is better and more dignified than having a number of mistresses. Islām holds you responsible for your actions. You cannot just enjoy women and avoid the responsibilities of fatherhood. This is inhuman and unjust.

There should be no one-parent families or illegitimate children in an ideal Islāmic society. It is only possible in a cultural climate of irresponsible and uncontrolled permissiveness. A woman who is going to be a second wife can refuse to marry the man on the grounds that he already has a wife. But if a woman happily consents to her husband marrying again and the second wife agrees, why should anyone else object to it?

The overwhelming majority of Muslims are monogamous — they have only one wife. The fact that some Muslims have more than one wife has become a matter for propaganda against Islām and such propaganda can give a misleading impression of the Islāmic way of life. This is especially so when non-practising Muslims are given prominence in this propaganda.

As opposed to polygamy, the case of polyandry (a woman having more than one husband) may be raised. The case of polyandry is impractical and it creates problems rather than solving them. How will paternity be decided? Which husband would claim the fatherhood of the child? How would inheritance be decided? Such questions have no answer in polyandry.

Furthermore, it is possible for a man to live with more than one wife and have children from all of them. But for a woman to be the wife of more than one husband seems almost impossible. A woman can bear children from only one husband at a time. Polyandry is forbidden in Islām.

Islām is a pragmatic way of life. It has responded to reality and necessity. It has also put a check on human tendencies and ensured balance. The system is full of wisdom and is perfectly scientific, fair and completely logical.

Allāh, the All-knowing, has prescribed what is best for us. We should not be apologetic in our approach. Islām provides the best answers to all problems. We cannot blame Islām if we do not know it or fail to understand it. We need to look at Islām as a whole, not only at a part of it. This is because Islām views life as a whole and does not divide it into different parts.

All areas of life are inter-related; the status of women, marriage and family life are essential aspects of the whole Islāmic system. One has to take a holistic view of Islām, there is no room to 'pick and choose'.

What did you learn? (8)

Key Stage 4 (15–16)

1. Discuss the role of marriage as the basis of the Islāmic family. Why does Islām not allow extramarital relationships? Give your reasons.
2. What status is given to women by Islām? How do men abuse this status?

Key Stage 5 (17–18)

1. Under what circumstances is polygamy allowed in Islām? Discuss the practicality and responsibility of this provision in Islām.
2. *"Women in Islām have been given both respect and dignity."* Discuss this statement with reference to their rights and duties. To what extent are Western misconceptions about Muslim women based on what they observe from Muslim men who are ignorant or negligent of real Islām, or on prejudicial coverage in the Western media?

Economic System of Islām 9

Islām is a complete way of life. No part of the life of an individual or a community is left out of Islām. The economic aspect is an important part of life, so Islām gives detailed guidelines for the conduct of our economic life. It concerns mainly how we earn and use our wealth. The Islāmic system is balanced and places everything in its right place.

Earning and spending money is essential for our living, but we do not live only for this. Man needs bread to live but he does not live for bread alone. We have a greater purpose in life. We are Allāh's agents *(Khalīfah)* on earth. We not only have a body but we also have a soul *(Rūḥ)* and a conscience. Without a conscience, our behaviour would be worse than wild animals and would create enormous problems in society.

Everything in Islām is for the benefit and welfare of humanity. The economic principles of Islām aim to establish a just society in which we behave responsibly and honestly, not selfishly fighting for the biggest possible share of something without regard for honesty, truth, decency, trust and responsibility.

The economic system of Islām is based on the following principles:

1. Earning and Expenditure by Ḥalāl Means

Muslims are not allowed to earn and spend in any way they like. Islām has laws, based on the *Qur'ān* and the *Sunnah*, to regulate earning and expenditure:

a. Earnings from the production, sale and distribution of alcoholic drinks are unlawful, as are earnings from gambling, lotteries and from *Ribā* (interest or usury) transactions (5:90–91; 2:275).

b. Earning by falsehood, deceit, fraud, and theft is unlawful *(Ḥarām)*. Taking orphans' property deceitfully has been particularly forbidden (2:188; 4:2; 6:152; 7:85; 83:1–5).

c. Hoarding food stuff and basic necessities, smuggling and the artificial creation of shortages are unlawful (3:180; 9:34–35).

d. Earnings from brothels and from other immoral sources which are harmful to society are also unlawful (24:23).

Islām strikes at the root of evil and wants to establish a just and fair society. A Muslim must earn his living in *Ḥalāl* ways and he should always bear in mind that whatever he does is known to Allāh. He will be accountable for his actions on the Day of Judgement. He cannot hide anything from the knowledge of Almighty Allāh.

Unlawful expenditure is not allowed in Islām. A Muslim should not spend his money irresponsibly. Rather, he should spend it wisely and thoughtfully. Extravagance and waste are strongly discouraged (7:31; 17:26; 19:27–31; 25:28).

Bank
interest
MANAGER
MONEY FROM POOR TO THE RICH

Halal Butcher
ISLAMIC WELFARE HOUSE
MONEY FROM RICH TO THE POOR
zakāh

2. Right to Property and Individual Liberty

In Islām a person has a right to his earnings. The Islāmic state does not interfere with the freedom of speech, work or earnings of an individual provided this freedom does not harm the greater good of society. Every individual will be answerable to Allāh for his or her actions on the Day of Judgement (4:7; 36:71; 16:111).

3. System of Zakāh (Welfare Contribution)

Compulsory payment of *Zakāh* is one of the basic principles of an Islāmic economy. It is one of the basic duties *('Ibādah)* of Islām. Every Muslim who has sufficient wealth must pay the fixed rate of *Zakāh* to the Islāmic state *(see Chapter 2). Zakāh* helps to narrow the gap between the rich and the poor. It is a form of social security. An ideal Islāmic state is responsible for providing the basic necessities of food, clothing, housing, medicine and education for every citizen. No one should have any fear of insecurity, poverty or hunger (9:60, 103; 98:5).

The voluntary giving of charity *(Ṣadaqah)* is greatly recommended, and giving to good causes to ensure human welfare has been particularly emphasized in Islām. It is a further means of helping the poorest and most vulnerable in society. It encourages those blessed by Allāh with more than they need, to show consideration for the less fortunate and exercise social responsibility.

4. Prohibition of Ribā (interest or usury)

An Islāmic economy prohibits all transactions involving *Ribā* (interest or usury). In Islām there is no distinction between *interest* and *usury*. Islām allows only a *zero* rate of interest, that is, *no* interest at all. Whatever the name used, interest or usury, it is prohibited in Islām.

Interest is neither a trade nor a profit. It is a means of exploitation and concentration of wealth. The *Qur'ān* says:

"They say, 'trade is like interest.' But Allāh has allowed trade and forbidden interest." (2:275)

"Whatever you pay as interest, so that it may increase in the property of (other) men, it does not increase with Allāh." (30:39)

"O you who believe, do not take interest, doubling and multiplying, and keep your duty to Allāh, so that you may prosper." (3:130)

"O you who believe, observe your duty to Allāh and give up what remains (due) from interest, if you are believers. But if you do not do it, then be warned of war from Allāh and His messenger; and if you repent, then you shall have your capital. Do not exploit and be not exploited." (2:278–279)

Interest *(Ribā)* is an integral part of modern free-market economies. Unlike *Zakāh*, which distributes wealth from the rich to the poor, interest takes wealth from the poor to the rich. Modern economies depend on interest; it is assumed to be impossible to live without it. This false assumption is challenged by the successful interest-free facilities offered by Islāmic banks and investment companies throughout the world, including the UK.

A fully-fledged interest-free economy is not yet a reality. It is a complex situation. Nevertheless, we should work towards an interest-free economy to ensure social justice and equal access to opportunities for everyone in the world. An interest-free economy is only possible when an Islāmic government carefully and systematically plans and implements the economic system of Islām. Political or state authority is essential to implement an Islāmic economic system.

5. Law of Inheritance (Mīrāth)

The Islāmic law of inheritance *(Mīrāth)* is a marvellous system that ensures the fair distribution of wealth after someone dies. It details the rights of relatives over the property of the deceased person. *Sūratun Nisā'* of the *Qur'ān* deals with the law of inheritance in great detail (4:7–12, 176).

Conclusion

Islām has laid down many more rules and guidelines about economic life. All human and natural resources should be put to good use in an Islāmic state. Corruption and all immoral pursuits must be rooted out, even if they are economically lucrative. Some individual freedoms may have to be sacrificed for the greater good of society.

Islām encourages simplicity, modesty, charity, mutual help and cooperation. It discourages miserliness, greed, extravagance and unnecessary waste.

We have discussed the main points of the Islāmic economic system. It is beyond the scope of this book to go into greater depth. Interested readers who would like to study further are encouraged to read some of the many books on Islāmic economics. You will find a list in the bibliography at the end of this book.

What did you learn? (9)

Key Stage 4 (15–16)

1. Explain the concept of *Zakāh* and contrast it with *Ribā* (interest). Why is *Ribā* so unfair to the poor?
2. What are the main principles of the Islāmic economic system?

Key Stage 5 (17–18)

1. *"Man does not live by bread alone." "The best things in life are free."* Discuss these statements.
2. Outline the principles of the economic system of Islām. Explain how it should lead to a more equal distribution of wealth.

Political System of Islām 10

Politics is a part of Islām. It cannot be separated from it. Indeed, the separation of religion and politics is meaningless in Islām. We have already learnt that Islām is a complete system of life, and politics is very much a part of our collective life. Just as Islām teaches us how to say *Ṣalāh*, observe *Ṣawm*, pay *Zakāh* and undertake *Ḥajj*, so it teaches us how to run a state, form a government, elect representatives, make treaties and conduct trade.

A detailed discussion of the Islāmic political system is not possible in this book, so we will have to content ourselves with its basic principles and main features. The interested reader will find references for further reading in the bibliography at the end of the book.

The Islāmic political system is based on the following main principles:

1. Sovereignty of Allāh

Sovereignty means the source of power and authority. In Islām, Allāh is the source of all powers and laws (3:154; 12:40; 25:2; 67:1). It is Allāh Who knows what is good and what is bad for His servants. His say is final. Human beings should not and must not change His Law. For example, the *Qur'ān* says, *"As for the thief, male and female, chop off their hands. It is the reward of their own actions and exemplary punishment from Allāh. Allāh is Mighty, Wise." (5:38)* According to Islām, this order cannot be changed by any ruler or government claiming to be Islāmic (5:44; 2:229). There are many laws in the *Qur'ān* concerning our life, and those laws must be put into practice by an Islāmic state for the greater good of all human beings.

2. Khilāfah of Mankind (Vicegerency of Man)

Man is the vicegerent, the agent or the representative of Allāh on earth (2:30; 6:165). Allāh is the sovereign and man is His representative. Man should do as Allāh commands him to do. Man can choose either to obey or disobey Allāh, but because of this freedom of choice he will be answerable to Allāh on the Day of Judgement. In the political sense, *Khilāfah* means that human beings should implement the will of Allāh on earth as His deputy or agent, on His behalf as a trust *(Amānah)*. An agent is always expected to behave as his master wants him to behave (10:14).

3. Legislation by Shūrā (Consultation)

Islām teaches us how to run a government, to legislate and to arrive at decisions by the process of *Shūrā*. *Shūrā* means "to take decisions by consultation and participation" (3:159; 42:38). This is an important part of the Islāmic political system. There is no room for tyranny in Islām. *Shūrā* must be based on the *Qur'ān* and the *Sunnah*. It must not contradict or attempt to overrule the *Qur'ān* and the *Sunnah*.

4. Accountability of Government

The Islāmic political system makes the ruler and the government responsible firstly to Allāh and then to the people. The ruler must work for the welfare of the people according to the *Qur'ān* and the *Sunnah* of Prophet *Muḥammad* ﷺ. In Islām the ruler is a servant of the people. Citizens of an Islāmic state have the right to question the ruler and the government about any matters that concern them. In turn, the people must obey their ruler, so long as he follows the *Qur'ān* and *Sunnah*.

Both the ruler and the ruled are the *Khalīfah* of Allāh. They will appear before Allāh and account for their actions on the Day of Judgement. The responsibility of the ruler is heavier than the ruled.

5. Independence of the Judiciary

In the Islāmic political system, the judiciary is independent of the executive. The head of the state, the government and any member or employee of the government can be called to the court when necessary. They would be treated no differently from other citizens. The *Qur'ān* has many injunctions about justice. One of the main functions of the Islāmic state is to ensure justice for all citizens (4:58, 135; 5:8). The ruler and the government have no right to interfere in the system of justice.

6. Equality Before the Law

The Islāmic political system ensures equality for all citizens before the law. It does not discriminate against anyone on the basis of language, colour, class, race, religion or sex. Allāh distinguishes between us on the basis of *Taqwā* (piety or fear of Allāh). One who loves and fears Allāh most is the best and noblest in Islām (49:13).

Conclusion

The duty of an ideal Islāmic state is to establish *Ṣalāh* and *Zakāh*; promote the right and forbid the wrong (22:44). The state is responsible for the welfare of all citizens — Muslims and non-Muslims alike. It must guarantee the basic necessities of life (food, clothing, housing, medicine and education). All citizens of the Islāmic state should enjoy freedom of belief, thought, conscience and speech. Every citizen should be free to develop his potential, improve his capacity, earn wealth and own such wealth within the limits set by the *Qur'ān* and the *Sunnah*. A citizen should enjoy the right to support or oppose any government policy which he thinks right or wrong with the following in mind:

a. The Islāmic state is duty bound to implement the laws of the *Qur'ān* and the *Sunnah*. The *Qur'ān* strongly denounces those who do not decide their matters by Allāh's revelations (5:42–50).
b. An ideal Islāmic state should ensure a fair distribution of wealth. Islām does not believe in equal distribution as it is against the law of creation and basic human nature and instinct. Islām ensures equitable distribution of wealth.

There is not a perfect Islāmic state in the world today. There are many Muslim countries. An Islāmic state is based on the model of the Prophet's ﷺ state in *Madīnah* while a Muslim state is one which has a majority Muslim population and some Islāmic features.

However, organised efforts are being made in many parts of the world to establish an Islāmic system of government to implement the laws of the *Qur'ān* and *Sunnah*. Notable among the organisations which have been working to Islāmise society are: *al-Ikhwānul Muslimūn* in the Middle East, *Jamā'at-e-Islāmi* in *Pakistan*, Bangladesh and Kashmir, *Adalet ve Kalkinma Partisi (AKP)* in Turkey, *Nahḍatul 'Ulamā' (NU)* in Indonesia, *Islāmic Salvation Front (FIS)* in Algeria, *National Islāmic Front* in Sudan (now defunct), *Parti Islām SeMalaysia (PAS)* in Malaysia, and *Ḥizb an-Nahḍah* in Tunisia. There are many more Islāmic organisations which have also been working towards the Islāmisation of societies.

The efforts for Islāmic revival in Egypt, Pakistan, Sudan, Iran, Turkey, Malaysia, Bangladesh, Algeria and elsewhere have generated great hope and enthusiasm among Muslim adults and youth all over the world. This hope can only become a reality when Muslims make actions match their words. Presently, there is a marked trend among the parties and organisations to present Islām in words more than in practice. But we must ensure our actions reflect what we profess. Only then will Almighty Allāh guarantee their success. It is hoped that a real Islāmic state will emerge from these efforts which will guide the world towards justice, happiness and peace.

What did you learn? (10)

Key Stage 4 (15–16)

1. *"Politics is part of religion in Islām."* Discuss this statement.
2. *"Muslims living in the West should be wary of getting involved in politics."* Do you agree with this? Give reasons for your answer.

Key Stage 5 (17–18)

1. Discuss the institution of *Shūrā* in Islām and the principle of *Khilāfah*. Why is it that religion and politics cannot be separated in Islām? Why do so many societies wish to separate them?
2. What should be done to establish a real Islāmic state in the world according to the model set by Prophet *Muḥammad* ﷺ? Consider modern countries that are said to be 'Islāmic', and discuss in what ways they fall short of the ideal.
3. Explain the concept of sovereignty in Islām. How does it contrast with the concept of sovereignty in a democracy?

Some other aspects of life 11

Food and Drink

Food and drink affect our health, growth and state of mind. Islām has given regulations about our food and drink. Islām aims to establish a healthy and moral society. It allows all wholesome and pure things to be taken as food and drink. The *Qur'ān* says:

"O Mankind, eat the lawful and good things from what is in the earth and do not follow the foot steps of the devil. Surely, he is your open enemy." (2:168)

It follows from this that Islām has forbidden only what is impure and harmful. Lawful things are called *Ḥalāl* and forbidden things called *Ḥarām* in *Sharī'ah* (Islāmic law).

Islām forbids eating the meat of the following:

a. dead animals (i.e. those which died 'naturally');
b. animals slain without invoking Allāh's name;
c. animals strangled to death;
d. pigs;
e. carnivorous animals;
f. animals devoured by wild beasts.

Islām also forbids the eating of *the blood of an animal* (2:173; 5:3; 6:145; 16:115).

Islām teaches respect and consideration for the life and welfare of animals. It is one of the many favours of Allāh that He has created animals for mankind to eat by His permission, provided we slaughter them in the way He has commanded. Islāmic law requires an animal to be slaughtered by a sharp knife penetrating the inner part of the animal's neck, ensuring it dies quickly and allowing the maximum drainage of blood. Allāh's name must be mentioned at the time of slaughter.

The meat and by-products of animals not slain in this way are *Ḥarām*. Efforts should be made to obtain *Ḥalāl* meat from Muslim butchers. If there is no Muslim butcher nearby, then the 'Kosher' meat of the Jews is regarded as *Ḥalāl* for Muslims.

There are now plenty of Muslim butchers in most of the European countries, USA, Canada, Australia and New Zealand. In case of doubt, Muslims can eat vegetarian food (without alcoholic ingredients).

Fish and vegetables are lawful. All kinds of intoxicating (alcoholic) drinks such as beer, wine and spirits are prohibited. Alcoholic drinks are not at all conducive to a healthy society. The *Qur'ān* says:

"O you who believe, intoxicants and gambling, idols and divining arrows are filthy tricks of Satan; avoid them so that you may prosper. Satan wants to incite enmity and hatred among you by means of wine and gambling and prevent you from remembering Allāh from Ṣalāh. So will you not give them up?" (5:90–91)

Drinking alcohol causes serious social problems in society. It leads to many vices and sins. Islām aims to root out all evils to ensure that society remains healthy and peaceful. Islām also forbids the taking of drugs except for medical purposes.

Muslims should begin meals by saying *Bismillāhir Rahmānir Raḥīm* (In the name of Allāh, the Most Merciful, the Most Kind), and finish by reciting the following *du'ā'*:

اَلْحَمْدُ لِلّٰهِ الَّذِىْ اَطْعَمَنَا وَسَقَانَا وَجَعَلَنَا مِنَ الْمُسْلِمِيْنَ

Alḥamdu lillāhil ladhī aṭ'amanā wa saqānā wa ja'alanā minal muslimīn.

All praise is for Allāh who gave us to eat and to drink and made us Muslims.

Prophet *Muḥammad* ﷺ asked us to eat with the right hand and to wash our hands before and after meals. It is better not to eat so much so as to fill the stomach. The Prophet ﷺ also asked us not to drink water and other soft drinks in one go; rather, we should pause whilst drinking and it is better to have three pauses.

The Islāmic system of life has very beneficial regulations. We should try to follow these rules as best as we can. We should not find excuses to avoid Islāmic laws and regulations, rather we must make serious efforts to follow Allāh's commands.

Dress

Islām asks us to look nice and decent. Allāh has created man in the best of forms and He wants His servants to dress nicely and decently. We should bear in mind that we are the best of all creatures and our dress should reflect this. Proper dress helps prevent indecency, immoral behaviour, and adds beauty to our personality.

The *Qur'ān* says: *"O children of Ādam, we have revealed to you clothing to conceal your private parts and as a thing of beauty. But the garment of Taqwā (piety) is the best of all." (7:26)*

Islām does not recommend any particular type of dress for us. However, there are guidelines which include:

1. *Men must cover their body at least from the navel to the knees.*
2. *Women must cover their whole body except the face, hands and feet while inside. But they are also required to cover their whole body including a part of the face while going out or meeting adult males, outside close relatives. Some Islāmic jurists allow the face to remain uncovered.*
3. *Men and women must not wear clothing that arouses base feelings. This includes clothing that is see-through, skin-tight or revealing.*
4. *Men are not allowed to wear pure silk, clothes decorated with gold or gold jewellery.*
5. *Men are not allowed to wear women's clothing and vice versa.*
6. *Muslims are not allowed to wear dress with symbols of other religions.*

Islām encourages simplicity and modesty. Dress expressing arrogance is disliked. The style of dress to wear depends on local custom and climatic conditions but the above guidelines still apply.

Festivals

Like all other religions, Islām has a number of special occasions of celebration and enjoyment. These occasions are observed with devotion to seek the pleasure of Allāh, not just for our own pleasure.

Festivals in Islām are occasions of thanksgiving, happiness and joy. The two major festivals in Islām each year are *'Īdul Fiṭr* and *'Īdul Aḍḥā.*

'Īdul Fiṭr is observed on the 1st of *Shawwāl* (the tenth month of the Islāmic calendar), the day after the month of *Ramaḍān.* On this day, after a month of fasting, Muslims express their joy and happiness by offering a congregational prayer, if possible in an open field, otherwise in Mosques or hired halls. They express their gratitude to Almighty Allāh for enabling them to observe a month of fasting. The day is generally observed as a holiday in Muslim countries. Special dishes are prepared and it is customary to visit friends and relatives and to give presents to children. Muslims generally wear their best clothes on this day.

'Īdul Aḍḥā is on the 10th of *Dhul Ḥijjah* (the twelfth month of the Islāmic calendar) and is followed by three further days of celebrating called *Aiyāmut Tashrīq. 'Īdul Aḍḥā* commemorates Prophet *Ibrāhīm's* (Abraham) readiness to sacrifice his son *Ismā'īl* (Ishmael) following the command of Allāh. Allāh accepted *Ibrāhīm's* devotion and obedience and asked him to sacrifice a ram instead. This occasion of great importance comes every year during the days of *Ḥajj* (Pilgrimage to *Makkah*) and is observed by offering congregational prayer, as in *'Īdul Fiṭr.*

After the prayer, Muslims who can afford it sacrifice animals like goats, sheep, cows or camels to seek Allāh's pleasure. The meat of the sacrificial animal is eaten and shared among relatives, neighbours and the poor. This sacrifice expresses the inner feeling of a Muslim that, if need be, he will sacrifice his most loved possession for Allāh. This is the lesson of the occasion.

We must remember that what Allāh wants is not the animal nor its meat or blood; rather He wants our devotion and submission to His command (22:37).

Other festive occasions include *Lailatul Qadr* (Night of Power), the day of *'Arafāt* (9th of *Dhul Ḥijjah*), and *'Āshūrā'* (10th of *Muḥarram*).

The *Ṣalātul Jumu'ah* on each Friday may also be regarded as a weekly festival for Muslims, when they gather together for congregational prayer.

Islāmic festivals are observed according to the Islamic calendar which is based on lunar months. The lunar year is shorter than the solar year by about eleven days. Festival dates are determined by the sighting of the new moon.

A practising Muslim in today's world genuinely feels unhappy when he sees injustice, inequality and oppression. Muslims in some parts of the world are under bad leadership and suffer from hunger and poverty. In other parts of the world Muslims are persecuted and killed for their beliefs. So, even on festival days, Muslims feel some sadness in their hearts when they think of those less fortunate than themselves.

Sometimes, in countries where Muslims are a minority, the sighting of the moon is a controversial issue and *'Īd* is observed on different days. The unity of Muslims is less visible when we do not celebrate together. Muslims should ask Almighty Allāh to help them to resolve this unhappy situation. When Allāh's mercy and blessings flow, peace and happiness will be established in society and Muslims will be able to enjoy their festivals which are meant to make them happy and joyful.

What did you learn? (11)

Key Stage 4 (15–16)

1. What are the dietary rules of Islām? Make a list of the things that Muslims are not allowed to eat.
2. What are the Islāmic regulations for dress? What is meant by modest dress and why is it important?
3. Write an essay on the festivals of Islām.

Key Stage 5 (17–18)

1. Discuss the significance of the Islāmic dress code for both men and women. In what ways might men dress immodestly?
2. Discuss the evil effects of alcoholism for society as a whole.
3. *"Why should we kill animals for food?"* In the light of the growth of vegetarianism, discuss the Islāmic attitude to eating meat.

Selected verses from the Qur'ān 12

إِنَّ هَٰذَا ٱلْقُرْءَانَ يَهْدِى لِلَّتِى هِىَ أَقْوَمُ وَيُبَشِّرُ
ٱلْمُؤْمِنِينَ ٱلَّذِينَ يَعْمَلُونَ ٱلصَّٰلِحَٰتِ أَنَّ لَهُمْ أَجْرًا كَبِيرًا ﴿٩﴾

"Surely, this Qur'ān guides to that which is most just, and gives good news to believers who practise good and they will get a great reward." (17:9)

وَأَنَّ هَٰذَا صِرَٰطِى مُسْتَقِيمًا فَٱتَّبِعُوهُ ۖ وَلَا تَتَّبِعُوا۟ ٱلسُّبُلَ
فَتَفَرَّقَ بِكُمْ عَن سَبِيلِهِۦ ۚ ذَٰلِكُمْ وَصَّىٰكُم بِهِۦ لَعَلَّكُمْ
تَتَّقُونَ ﴿١٥٣﴾

"And He (commands you, saying): This is My straight path, so follow it. Do not follow other paths, which will separate you from His path. Thus He has ordered you so that you may be truly obedient (Muttaqūn)." (6:153)

Tawḥīd

ٱللَّهُ لَآ إِلَٰهَ إِلَّا هُوَ
ٱلْحَىُّ ٱلْقَيُّومُ ۚ لَا تَأْخُذُهُۥ سِنَةٌ وَلَا نَوْمٌ ۚ لَّهُۥ مَا فِى ٱلسَّمَٰوَٰتِ وَمَا
فِى ٱلْأَرْضِ ۗ مَن ذَا ٱلَّذِى يَشْفَعُ عِندَهُۥٓ إِلَّا بِإِذْنِهِۦ ۚ يَعْلَمُ مَا بَيْنَ
أَيْدِيهِمْ وَمَا خَلْفَهُمْ ۖ وَلَا يُحِيطُونَ بِشَىْءٍ مِّنْ عِلْمِهِۦٓ إِلَّا بِمَا
شَآءَ ۚ وَسِعَ كُرْسِيُّهُ ٱلسَّمَٰوَٰتِ وَٱلْأَرْضَ ۖ وَلَا يَـُٔودُهُۥ حِفْظُهُمَا ۚ
وَهُوَ ٱلْعَلِىُّ ٱلْعَظِيمُ ﴿٢٥٥﴾

"Allāh! There is none worthy of worship except Him,
the Living, the Ever Lasting!
Slumber does not overtake Him nor does sleep,
Whatever is in the Heavens and in the Earth belongs to Him.
Who is there to plead to Him except with His permission?
He knows what lies before them and what is behind them,
while they grasp nothing of His knowledge except what He wills.
His Authority (Kursī) extends over Heaven and Earth;
Preserving them both does not overburden Him.
*He is the Most High, the Most Great." (2:255)**

Risālah

وَلَقَدْ بَعَثْنَا فِى كُلِّ أُمَّةٍ رَّسُولًا أَنِ ٱعْبُدُوا۟ ٱللَّهَ
وَٱجْتَنِبُوا۟ ٱلطَّٰغُوتَ ۖ ... ﴿٣٦﴾

"And surely, We have sent a messenger to every nation (proclaiming) serve Allāh (Alone) and turn away from false gods (Taghūt)…" (16:36)

لَقَدْ مَنَّ ٱللَّهُ عَلَى ٱلْمُؤْمِنِينَ إِذْ بَعَثَ فِيهِمْ رَسُولًا مِّنْ أَنفُسِهِمْ
يَتْلُوا۟ عَلَيْهِمْ ءَايَٰتِهِۦ وَيُزَكِّيهِمْ وَيُعَلِّمُهُمُ ٱلْكِتَٰبَ
وَٱلْحِكْمَةَ وَإِن كَانُوا۟ مِن قَبْلُ لَفِى ضَلَٰلٍ مُّبِينٍ ﴿١٦٤﴾

"Allāh has favoured the believers by sending them a messenger from among themselves, to recite His verses to them, to purify them, and teach them the book and wisdom whereas previously they were in clear error." (3:164)

---

* (This verse is called *Ayatul Kursī.*)

ٱلْكَٰفِرُونَ ﴿٨﴾ هُوَ ٱلَّذِىٓ أَرْسَلَ رَسُولَهُۥ بِٱلْهُدَىٰ وَدِينِ ٱلْحَقِّ لِيُظْهِرَهُۥ
عَلَى ٱلدِّينِ كُلِّهِۦ وَلَوْ كَرِهَ ٱلْمُشْرِكُونَ ﴿٩﴾

"He it is Who has sent His messenger with the guidance and the religion of truth, that He make it victorious over every other religion, however much the idolaters may dislike." (61:9)

Ākhirah

يَٰٓأَيُّهَا ٱلنَّاسُ إِن كُنتُمْ فِى
رَيْبٍ مِّنَ ٱلْبَعْثِ فَإِنَّا خَلَقْنَٰكُم مِّن تُرَابٍ ثُمَّ مِن نُّطْفَةٍ ثُمَّ
مِنْ عَلَقَةٍ ثُمَّ مِن مُّضْغَةٍ مُّخَلَّقَةٍ وَغَيْرِ مُخَلَّقَةٍ لِّنُبَيِّنَ لَكُمْ
وَنُقِرُّ فِى ٱلْأَرْحَامِ مَا نَشَآءُ إِلَىٰٓ أَجَلٍ مُّسَمًّى ثُمَّ نُخْرِجُكُمْ
طِفْلًا ثُمَّ لِتَبْلُغُوٓا۟ أَشُدَّكُمْ ۖ وَمِنكُم مَّن يُتَوَفَّىٰ
وَمِنكُم مَّن يُرَدُّ إِلَىٰٓ أَرْذَلِ ٱلْعُمُرِ لِكَيْلَا يَعْلَمَ مِنۢ
بَعْدِ عِلْمٍ شَيْـًٔا ۚ وَتَرَى ٱلْأَرْضَ هَامِدَةً فَإِذَآ أَنزَلْنَا عَلَيْهَا
ٱلْمَآءَ ٱهْتَزَّتْ وَرَبَتْ وَأَنۢبَتَتْ مِن كُلِّ زَوْجٍۭ بَهِيجٍ ﴿٥﴾
ذَٰلِكَ بِأَنَّ ٱللَّهَ هُوَ ٱلْحَقُّ وَأَنَّهُۥ يُحْىِ ٱلْمَوْتَىٰ وَأَنَّهُۥ عَلَىٰ كُلِّ شَىْءٍ قَدِيرٌ ﴿٦﴾
وَأَنَّ ٱلسَّاعَةَ ءَاتِيَةٌ لَّا رَيْبَ فِيهَا وَأَنَّ ٱللَّهَ يَبْعَثُ مَن فِى ٱلْقُبُورِ ﴿٧﴾

"O mankind! If you are in doubt about the Resurrection
then consider that We have created you from dust, then from a drop of seed,
then from something that clings, then from a lump of flesh shapely and shapeless,
so that We may make (our power) clear to you.
And We cause what We wish to remain in the wombs for an appointed time,
and afterwards We bring you forth as babies,
then (give you growth) that you attain your full strength.
And among you there is he who dies (young),
and among you there is he who is brought to the most pitiable time of life (senility),
so that, after knowledge, he knows not (because of infirmity).
And you (Muḥammad) see the earth barren, but when We send down rain thereon,
it thrills and swells and puts forth every lovely kind of growth.
This is all because of Allāh. He is the Truth.
Surely, He makes the dead alive and surely He has the power to do everything;
there is no doubt that the Hour will come
and truly Allāh will raise those who are in graves." (22:5–7)

وَقَالَ ٱلَّذِينَ كَفَرُوٓاْ
أَءِذَا كُنَّا تُرَٰبًا وَءَابَآؤُنَآ أَئِنَّا لَمُخۡرَجُونَ ﴿٦٧﴾

"Those who disbelieve say: when we have become dust like our forefathers, shall we truly be raised up again?" (27:67)

أَفَحَسِبۡتُمۡ أَنَّمَا خَلَقۡنَٰكُمۡ عَبَثًا وَأَنَّكُمۡ
إِلَيۡنَا لَا تُرۡجَعُونَ ﴿١١٥﴾

"Do you think then that We have created you for nothing and that you would not be returned to Us?" (23:115)

وَخَلَقَ ٱللَّهُ ٱلسَّمَٰوَٰتِ وَٱلۡأَرۡضَ بِٱلۡحَقِّ
وَلِتُجۡزَىٰ كُلُّ نَفۡسِۢ بِمَا كَسَبَتۡ وَهُمۡ لَا يُظۡلَمُونَ ﴿٢٢﴾

"Allāh has created the Heavens and Earth with truth and that everyone may be repaid what it has earned. And they will not be wronged." (45:22)

Qualities of a Mu'min

قَدۡ أَفۡلَحَ ٱلۡمُؤۡمِنُونَ ﴿١﴾ ٱلَّذِينَ هُمۡ فِي صَلَاتِهِمۡ خَٰشِعُونَ ﴿٢﴾
وَٱلَّذِينَ هُمۡ عَنِ ٱللَّغۡوِ مُعۡرِضُونَ ﴿٣﴾ وَٱلَّذِينَ هُمۡ لِلزَّكَوٰةِ
فَٰعِلُونَ ﴿٤﴾ وَٱلَّذِينَ هُمۡ لِفُرُوجِهِمۡ حَٰفِظُونَ ﴿٥﴾ إِلَّا عَلَىٰٓ
أَزۡوَٰجِهِمۡ أَوۡ مَا مَلَكَتۡ أَيۡمَٰنُهُمۡ فَإِنَّهُمۡ غَيۡرُ مَلُومِينَ ﴿٦﴾
فَمَنِ ٱبۡتَغَىٰ وَرَآءَ ذَٰلِكَ فَأُوْلَٰٓئِكَ هُمُ ٱلۡعَادُونَ ﴿٧﴾ وَٱلَّذِينَ هُمۡ
لِأَمَٰنَٰتِهِمۡ وَعَهۡدِهِمۡ رَٰعُونَ ﴿٨﴾ وَٱلَّذِينَ هُمۡ عَلَىٰ صَلَوَٰتِهِمۡ
يُحَافِظُونَ ﴿٩﴾ أُوْلَٰٓئِكَ هُمُ ٱلۡوَٰرِثُونَ ﴿١٠﴾ ٱلَّذِينَ يَرِثُونَ
ٱلۡفِرۡدَوۡسَ هُمۡ فِيهَا خَٰلِدُونَ ﴿١١﴾

"Successful indeed are the believers,
who are humble in their prayers (Ṣalāh),
who avoid vain talk,
And who practise the system of Zakāh;
And who guard their modesty except from their wives or the (slaves)
that their right hands possess for then they are not blameworthy,

But whoever wants beyond that such are the transgressors —
And who faithfully observe their trusts and undertakings,
And who are mindful of their prayers (Ṣalāh).
These are indeed the inheritors
Who will inherit the Paradise wherein they will live forever." (23:1–11)

يَـٰٓأَيُّهَا ٱلَّذِينَ ءَامَنُوا۟ ٱتَّقُوا۟ ٱللَّهَ حَقَّ تُقَاتِهِۦ وَلَا تَمُوتُنَّ إِلَّا وَأَنتُم
مُّسْلِمُونَ ﴿١٠٢﴾

"O believers, fear Allāh as He should be feared and do not die except as Muslims." (3:102)

Luqmān's* Advice to his Son

وَإِذْ قَالَ لُقْمَـٰنُ لِٱبْنِهِۦ وَهُوَ يَعِظُهُۥ يَـٰبُنَىَّ لَا تُشْرِكْ بِٱللَّهِ ۖ
إِنَّ ٱلشِّرْكَ لَظُلْمٌ عَظِيمٌ ﴿١٣﴾

"And (remember) when Luqmān said to his son when he was advising him: 'O my son! Do not make any partner to Allāh. Truly, making anyone partner to Allāh is a terrible sin (great ẓulm).'" (31:13)

يَـٰبُنَىَّ أَقِمِ ٱلصَّلَوٰةَ وَأْمُرْ
بِٱلْمَعْرُوفِ وَٱنْهَ عَنِ ٱلْمُنكَرِ وَٱصْبِرْ عَلَىٰ مَآ أَصَابَكَ ۖ إِنَّ ذَٰلِكَ
مِنْ عَزْمِ ٱلْأُمُورِ ﴿١٧﴾ وَلَا تُصَعِّرْ خَدَّكَ لِلنَّاسِ وَلَا تَمْشِ فِى ٱلْأَرْضِ
مَرَحًا ۖ إِنَّ ٱللَّهَ لَا يُحِبُّ كُلَّ مُخْتَالٍ فَخُورٍ ﴿١٨﴾ وَٱقْصِدْ فِى مَشْيِكَ
وَٱغْضُضْ مِن صَوْتِكَ ۚ إِنَّ أَنكَرَ ٱلْأَصْوَٰتِ لَصَوْتُ ٱلْحَمِيرِ ﴿١٩﴾

"'O my son! Establish Ṣalāh and command for the right and forbid the evil
and persevere in whatever difficulty you are in.
Surely, this is one of those things which have been strongly recommended.
Do not turn your face in disgust from people, nor walk arrogantly on the land.
Allāh does not love the arrogant boasters. Be modest in your behaviour and lower your voice.
Truly the harshest of all voices is the voice of the ass.'" (31:17–19)

---

* *Luqmān* was famous for his sound intelligence and wisdom in Arabia. He was most probably an Arabic-speaking African.

Duties and Obligations

Duty Towards Parents

...وَبِالْوَالِدَيْنِ إِحْسَانًا وَذِي الْقُرْبَىٰ وَالْيَتَامَىٰ
وَالْمَسَاكِينِ وَقُولُوا لِلنَّاسِ حُسْنًا... ﴿٨٣﴾

"...Be kind to your parents and the relatives and the orphans,
and those in need and speak nicely to people...." (2:83)

وَوَصَّيْنَا الْإِنسَانَ بِوَالِدَيْهِ حَمَلَتْهُ أُمُّهُ وَهْنًا عَلَىٰ وَهْنٍ
وَفِصَالُهُ فِي عَامَيْنِ أَنِ اشْكُرْ لِي وَلِوَالِدَيْكَ إِلَيَّ الْمَصِيرُ ﴿١٤﴾

"And We have made it a duty for man to be good to his parents.
His mother bears him with one fainting spell after another fainting spell,
while his weaning takes two years.
Thank Me as well as your parents; towards Me lies the final destination." (31:14)

وَقَضَىٰ رَبُّكَ أَلَّا تَعْبُدُوا إِلَّا إِيَّاهُ وَبِالْوَالِدَيْنِ إِحْسَانًا ۚ إِمَّا
يَبْلُغَنَّ عِندَكَ الْكِبَرَ أَحَدُهُمَا أَوْ كِلَاهُمَا فَلَا تَقُل لَّهُمَا
أُفٍّ وَلَا تَنْهَرْهُمَا وَقُل لَّهُمَا قَوْلًا كَرِيمًا ﴿٢٣﴾ وَاخْفِضْ
لَهُمَا جَنَاحَ الذُّلِّ مِنَ الرَّحْمَةِ وَقُل رَّبِّ ارْحَمْهُمَا كَمَا رَبَّيَانِي
صَغِيرًا ﴿٢٤﴾

"Your Lord has ordered that you worship none but Him and (show) kindness to your parents,
whether either of them or both of them attain old age in your life, never say to them, 'Ough'
nor be harsh to them, but speak to them kindly.
And serve them with tenderness and humility and say:
My Lord, have mercy on them, just as they cared for me as a little child." (17:23–24)

وَوَصَّيْنَا الْإِنسَانَ
بِوَالِدَيْهِ حُسْنًا ۖ وَإِن جَاهَدَاكَ لِتُشْرِكَ بِي مَا لَيْسَ لَكَ بِهِ عِلْمٌ
فَلَا تُطِعْهُمَا ۚ إِلَيَّ مَرْجِعُكُمْ فَأُنَبِّئُكُم بِمَا كُنتُمْ تَعْمَلُونَ ﴿٨﴾

"We have made it a duty on man to be kind to his parents,
but if they try to make you associate anything with Me which you have no knowledge of,
do not obey them. To Me is your return and I shall tell you what you used to do." (29:8)

Relatives, Neighbours and the Needy

وَءَاتِ ذَا ٱلْقُرْبَىٰ حَقَّهُۥ
وَٱلْمِسْكِينَ وَٱبْنَ ٱلسَّبِيلِ وَلَا تُبَذِّرْ تَبْذِيرًا ﴿٢٦﴾

"Give your relatives their due and also the needy and the traveller in need and do not squander (your wealth) irresponsibly." (17:26)

إِنَّ ٱللَّهَ يَأْمُرُ بِٱلْعَدْلِ وَٱلْإِحْسَـٰنِ وَإِيتَآئِ ذِى ٱلْقُرْبَىٰ ... ﴿٩١﴾

"Allāh commands justice, kindness and giving (their due) to near relatives..." (16:90)

وَإِذَا حَضَرَ ٱلْقِسْمَةَ أُو۟لُوا۟ ٱلْقُرْبَىٰ وَٱلْيَتَـٰمَىٰ وَٱلْمَسَـٰكِينُ
فَٱرْزُقُوهُم مِّنْهُ وَقُولُوا۟ لَهُمْ قَوْلًا مَّعْرُوفًا ﴿٨﴾

"And when near relatives, orphans and the needy are present at the division (of inheritance), provide for them out of it and speak politely to them." (4:8)

... وَبِٱلْوَٰلِدَيْنِ إِحْسَـٰنًا وَبِذِى ٱلْقُرْبَىٰ وَٱلْيَتَـٰمَىٰ
وَٱلْمَسَـٰكِينِ وَٱلْجَارِ ذِى ٱلْقُرْبَىٰ وَٱلْجَارِ ٱلْجُنُبِ ... ﴿٣٦﴾

"...And (show) kindness to (your) parents and to near relatives, orphans, the needy and to the neighbour who is your relative and the neighbour who is not your relative..." (4:36)

أَرَءَيْتَ ٱلَّذِى يُكَذِّبُ بِٱلدِّينِ ﴿١﴾ فَذَٰلِكَ ٱلَّذِى
يَدُعُّ ٱلْيَتِيمَ ﴿٢﴾ وَلَا يَحُضُّ عَلَىٰ طَعَامِ ٱلْمِسْكِينِ ﴿٣﴾

"Have you seen him who rejects the Judgement? That is the person who pushes the orphan aside and does not encourage feeding the needy." (107:1–3)

Orphans

فَأَمَّا ٱلْيَتِيمَ فَلَا تَقْهَرْ ﴿٩﴾

"Therefore, do not treat the orphan with oppression." (93:9)

إِنَّ ٱلَّذِينَ يَأْكُلُونَ أَمْوَٰلَ ٱلْيَتَـٰمَىٰ ظُلْمًا إِنَّمَا يَأْكُلُونَ فِى
بُطُونِهِمْ نَارًا ۖ وَسَيَصْلَوْنَ سَعِيرًا ﴿١٠﴾

"Those who live on orphans' property without having any right to do so only suck up fire into their bellies, and they will (eventually) roast in a blaze." (4:10)

وَءَاتُوا۟ ٱلْيَتَـٰمَىٰٓ أَمْوَٰلَهُمْ ۖ وَلَا تَتَبَدَّلُوا۟ ٱلْخَبِيثَ بِٱلطَّيِّبِ ۖ ... ﴿٢﴾

"Give orphans their property and do not exchange something bad for something good..." (4:2)

وَلَا تَقْرَبُوا۟ مَالَ ٱلْيَتِيمِ إِلَّا بِٱلَّتِى هِىَ أَحْسَنُ حَتَّىٰ يَبْلُغَ أَشُدَّهُۥ ۖ ... ﴿١٥٢﴾

"Do not approach an orphan's estate before he comes of age except to improve it..." (6:152; 17:34)

Social Manners

Brotherhood

إِنَّمَا ٱلْمُؤْمِنُونَ إِخْوَةٌ فَأَصْلِحُوا۟ بَيْنَ أَخَوَيْكُمْ ۚ وَٱتَّقُوا۟ ٱللَّهَ لَعَلَّكُمْ تُرْحَمُونَ ﴿١٠﴾

"Believers are but brothers, so set things right between your brothers and observe your duty to Allāh so that you may obtain mercy." (49:10)

Greetings

وَإِذَا جَآءَكَ ٱلَّذِينَ يُؤْمِنُونَ بِـَٔايَـٰتِنَا فَقُلْ سَلَـٰمٌ عَلَيْكُمْ ۖ ... ﴿٥٤﴾

"When those who believe in Our signs come to you, say: peace be upon you..." (6:54)

وَإِذَا حُيِّيتُم بِتَحِيَّةٍ فَحَيُّوا۟
بِأَحْسَنَ مِنْهَآ أَوْ رُدُّوهَآ ۗ إِنَّ ٱللَّهَ كَانَ عَلَىٰ كُلِّ شَىْءٍ حَسِيبًا ﴿٨٦﴾

"When you are welcomed with a greeting, then answer back with something finer than it or (at least) return it. Truly Allāh takes count of all things." (4:86)

... فَإِذَا دَخَلْتُم بُيُوتًا فَسَلِّمُوا۟ عَلَىٰٓ أَنفُسِكُمْ
تَحِيَّةً مِّنْ عِندِ ٱللَّهِ مُبَـٰرَكَةً طَيِّبَةً ۚ ... ﴿٦١﴾

"...When you enter houses salute one another with a greeting from Allāh, blessed and sweet..." (24:61)

Co-operation

... وَتَعَاوَنُوا۟ عَلَى ٱلْبِرِّ وَٱلتَّقْوَىٰ ۖ وَلَا تَعَاوَنُوا۟ عَلَى ٱلْإِثْمِ وَٱلْعُدْوَٰنِ ۚ ... ﴿٢﴾

"...Co-operate with one another for virtue and piety and do not co-operate with one another for sin and transgression..." (5:2)

وَٱعْتَصِمُوا۟ بِحَبْلِ ٱللَّهِ جَمِيعًا وَلَا تَفَرَّقُوا۟ ۚ ... ﴿١٠٣﴾

"And hold fast together to Allāh's rope (Islām) and do not be divided..." (3:103)

وَٱلْمُؤْمِنُونَ وَٱلْمُؤْمِنَـٰتُ بَعْضُهُمْ
أَوْلِيَآءُ بَعْضٍ ۚ يَأْمُرُونَ بِٱلْمَعْرُوفِ وَيَنْهَوْنَ عَنِ ٱلْمُنكَرِ
وَيُقِيمُونَ ٱلصَّلَوٰةَ وَيُؤْتُونَ ٱلزَّكَوٰةَ وَيُطِيعُونَ ٱللَّهَ وَرَسُولَهُۥٓ ۚ ... ﴿٧١﴾

"And the believers, men and women, are friends of one another, they command for the right and forbid the wrong, establish Ṣalāh and pay Zakāh and obey Allāh and His messenger..." (9:71)

Meetings

يَٰٓأَيُّهَا ٱلَّذِينَ

ءَامَنُوٓا۟ إِذَا قِيلَ لَكُمْ تَفَسَّحُوا۟ فِى ٱلْمَجَٰلِسِ فَٱفْسَحُوا۟ يَفْسَحِ

ٱللَّهُ لَكُمْ ۖ وَإِذَا قِيلَ ٱنشُزُوا۟ فَٱنشُزُوا۟ يَرْفَعِ ٱللَّهُ ٱلَّذِينَ ءَامَنُوا۟

مِنكُمْ وَٱلَّذِينَ أُوتُوا۟ ٱلْعِلْمَ دَرَجَٰتٍ ۚ وَٱللَّهُ بِمَا تَعْمَلُونَ خَبِيرٌ ﴿١١﴾

"O you who believe, when you are asked to make room in meetings, then make room.
Allāh will make room for you (in the Ākhirah).
And when it is said, "Move up" then move on.
Allāh will raise in rank those of you who believe as well as those who are given knowledge.
Allāh knows whatever you do." (58:11)

إِنَّمَا ٱلْمُؤْمِنُونَ ٱلَّذِينَ ءَامَنُوا۟ بِٱللَّهِ وَرَسُولِهِۦ وَإِذَا كَانُوا۟ مَعَهُۥ

عَلَىٰٓ أَمْرٍ جَامِعٍ لَّمْ يَذْهَبُوا۟ حَتَّىٰ يَسْتَـْٔذِنُوهُ ۚ إِنَّ ٱلَّذِينَ يَسْتَـْٔذِنُونَكَ

أُو۟لَٰٓئِكَ ٱلَّذِينَ يُؤْمِنُونَ بِٱللَّهِ وَرَسُولِهِۦ ۚ ... ﴿٦٢﴾

"Truly they are the believers who believe in Allāh and His messenger
and when they are with him on some common matter,
they should not leave until they have asked him for permission to do so.
Those who ask for such permission
are the ones who believe in Allāh and His messenger…" (24:62)

Talking

وَٱقْصِدْ فِى مَشْيِكَ

وَٱغْضُضْ مِن صَوْتِكَ ۚ إِنَّ أَنكَرَ ٱلْأَصْوَٰتِ لَصَوْتُ ٱلْحَمِيرِ ﴿١٩﴾

"Be modest in your behaviour and lower your voice.
Truly the harshest of all voices is the voice of the ass." (31:19)

Seek Permission Before Entering Someone's House

يَٰٓأَيُّهَا ٱلَّذِينَ

ءَامَنُوا۟ لَا تَدْخُلُوا۟ بُيُوتًا غَيْرَ بُيُوتِكُمْ حَتَّىٰ تَسْتَأْنِسُوا۟

وَتُسَلِّمُوا۟ عَلَىٰٓ أَهْلِهَا ۚ ذَٰلِكُمْ خَيْرٌ لَّكُمْ لَعَلَّكُمْ تَذَكَّرُونَ ﴿٢٧﴾

فَإِن لَّمْ تَجِدُوا۟ فِيهَآ أَحَدًا فَلَا تَدْخُلُوهَا حَتَّىٰ يُؤْذَنَ لَكُمْ ... ﴿٢٨﴾

"O you who believe! Do not enter houses other than your own
without first seeking permission and greeting the people inside.
That is better for you so that you may be heedful.
And if you find no one therein, still do not enter until permission has been given…"
(24:27–28)

Keeping a Promise

يَـٰٓأَيُّهَا ٱلَّذِينَ ءَامَنُوٓا۟ أَوْفُوا۟ بِٱلْعُقُودِ ... (١)

"O you who believe, fulfil your contracts (promises, covenants)…" (5:1)

... وَأَوْفُوا۟ بِٱلْعَهْدِ ۖ إِنَّ ٱلْعَهْدَ كَانَ مَسْـُٔولًا (٣٤)

"…Keep your promise, every promise will be enquired into." (17:34)

مِّنَ ٱلْمُؤْمِنِينَ رِجَالٌ صَدَقُوا۟ مَا عَـٰهَدُوا۟ ٱللَّهَ عَلَيْهِ ... (٢٣)

"Among the believers are men who are true to the contract they made with Allāh…"
(33:23)

وَٱلْمُوفُونَ بِعَهْدِهِمْ إِذَا عَـٰهَدُوا۟ ... (١٧٧)

"…And (the pious are those) who honour their contracts when they make them…"
(2:177)

Basic Virtues

Honesty

وَأَوْفُوا۟ ٱلْكَيْلَ إِذَا كِلْتُمْ وَزِنُوا۟ بِٱلْقِسْطَاسِ ٱلْمُسْتَقِيمِ ... (٣٥)

"And give full measure when measuring out, and weigh with proper scales…" (17:35)

وَأَقِيمُوا۟ ٱلْوَزْنَ بِٱلْقِسْطِ وَلَا تُخْسِرُوا۟ ٱلْمِيزَانَ (٩)

"And give just weight and do not weigh unfairly." (55:9)

... وَإِذَا قُلْتُمْ فَٱعْدِلُوا۟ وَلَوْ كَانَ ذَا قُرْبَىٰ ... (١٥٢)

"Whenever you speak, speak justly even if a near relative is concerned…" (6:152)

Truthfulness

يَـٰٓأَيُّهَا ٱلَّذِينَ ءَامَنُوا۟ ٱتَّقُوا۟ ٱللَّهَ وَكُونُوا۟ مَعَ ٱلصَّـٰدِقِينَ (١١٩)

"O you who believe! Fear Allāh and stand by those who are truthful." (9:119)

لِّيَجْزِيَ ٱللَّهُ ٱلصَّـٰدِقِينَ بِصِدْقِهِمْ وَيُعَذِّبَ ٱلْمُنَـٰفِقِينَ
إِن شَآءَ أَوْ يَتُوبَ عَلَيْهِمْ... ﴿٢٤﴾

"That Allāh may reward the truthful for their truth and punish the hypocrites, if He wills..." (33:24)

إِنَّ ٱلْمُسْلِمِينَ وَٱلْمُسْلِمَـٰتِ وَٱلْمُؤْمِنِينَ وَٱلْمُؤْمِنَـٰتِ
وَٱلْقَـٰنِتِينَ وَٱلْقَـٰنِتَـٰتِ وَٱلصَّـٰدِقِينَ وَٱلصَّـٰدِقَـٰتِ...
...أَعَدَّ ٱللَّهُ لَهُم مَّغْفِرَةً وَأَجْرًا عَظِيمًا ﴿٣٥﴾

"Truly Muslim men and Muslim women, believing men and believing women and obedient men and obedient women, and the truthful men and the truthful women... Allāh has promised them forgiveness and a great reward." (33:35)

قَالَ ٱللَّهُ هَـٰذَا يَوْمُ
يَنفَعُ ٱلصَّـٰدِقِينَ صِدْقُهُمْ ۚ لَهُمْ جَنَّـٰتٌ تَجْرِى مِن تَحْتِهَا ٱلْأَنْهَـٰرُ
خَـٰلِدِينَ فِيهَآ أَبَدًا ۚ رَّضِىَ ٱللَّهُ عَنْهُمْ وَرَضُوا۟ عَنْهُ ۚ ذَٰلِكَ ٱلْفَوْزُ ٱلْعَظِيمُ ﴿١١٩﴾

"Allāh said: This is the day (Day of Judgement) on which the truthful will benefit from their truthfulness, for them are the gardens underneath which the rivers flow where they will live forever. Allāh is pleased with them and they are pleased with Him. That is the greatest success." (5:119)

Patience, Steadfastness and Forgiveness

...ٱسْتَعِينُوا۟ بِٱللَّهِ وَٱصْبِرُوٓا۟ ۖ إِنَّ ٱلْأَرْضَ لِلَّهِ يُورِثُهَا مَن
يَشَآءُ مِنْ عِبَادِهِۦ... ﴿١٢٨﴾

"...Seek help from Allāh and be patient, the earth belongs to Allāh. He gives it as heritage to whom He wills from among His slaves..." (7:128)

...رَبَّنَآ أَفْرِغْ عَلَيْنَا صَبْرًا وَثَبِّتْ أَقْدَامَنَا
وَٱنصُرْنَا عَلَى ٱلْقَوْمِ ٱلْكَـٰفِرِينَ ﴿٢٥٠﴾

"...Our Lord, fill us full of patience and make our feet firm. Help us against the disbelievers." (2:250)

$$\text{وَلَمَن صَبَرَ وَغَفَرَ إِنَّ ذَٰلِكَ لَمِنْ عَزْمِ ٱلْأُمُورِ ﴿٤٣﴾}$$

"And anyone who acts patiently and forgives,
that truly would be from the things recommended by Allāh." (42:43)

$$\text{وَٱصْبِرْ عَلَىٰ مَا يَقُولُونَ وَٱهْجُرْهُمْ هَجْرًا جَمِيلًا ﴿١٠﴾}$$

"Tolerate patiently what (unbelievers) say and part from them in a polite manner." (73:10)

$$\text{يَٰٓأَيُّهَا ٱلَّذِينَ ءَامَنُوا۟ ٱسْتَعِينُوا۟ بِٱلصَّبْرِ وَٱلصَّلَوٰةِ إِنَّ ٱللَّهَ مَعَ ٱلصَّٰبِرِينَ ﴿١٥٣﴾}$$

"O you who believe! Seek help in steadfastness (patience) and prayer.
Surely Allāh is with those who are steadfast (patient)." (2:153)

$$\text{... وَٱلصَّٰبِرِينَ فِى ٱلْبَأْسَآءِ وَٱلضَّرَّآءِ وَحِينَ ٱلْبَأْسِ أُو۟لَٰٓئِكَ ٱلَّذِينَ صَدَقُوا۟ وَأُو۟لَٰٓئِكَ هُمُ ٱلْمُتَّقُونَ ﴿١٧٧﴾}$$

"...and those who are steadfast in poverty and illness and during the time of battle. Such
are they who are on the right track and such are Allāh-fearing (Muttaqūn)." (2:177)

$$\text{يَٰٓأَيُّهَا ٱلَّذِينَ ءَامَنُوا۟ ٱصْبِرُوا۟ وَصَابِرُوا۟ وَرَابِطُوا۟ وَٱتَّقُوا۟ ٱللَّهَ لَعَلَّكُمْ تُفْلِحُونَ ﴿٢٠٠﴾}$$

"O you who believe, endure and outdo all others in endurance, be firm in the battlefield,
and observe your duty to Allāh, so that you may be successful." (3:200)

$$\text{فَٱصْبِرْ صَبْرًا جَمِيلًا ﴿٥﴾}$$

"Be patient (O Muḥammad) with the finest patience." (70:5)

$$\text{فَٱصْبِرْ كَمَا صَبَرَ أُو۟لُوا۟ ٱلْعَزْمِ مِنَ ٱلرُّسُلِ ... ﴿٣٥﴾}$$

"Then have patience (O Muḥammad)
as the most determined of the messengers (before you) had patience..." (46:35)

$$\text{خُذِ ٱلْعَفْوَ وَأْمُرْ بِٱلْعُرْفِ وَأَعْرِضْ عَنِ ٱلْجَٰهِلِينَ ﴿١٩٩﴾}$$

"Practise forgiveness, command decency and avoid ignorant people." (7:199)

Punctuality and Time-keeping

$$\text{... إِنَّ ٱلصَّلَوٰةَ كَانَتْ عَلَى ٱلْمُؤْمِنِينَ كِتَٰبًا مَّوْقُوتًا ﴿١٠٣﴾}$$

"...Surely Ṣalāh at fixed hours has been ordained on the believers." (4:103)

Courage

ٱلَّذِينَ قَالَ لَهُمُ ٱلنَّاسُ إِنَّ ٱلنَّاسَ قَدْ جَمَعُوا۟ لَكُمْ فَٱخْشَوْهُمْ
فَزَادَهُمْ إِيمَـٰنًا وَقَالُوا۟ حَسْبُنَا ٱللَّهُ وَنِعْمَ ٱلْوَكِيلُ ﴿١٧٣﴾

"Those to whom people said: Truly the people have gathered against you, so fear them. (The threat of danger) but it increased their faith and they said: Allāh is enough for us! Most Excellent is He in Whom we trust." (3:173)

وَلَمَّا رَءَا ٱلْمُؤْمِنُونَ ٱلْأَحْزَابَ قَالُوا۟ هَـٰذَا مَا وَعَدَنَا ٱللَّهُ وَرَسُولُهُۥ
وَصَدَقَ ٱللَّهُ وَرَسُولُهُۥ ۚ وَمَا زَادَهُمْ إِلَّآ إِيمَـٰنًا وَتَسْلِيمًا ﴿٢٢﴾

"And when the true believers saw the troops they said: That is that which Allāh and His messenger promised us. Allāh and His messengers told the truth. It strengthened their faith and obedience." (33:22)

Kindness, politeness and mercy

فَبِمَا رَحْمَةٍ مِّنَ
ٱللَّهِ لِنتَ لَهُمْ ۖ وَلَوْ كُنتَ فَظًّا غَلِيظَ ٱلْقَلْبِ لَٱنفَضُّوا۟ مِنْ حَوْلِكَ ۖ
فَٱعْفُ عَنْهُمْ وَٱسْتَغْفِرْ لَهُمْ وَشَاوِرْهُمْ فِى ٱلْأَمْرِ ... ﴿١٥٩﴾

"It is because of mercy from Allāh that you (Muḥammad) were so gentle with them, for if you had been harsh and cruel-hearted they would have broken away from around you. Pardon them, seek forgiveness for them and consult them about the matter…" (3:159)

... وَأَحْسِن كَمَآ أَحْسَنَ ٱللَّهُ إِلَيْكَ ۖ ... ﴿٧٧﴾

"…Be kind (or do good) as Allāh has been kind (good) to you…" (28:77)

وَقُل رَّبِّ ٱغْفِرْ وَٱرْحَمْ وَأَنتَ خَيْرُ ٱلرَّٰحِمِينَ ﴿١١٨﴾

"And say (O Muḥammad), 'My Lord, forgive and have mercy, and You are the best of those who show mercy!'" (23:118)

Trustworthiness

إِنِّي لَكُمْ رَسُولٌ أَمِينٌ ﴿١٠٧﴾ فَاتَّقُوا اللَّهَ وَأَطِيعُونِ ﴿١٠٨﴾

"Surely, I am a trustworthy messenger to you, so observe your duty to Allāh and obey me."
(26:107–108)

إِنَّ اللَّهَ يَأْمُرُكُمْ أَنْ تُؤَدُّوا الْأَمَانَاتِ إِلَىٰ أَهْلِهَا ... ﴿٥٨﴾

"Allāh orders you to restore things entrusted (to you) to their owners..." (4:58)

Justice

لَقَدْ أَرْسَلْنَا رُسُلَنَا بِالْبَيِّنَاتِ وَأَنْزَلْنَا مَعَهُمُ الْكِتَابَ
وَالْمِيزَانَ لِيَقُومَ النَّاسُ بِالْقِسْطِ ... ﴿٢٥﴾

"We surely sent Our messengers with clear proofs
and revealed with them books and the balance (justice),
so that people may deal with justice..." (57:25)

إِنَّ اللَّهَ يَأْمُرُ بِالْعَدْلِ وَالْإِحْسَانِ ... ﴿٩٠﴾

"Allāh commands justice and fairness..." (16:90)

... وَلَا يَجْرِمَنَّكُمْ شَنَآنُ قَوْمٍ عَلَىٰ
أَلَّا تَعْدِلُوا ۚ اعْدِلُوا هُوَ أَقْرَبُ لِلتَّقْوَىٰ ... ﴿٨﴾

"...Let not the enmity and hatred of others make you avoid justice.
Be just, that is nearer to piety..." (5:8)

Ḥijāb and Chastity

قُلْ لِلْمُؤْمِنِينَ يَغُضُّوا مِنْ أَبْصَارِهِمْ وَيَحْفَظُوا فُرُوجَهُمْ ۚ
ذَٰلِكَ أَزْكَىٰ لَهُمْ ۗ إِنَّ اللَّهَ خَبِيرٌ بِمَا يَصْنَعُونَ ﴿٣٠﴾

"Tell the believing men to lower their gaze (from looking at forbidden things)
and guard their private parts (from illegal sexual acts).
That is purer for them. Surely Allāh knows what they do." (24:30)

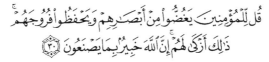

وَقُل لِّلْمُؤْمِنَٰتِ
يَغْضُضْنَ مِنْ أَبْصَٰرِهِنَّ وَيَحْفَظْنَ فُرُوجَهُنَّ وَلَا يُبْدِينَ
زِينَتَهُنَّ إِلَّا مَا ظَهَرَ مِنْهَا ۖ وَلْيَضْرِبْنَ بِخُمُرِهِنَّ عَلَىٰ جُيُوبِهِنَّ ۖ
وَلَا يُبْدِينَ زِينَتَهُنَّ إِلَّا لِبُعُولَتِهِنَّ أَوْ ءَابَآئِهِنَّ أَوْ
ءَابَآءِ بُعُولَتِهِنَّ أَوْ أَبْنَآئِهِنَّ أَوْ أَبْنَآءِ بُعُولَتِهِنَّ
أَوْ إِخْوَٰنِهِنَّ أَوْ بَنِىٓ إِخْوَٰنِهِنَّ أَوْ بَنِىٓ أَخَوَٰتِهِنَّ أَوْ نِسَآئِهِنَّ
أَوْ مَا مَلَكَتْ أَيْمَٰنُهُنَّ أَوِ ٱلتَّٰبِعِينَ غَيْرِ أُو۟لِى ٱلْإِرْبَةِ مِنَ
ٱلرِّجَالِ أَوِ ٱلطِّفْلِ ٱلَّذِينَ لَمْ يَظْهَرُوا۟ عَلَىٰ عَوْرَٰتِ ٱلنِّسَآءِ ۖ
وَلَا يَضْرِبْنَ بِأَرْجُلِهِنَّ لِيُعْلَمَ مَا يُخْفِينَ مِن زِينَتِهِنَّ ۚ وَتُوبُوٓا۟
إِلَى ٱللَّهِ جَمِيعًا أَيُّهَ ٱلْمُؤْمِنُونَ لَعَلَّكُمْ تُفْلِحُونَ ﴿٣١﴾

"And tell the believing women to lower their gaze and guard their private parts
and not show off their beauty except which is apparent,
to draw cloaks (head coverings) over their juyūb (bosoms, bodies, necks and heads)
and not to reveal their feminine beauty except to their husbands or fathers
or husband's father or their sons or their husband's sons
or their brothers or their brother's sons or sisters or their women or their maids
or old male attendants having no sexual vigour
or small children who have no sense of women's private parts.
And let them not stamp their feet so as to reveal what they hide of their beauty.
And turn to Allāh together, O believers! In order that you may prosper." (24:31)

يَٰٓأَيُّهَا ٱلنَّبِىُّ قُل لِّأَزْوَٰجِكَ وَبَنَاتِكَ وَنِسَآءِ ٱلْمُؤْمِنِينَ يُدْنِينَ
عَلَيْهِنَّ مِن جَلَٰبِيبِهِنَّ ۚ ذَٰلِكَ أَدْنَىٰٓ أَن يُعْرَفْنَ فَلَا يُؤْذَيْنَ ۗ وَكَانَ
ٱللَّهُ غَفُورًا رَّحِيمًا ﴿٥٩﴾

"O prophet! Tell your wives and your daughters and the women of the believers
to draw their cloaks close round them (when they go out).
That will be better, so that they may be recognised and not to be annoyed.
Allāh is ever Forgiving and Merciful." (33:59)

Bringing About Social Change

...إِنَّ ٱللَّهَ لَا يُغَيِّرُ مَا بِقَوْمٍ حَتَّىٰ يُغَيِّرُوا۟ مَا بِأَنفُسِهِمْ ۗ ... ﴿١١﴾

"...Surely Allāh does not change the condition of a people
as long as they do not change what is in themselves..." (13:11)

Generosity

لَن تَنَالُوا۟ ٱلْبِرَّ حَتَّىٰ تُنفِقُوا۟ مِمَّا تُحِبُّونَ ۚ ... ﴿٩٢﴾

"You will not attain righteousness (al-Birr)
until you spend what you hold is dear to you..." (3:92)

ٱلَّذِينَ يُنفِقُونَ أَمْوَٰلَهُم
بِٱلَّيْلِ وَٱلنَّهَارِ سِرًّا وَعَلَانِيَةً فَلَهُمْ أَجْرُهُمْ عِندَ
رَبِّهِمْ وَلَا خَوْفٌ عَلَيْهِمْ وَلَا هُمْ يَحْزَنُونَ ﴿٢٧٤﴾

"Those who spend their wealth (for the sake of Allāh) night and day,
both secretly and openly, will get their reward from their Lord,
they shall have no cause to fear nor shall they grieve." (2:274)

Reliance on Allāh

إِن يَنصُرْكُمُ ٱللَّهُ
فَلَا غَالِبَ لَكُمْ ۖ وَإِن يَخْذُلْكُمْ فَمَن ذَا ٱلَّذِى يَنصُرُكُم مِّنۢ
بَعْدِهِۦ ۗ وَعَلَى ٱللَّهِ فَلْيَتَوَكَّلِ ٱلْمُؤْمِنُونَ ﴿١٦٠﴾

"If Allāh is your helper none can overcome you and if He does not help you,
who is there to help you? And on Allāh let the believers rely." (3:160)

...وَمَن يَتَوَكَّلْ عَلَى ٱللَّهِ فَهُوَ حَسْبُهُۥٓ ۚ ... ﴿٣﴾

"... and he who relies on Allāh, He is enough for him..." (65:3)

Bad Conduct & Prohibitions

Lying

...فَٱجۡتَنِبُواْ
ٱلرِّجۡسَ مِنَ ٱلۡأَوۡثَٰنِ وَٱجۡتَنِبُواْ قَوۡلَ ٱلزُّورِ ﴿٣٠﴾

"... Give up the filth of worshipping idols and stop lying." (22:30)

...لَعۡنَتَ ٱللَّهِ عَلَيۡهِ إِن كَانَ مِنَ ٱلۡكَٰذِبِينَ ﴿٧﴾

"... Allāh's curse will be on him if he is of those who tell a lie." (24:7)

Backbiting, Spying and Suspicion

يَٰٓأَيُّهَا ٱلَّذِينَ ءَامَنُواْ ٱجۡتَنِبُواْ كَثِيرٗا مِّنَ ٱلظَّنِّ إِنَّ بَعۡضَ ٱلظَّنِّ إِثۡمٞۖ
وَلَا تَجَسَّسُواْ وَلَا يَغۡتَب بَّعۡضُكُم بَعۡضًاۚ أَيُحِبُّ أَحَدُكُمۡ أَن
يَأۡكُلَ لَحۡمَ أَخِيهِ مَيۡتٗا فَكَرِهۡتُمُوهُۚ وَٱتَّقُواْ ٱللَّهَۚ إِنَّ ٱللَّهَ تَوَّابٞ
رَّحِيمٞ ﴿١٢﴾

"O you who believe! Avoid much suspicion for indeed some suspicions are sins.
And spy not, neither backbite one another.
Would one of you love to eat the flesh of his dead brother?
You hate that (so hate backbiting)! And keep your duty to Allāh.
Surely, Allāh is Forgiving and the most Kind." (49:12)

Cheating and Fraud

وَيۡلٞ لِّلۡمُطَفِّفِينَ ﴿١﴾ ٱلَّذِينَ إِذَا ٱكۡتَالُواْ عَلَى ٱلنَّاسِ يَسۡتَوۡفُونَ ﴿٢﴾
وَإِذَا كَالُوهُمۡ أَو وَّزَنُوهُمۡ يُخۡسِرُونَ ﴿٣﴾

"The cheaters will suffer terribly.
Those who insist on full measure when they have people measure something for them;
but when they have to measure or weigh things for others, they give less than their due."
(83:1–3)

Extravagance

...وَلَا تُبَذِّرۡ تَبۡذِيرًا ﴿٢٦﴾ إِنَّ ٱلۡمُبَذِّرِينَ
كَانُوٓاْ إِخۡوَٰنَ ٱلشَّيَٰطِينِۖ وَكَانَ ٱلشَّيۡطَٰنُ لِرَبِّهِۦ كَفُورٗا ﴿٢٧﴾

"... Do not squander (your money) extravagantly.
Truly the extravagant are the brothers of devils, and the devil is ever ungrateful to his Lord."
(17:26–27)

Arrogance

وَلَا تَمْشِ فِي ٱلْأَرْضِ مَرَحًا إِنَّكَ لَن تَخْرِقَ ٱلْأَرْضَ وَلَن تَبْلُغَ
ٱلْجِبَالَ طُولًا ﴿٣٧﴾

"Do not walk in the earth arrogantly.
Surely, you can never split the earth apart nor rival the mountains in height." (17:37)

...وَٱللَّهُ لَا يُحِبُّ كُلَّ مُخْتَالٍ فَخُورٍ ﴿٢٣﴾

"... Allāh does not love arrogant boasters." (57:23)

Hoarding

وَلَا يَحْسَبَنَّ ٱلَّذِينَ يَبْخَلُونَ بِمَآ ءَاتَىٰهُمُ ٱللَّهُ مِن فَضْلِهِۦ هُوَ خَيْرًا
لَّهُم بَلْ هُوَ شَرٌّ لَّهُمْ سَيُطَوَّقُونَ مَا بَخِلُوا۟ بِهِۦ يَوْمَ ٱلْقِيَٰمَةِ... ﴿١٨٠﴾

"And let the hoarders not think that what Allāh has bestowed upon them from His bounty
is better for them. But it is worse for them.
That which they hoard will be a burden for them on the Day of Judgement..." (3:180)

...وَٱلَّذِينَ يَكْنِزُونَ ٱلذَّهَبَ وَٱلْفِضَّةَ وَلَا يُنفِقُونَهَا
فِي سَبِيلِ ٱللَّهِ فَبَشِّرْهُم بِعَذَابٍ أَلِيمٍ ﴿٣٤﴾

"...Those who hoard gold and silver and do not spend them for Allāh's sake,
announce to them a painful punishment." (9:34)

Mischief and Corruption

...كُلُوا۟ وَٱشْرَبُوا۟ مِن رِّزْقِ ٱللَّهِ وَلَا تَعْثَوْا۟ فِي ٱلْأَرْضِ مُفْسِدِينَ ﴿٦٠﴾

"... Eat and drink that which Allāh has given you
and do not act corruptly making mischief in the earth." (2:60)

Mockery and Ridicule

يَٰٓأَيُّهَا ٱلَّذِينَ ءَامَنُوا۟ لَا يَسْخَرْ قَوْمٌ مِّن قَوْمٍ
عَسَىٰٓ أَن يَكُونُوا۟ خَيْرًا مِّنْهُمْ ... ﴿١١﴾

"O you who believe! No people should mock or ridicule other people, for the ridiculed ones may be better than those who ridicule them..." (49:11)

Hypocrisy

وَمِنَ ٱلنَّاسِ مَن يَقُولُ ءَامَنَّا بِٱللَّهِ وَبِٱلْيَوْمِ ٱلْءَاخِرِ وَمَا هُم بِمُؤْمِنِينَ ﴿٨﴾

"And, there are people who say: we believe in Allāh and the Last Day but actually they do not believe." (2:8)

إِذَا جَآءَكَ ٱلْمُنَٰفِقُونَ قَالُوا۟ نَشْهَدُ إِنَّكَ لَرَسُولُ ٱللَّهِ وَٱللَّهُ يَعْلَمُ
إِنَّكَ لَرَسُولُهُۥ وَٱللَّهُ يَشْهَدُ إِنَّ ٱلْمُنَٰفِقِينَ لَكَٰذِبُونَ ﴿١﴾

"When the hypocrites come to you (O Muhammad) they say: 'We testify that you are indeed Allāh's messenger', and Allāh knows that you are His messenger, and Allāh declares that the hypocrites are liars indeed." (63:1)

Abortion and Fear of Poverty

وَلَا تَقْتُلُوٓا۟ أَوْلَٰدَكُمْ خَشْيَةَ إِمْلَٰقٍ نَّحْنُ نَرْزُقُهُمْ وَإِيَّاكُمْ
إِنَّ قَتْلَهُمْ كَانَ خِطْـًٔا كَبِيرًا ﴿٣١﴾

"Do not kill your children in fear of poverty, We shall provide for them and you. Killing them is a big sin." (17:31)

Interest and Usury

...وَأَحَلَّ ٱللَّهُ ٱلْبَيْعَ وَحَرَّمَ ٱلرِّبَوٰا۟ ... ﴿٢٧٥﴾

"...Allāh has permitted trading and forbidden interest and usury..." (2:275)

Wine and Gambling

يَٰٓأَيُّهَا ٱلَّذِينَ ءَامَنُوٓا۟ إِنَّمَا ٱلْخَمْرُ وَٱلْمَيْسِرُ وَٱلْأَنصَابُ وَٱلْأَزْلَٰمُ رِجْسٌ
مِّنْ عَمَلِ ٱلشَّيْطَٰنِ فَٱجْتَنِبُوهُ لَعَلَّكُمْ تُفْلِحُونَ ﴿٩٠﴾

"O you who believe! Wine (all kinds of alcoholic drinks) and gambling, stone altars and divining arrows are only a filthy work of Satan; give them up so that you may prosper." (5:90)

Fornication and Adultery

وَلَا تَقْرَبُوا۟ ٱلزِّنَىٰٓ ۖ إِنَّهُۥ كَانَ فَٰحِشَةً وَسَآءَ سَبِيلًا ﴿٣٢﴾

"And keep away from illegal sexual intercouse.
Surely, it is a hateful filthy work and a very bad thing." (17:32)

ٱلزَّانِيَةُ وَٱلزَّانِى فَٱجْلِدُوا۟ كُلَّ وَٰحِدٍ مِّنْهُمَا مِا۟ئَةَ جَلْدَةٍ ... ﴿٢﴾

"The man and the woman who commit illegal sexual intercourse,
flog each one of them with a hundred lashes..." (24:2)

Theft

وَٱلسَّارِقُ وَٱلسَّارِقَةُ فَٱقْطَعُوٓا۟
أَيْدِيَهُمَا جَزَآءًۢ بِمَا كَسَبَا نَكَٰلًا مِّنَ ٱللَّهِ ۗ وَٱللَّهُ عَزِيزٌ حَكِيمٌ ﴿٣٨﴾

"As for the thief, both male and female, chop off their hands.
It is the reward of their own deeds and exemplary punishment from Allāh.
Allāh is the Mighty and the Most Wise." (5:38)

What did you learn? (12)

Key Stage 4 (15–16)

1. What does the *Qur'ān* teach about *Tawḥīd*, *Risālah* and *Ākhirah?* Find out as many verses as you can on these three topics from the *Qur'ān*.
2. Summarise the advice *Luqmān* gave to his son.
3. What are the duties of a Muslim towards parents, relatives, neighbours and the needy? Use verses from the *Qur'ān* to justify your answer.
4. What lessons do we learn from the *Qur'ān* about social manners?
5. List ten basic virtues which Allāh expects Muslims to acquire.

Key Stage 5 (17–18)

1. *"Islam is a complete way of life. It is not just a matter of praying or doing things 'parrot fashion'."* Justify this using references from the *Qur'ān*.
2. *"Muslims should not just be recognised by their beards and ḥijābs, but by their manners and behaviour."* Discuss.

Selections from the Aḥādīth 13

Ḥ*adīth* (pl. *Aḥādīth*) means news or information. It has a special meaning in Islām. It refers to the sayings and doings of Prophet *Muḥammad* ﷺ and the actions he approved.

Duties and Obligations

Jihād

"The most excellent man is the one who works hard in the way of Allāh with his life and property." *(al-Bukhārī)*

"The best *Jihād* is to speak the truth before a tyrant ruler." *(al-Bukhārī)*

Īmān, Islām and Iḥsān

"Faith *(Īmān)* is that you believe in Allāh *(Tawḥīd)* and His angels and His messengers *(Risālah)* and in the life after death *(Ākhirah)*.

Islām is that you worship Allāh and not associate anyone with Him, keep up *Ṣalāh*, pay *Zakāh*, and observe *Ṣawm* in *Ramaḍān*.

Iḥsān is that you worship Allāh as if you see Him and if you do not see Him, surely He sees you." *(al-Bukhārī)*.

Love of the Prophet ﷺ

"None of you has faith unless I am dearer to him than his father, and his son and all mankind." *(al-Bukhārī)*

Ṣalāh and Ṭahārah

"The key to Paradise is *Ṣalāh* and the key to *Ṣalāh* is *Ṭahārah* (purification)." *(Mishkāt)*

Parents

"A man asked the Prophet ﷺ, "O messenger of Allāh! Who deserves the best care from me? The Prophet ﷺ said, "Your mother." The man asked, "Who then?" The Prophet ﷺ said, "Your mother." The man asked once again, "Who then?" the Prophet ﷺ said, "Your mother." *(al-Bukhārī)*

A man came to the Prophet ﷺ and said, "Messenger of Allāh, I desire to go on a military expedition and I have come to consult you." The Prophet ﷺ asked him if he had a mother, and when he replied that he had, the Prophet ﷺ said, "Stay with her, for Paradise is at her feet." (an-Nasā'ī)

"A father's pleasure is Allāh's pleasure, a father's displeasure is Allāh's displeasure." *(at-Tirmidhī)*

Wife

"The most perfect of the believers is the best of you in character, and the best of you are those among you who are best to their wives." *(at-Tirmidhī)*

Children

"He is not of us who has no compassion for our little ones and does not honour our old ones." *(at-Tirmidhī)*

"No father can give his child anything better than good manners." *(at-Tirmidhī)*

"Be careful of your duty to Allāh and be fair and just to your children." *(al-Bukhārī)*

"Whoever properly brings up two daughters until they reach maturity, that man and myself (the Prophet) will be as close in paradise as two adjacent fingers." *(Muslim)*

Guests

"He who believes in Allāh and the Last Day should honour his guest." *(al-Bukhārī)*

Neighbours

"By Allāh, he has no faith (the Prophet ﷺ repeated it three times) whose neighbours are not safe from his wickedness." *(al-Bukhārī)*

"He is not a believer who eats his fill while his neighbour remains hungry by his side." *(al-Baihaqī)*

"*Jibrā'īl* has been recommending good treatment towards the neighbours so much that I thought he would give them the right to inherit." *(al-Bukhārī)*

Orphans

"The best house among the Muslims is the house in which an orphan is well treated and the worst house among Muslims is the house in which an orphan is badly treated." *(Ibn Mājah)*

The needy

"One who tries to help the widow and the poor is like a warrior in the way of Allāh." *(al-Bukhārī)*

Basic Qualities

Intention (Niyyah)

"Actions shall be judged only by intention, a man shall get what he intends." *(al-Bukhārī)*

Truthfulness

"Guarantee me six things and I shall assure you of Paradise. When you speak, speak the truth, keep your promise, discharge your trust, guard your chastity and lower your gaze and withhold your hands from high-handedness." *(al-Baihaqī)*

"Surely truth leads to virtue, and virtue leads to Paradise." *(al-Bukhārī)*

Keeping promises

"Do not quarrel with your brother Muslim, nor jest with him nor make him a promise which you cannot keep." *(at-Tirmidhī)*

Tolerance

"There are two traits in me which Allāh likes, toleration and deliberation in undertakings." *(Aḥmad, at-Tirmidhī)*

Politeness

"Allāh is polite and likes politeness." *(condensed from Muslim)*

Modesty

"Modesty *(ḥayā')* is part of faith." *(al-Bukhārī, Muslim)*

Brotherhood

"Each of you is a mirror of his brother, if you see something wrong in your brother, you must tell him to get rid of it." *(at-Tirmidhī)*

"Believers are like the parts of a building to one another — each part supporting the others." *(al-Bukhārī)*

"None of you can be a believer unless he loves for his brother what he loves for himself." *(al-Bukhārī)*
"A Muslim is he from whose tongue and hands, other Muslims are safe." *(al-Bukhārī)*

Charity

"Every good action is a charity and it is a good action to meet a friend with a smiling face." *(al-Bukhārī)*

"There is a man who gives charity and he conceals it so much that his left hand does not know what his right hand spends." *(al-Bukhārī)*

"Removing from a road that which is harmful is charity." *(al-Bukhārī)*

Contentment

"Wealth does not come from abundance of goods but from a contented heart." *(al-Bukhārī, Muslim)*

Learning

"The best of you is he who has learnt the *Qur'ān* and then taught it." *(al-Bukhārī)*

"The seeking of knowledge is a must for every Muslim man and woman." *(Mishkāt)*

"The learned are the successors of the prophets. They leave behind knowledge as inheritance. One who inherits it obtains a great fortune." *(al-Bukhārī)*

Kindness

"Allāh is not kind to him who is not kind to people." *(al-Bukhārī, Muslim)*

"Those who are kind and considerate to Allāh's creatures, Allāh bestows His kindness and affection on them. Show kindness to the creatures on the earth so that Allāh may be kind to you." *(Abu Dāwūd, at-Tirmidhī)*

Thankfulness

"He who does not thank people does not thank Allāh." *(at-Tirmidhī)*

Steadfastness

Sufyān bin 'Abdullāh said, "I asked: 'O Messenger of Allāh, tell me something about Islām which I can ask of no one but you.' He said: 'Say, I believe in Allāh — and thereafter be upright.'" *(Muslim)*

Repentance (Tawbah)

"By Allāh, I *(Muḥammad)* ask Allāh's forgiveness and turn to Him in repentance more than seventy times a day." *(al-Bukhārī)*

Gifts

"Give gifts to one another, for gifts take away malice." *(Mishkāt)*

"The messenger of Allāh used to accept gifts and give gifts in return." *(al-Bukhārī)*

Visiting the sick

"Visit the sick, feed the hungry and free the captives." *(al-Bukhārī)*

Manners

Meeting and greeting

"When one of you arrives at a meeting where people are seated, he should say *salām* to them. And when he wishes to leave, he should say *salām* to them. " *(Abū Dāwūd)*

"Do not sit between two men without the permission of both of them." *(Abū Dāwūd)*

"Meetings are like trusts, except three kinds of meeting: for shedding prohibited blood, or for committing adultery or for taking property unlawfully." *(Abū Dāwūd)*

"When one of you meets his brother, he should say *salām* to him." *(Abū Dāwūd)*

"The young should say *salām* to the old, the passer-by to the one sitting and the small group to the large one." *(al-Bukhārī)*

"The best (way) of saying *salām* is shaking hands." *(at-Tirmidhī)*

Talking

"He who truly believes in Allāh and the last day should speak good or keep silent." *(al-Bukhārī, Muslim)*

"He who keeps silent, remains safe." *(at-Tirmidhī)*

Eating and drinking

"The blessing of food is to wash hands at the beginning and washing after taking it." *(Mishkāt)*

"Say Allāh's name *(Bismillāh)* and eat with your right hand and eat from near you." *(al-Bukhārī)*

"When one drinks, he should not breathe into the vessel (glass)." *(al-Bukhārī)*

Clothing

"Eat and drink, give *ṣadaqah* and wear good clothes as long as these do not involve excess or arrogance." *(an-Nasā'ī, Ibn Mājah)*

"Indeed, he who wears silk in this world (will) have no share in it in the life after death." *(al-Bukhārī and Muslim)*

"Gold and silk are lawful to the women of my *Ummah* and forbidden to the men." *(at-Tirmidhī, an-Nasā'ī)*

"Allāh's messenger cursed the men who put on women's clothes and the women who put on men's clothes." (*Abū Dāwūd*)

"The Prophet ﷺ said to *Aṣmā'*, the daughter of *Abū Bakr*, 'When a woman reaches puberty, it is not right that any part of her body (should) be seen but this and this,' and he pointed to his face and two hands." *(Abū Dāwūd)*

Leave that which does not concern you

"An excellent Islāmic practice is to give up what is not one's business." (*Mālik, Aḥmad*)

Bad Conduct

Lying

"Woe to him who tells lies to make people laugh! Woe to him! Woe to him!" *(Aḥmad, at-Tirmidhī)*

"It is great treachery that you tell your brother something he accepts as truth from you, but you are lying." (*Abū Dāwūd)*

Backbiting

"If anybody pledges to me that he will keep his tongue under control, guard his chastity, will not speak ill of others nor indulge in slander and backbiting and refrain from adultery and similar sins, I shall assure him of Paradise." *(al-Bukhārī)*

Suspicion

"Beware of suspicion, for suspicion may be based on false information, do not spy on another, do not disclose others' hidden defects." (*al-Bukhārī)*

Jealousy

"Keep away from jealousy for as fire burns wood, so jealousy consumes good actions." (*Abū Dāwūd)*

"Nothing is more atrocious than injuring unjustly a Muslim's reputation." (*at-Tirmidhī)*

Anger

"He is not strong who throws down another, but he is who controls his anger." *(al-Bukhārī, Muslim)*

"If anger rouses anyone, he should sit down and if that does not help, he should lie down." (*at-Tirmidhī*)

Pride

"If anyone has got an atom of pride in his heart, he will not enter Paradise." *(al-Bukhārī)*

Abuse

"Abusing a Muslim is sinful and killing him is disbelief *(kufr)*." *(al-Bukhārī, Muslim)*

Hypocrisy

"The signs of the hypocrite are three: When he speaks, he lies; when he promises, he breaks it; when any trust is kept with him, he misuses it." *(al-Bukhārī)*

Taunting

"A believer neither taunts, nor curses nor speaks foul nor chats nor babbles." (*at-Tirmidhī*)

"Do not rejoice over the distress of a brother Muslim for Allāh may relieve his distress and put you in his position." *(at-Tirmidhī)*

Sickness of heart

"Beware, in everybody there is a piece of flesh, if it is healthy, the whole body is healthy, and if it is sick, the whole body is sick. Beware, it is the heart." *(al-Bukhārī, Muslim)*

What did you learn? (13)

Key Stage 4 (15–16)

1. Give some examples of the sayings of the Prophet ﷺ about duties and obligations.
2. Write down ten *Aḥādīth* which ask us to avoid bad habits and conduct.
3. Give examples from the Prophet's ﷺ life in which he was steadfast, kind, and truthful. Include sayings of the Prophet ﷺ about these qualities.

Key Stage 5 (17–18)

1. Explain the concept of brotherhood/sisterhood in the context of the Prophet's ﷺ sayings.
2. Why was the Prophet ﷺ known as *'The Living Qur'ān'?*

Muslim Countries of the World 14

Population and Resources

Muslims, wherever they are, form one nation *(Millātun Wāḥidah)*. It is faith that binds people together in Islām, not the geographical territory, colour, race or language. Citizenship of an Islāmic state may be determined by geographical boundaries.

There are 53 Muslim countries in the world on the basis of a majority of the population. The total Muslim population in the world is nearly 1.4 billion, which is a formidable human power.

The Muslim countries together produce two-thirds of the world's oil, about 70 per cent of the rubber, about 75 per cent of the jute, 67 per cent of the spices, two-thirds of the palm-oil, 50 per cent of the phosphate and 40 per cent of the tin. They also produce a large quantity of the world's cotton, tea, coffee, wool, uranium, manganese, cobalt and many other commodities and minerals. There is also a huge amount of natural gas in the Muslim countries.

If we look at a world map, we find the Muslim countries situated at strategically important positions. 60 per cent of the Mediterranean Sea is bounded by Muslim countries. The Red Sea and the Gulf are fully within the Muslim region.

In the course of history, Muslims lost their essential unity; it should be restored once again for the greater good of all mankind.

Muslims, who once contributed tremendously to the science and civilisation of the world, could do so once again if they unite on the basis of Islām. Real human progress can only be achieved by the faithful observance of the teachings of Islām. We should consciously try to restore the glory of Islām and make the present day problem-torn world a happy and peaceful place to live in. Pride in the past will be meaningful if the present can be shaped in the light of the past with a promise for the future. The Muslim *Millāh* has the potential and the need is for the faithful practice of the teachings of Islām.

Muslim Majority Countries

	Name	*Area (sq. km)*	*Total population (in millions)*	*Proportion of Muslims (%)*	*Number of Muslims*
1	Afghanistan	652,225	27.8	99	27,478,000
2	Albania	28,748	3.5	70	2,481,000
3	Algeria	2,381,740	32.3	99	31,955,000
4	Azerbaijan	86,600	7.8	93	7,284,000
5	Bahrain	665	0.7	100	656,000
6	Bangladesh	144,000	133.4	83	110,703,000
7	Bosnia & Herzegovina	51,129	4.0	40	1,586,000
8	Brunei	5,765	0.4	67	235,000
9	Burkina Faso	274,200	12.6	50	6,302,000
10	Chad	1,284,000	9.0	54	4,859,000
11	Comoros	2,170	0.6	98	602,000
12	Côte d'Ivoire	322,460	16.8	40	6,722,000
13	Djibouti	23,000	0.5	94	444,000
14	Egypt	1,001,450	70.7	94	66,470,000
15	Eritrea	121,320	4.5	50	2,233,000
16	Ethiopia	1,127,127	67.7	50	33,837,000
17	Gambia, The	11,300	1.5	90	1,310,000
18	Guinea	245,857	7.8	85	6,609,000
19	Guinea-Bissau	36,120	1.3	45	605,000
20	Indonesia	1,919,440	231.3	88	203,569,000
21	Iran	1,648,000	66.6	99	65,956,000
22	Iraq	437,072	24.0	97	23,282,000
23	Jordan	92,300	5.3	94	4,989,000
24	Kazakhstan	2,717,300	16.7	47	7,869,000
25	Kuwait	17,820	2.1	85	1,795,000
26	Kyrgyzstan	198,500	4.8	75	3,617,000
27	Lebanon	10,400	3.7	70	2,574,000
28	Libya	1,759,540	5.4	97	5,208,000
29	Malaysia	329,750	22.7	60	13,597,000
30	Maldives	300	0.3	100	320,000
31	Mali	1,240,000	11.3	90	10,206,000
32	Mauritania	1,030,700	2.8	100	2,829,000
33	Morocco	446,550	31.2	99	30,763,000

34	Niger	1,267,000	10.6	90	9,576,000
35	Nigeria	923,770	129.9	50	64,967,000
36	Oman	309,500	2.7	100	2,713,000
37	Pakistan	796,095	147.7	97	143,234,000
38	Palestinian Authority*	6,237	3.7	98	3,660,000
39	Qatar	11,437	0.8	95	754,000
40	Saudi Arabia	1,960,582	23.5	100	23,513,000
41	Senegal	196,190	10.6	94	9,954,000
42	Sierra Leone	71,740	5.6	70	3,930,000
43	Somalia	637,657	7.8	100	7,753,000
44	Sudan	2,505,810	37.1	79	29,301,000
45	Syria	185,180	17.2	90	15,440,000
46	Tajikistan	143,100	6.7	90	6,048,000
47	Tanzania	945,087	37.2	40	14,875,000
48	Tunisia	163,610	9.8	98	9,619,000
49	Turkey	780,580	67.3	100	67,174,000
50	Turkmenistan	488,100	4.7	89	4,173,000
51	United Arab Emirates	83,600	3.3	96	3,168,000
52	Uzbekistan	447,400	25.6	88	22,496,000
53	Western Sahara	266,000	0.3	100	256,000
54	Yemen	527,970	18.7	100	18,701,000

Sources:

1. Figures supplied by the London embassies of some of the above countries in the year 2002.
2. The World Factbook 2002, CIA.
3. International Religious Freedom Report for 2002, US Dept. of State.

Population figures and the proportion of Muslims are approximate, and have been rounded off for inclusion in the table. Calculation of the number of Muslims is based on figures before rounding, and are themselves rounded off to the nearest thousand.

* The territories of the Palestinian Authority (including the West Bank, the Gaza Strip and East Jerusalem) are still being negotiated with Israel.

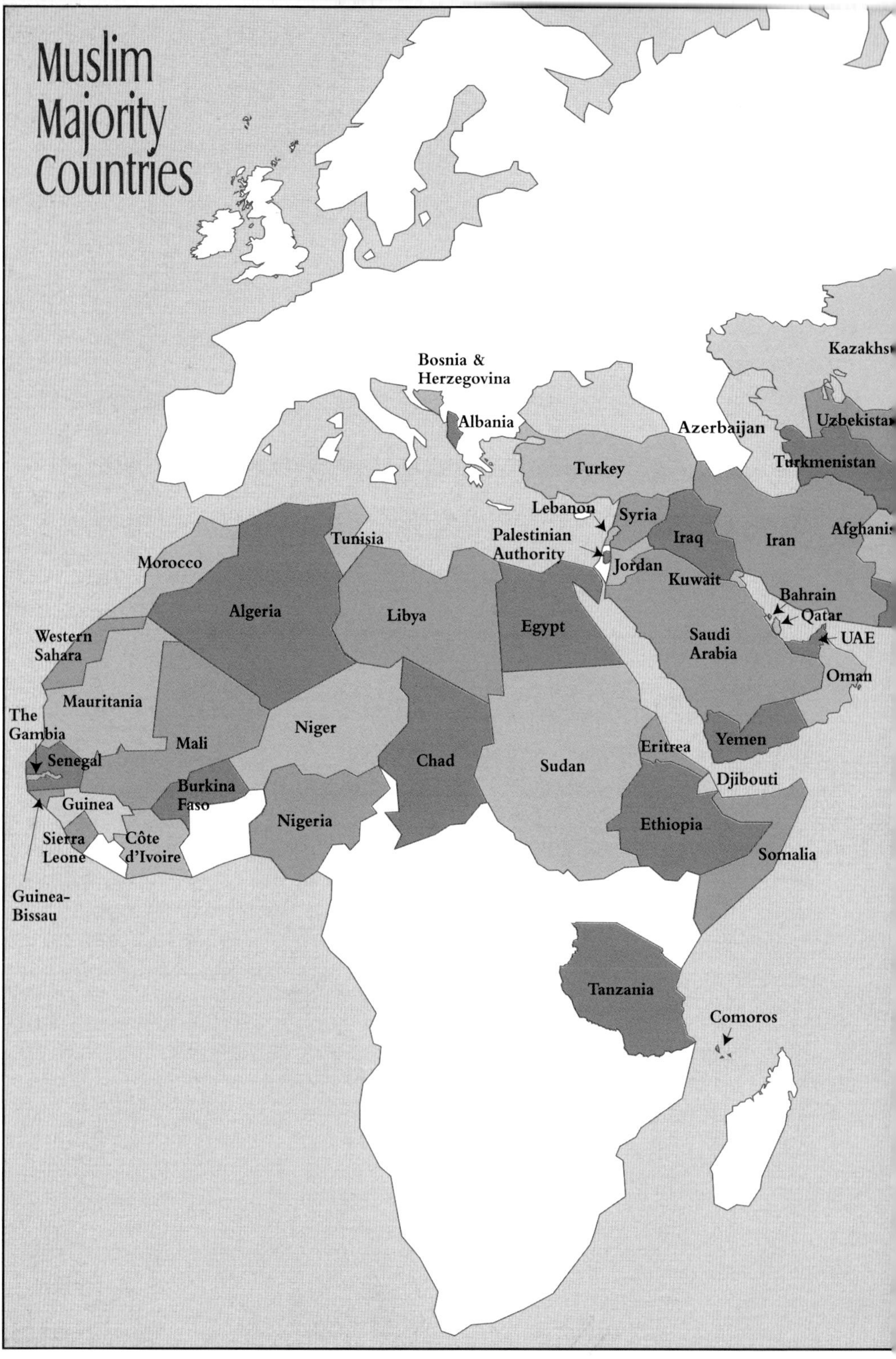
Muslim Majority Countries
Bosnia & Herzegovina
Albania
Azerbaijan
Kazakhs
Uzbekista
Turkmenistan
Turkey
Lebanon
Syria
Palestinian Authority
Iraq
Iran
Afghanis
Jordan
Kuwait
Bahrain
Qatar
UAE
Tunisia
Morocco
Algeria
Libya
Egypt
Saudi Arabia
Oman
Western Sahara
Mauritania
The Gambia
Senegal
Mali
Niger
Chad
Sudan
Eritrea
Yemen
Djibouti
Burkina Faso
Guinea
Nigeria
Ethiopia
Sierra Leone
Côte d'Ivoire
Somalia
Guinea-Bissau
Tanzania
Comoros

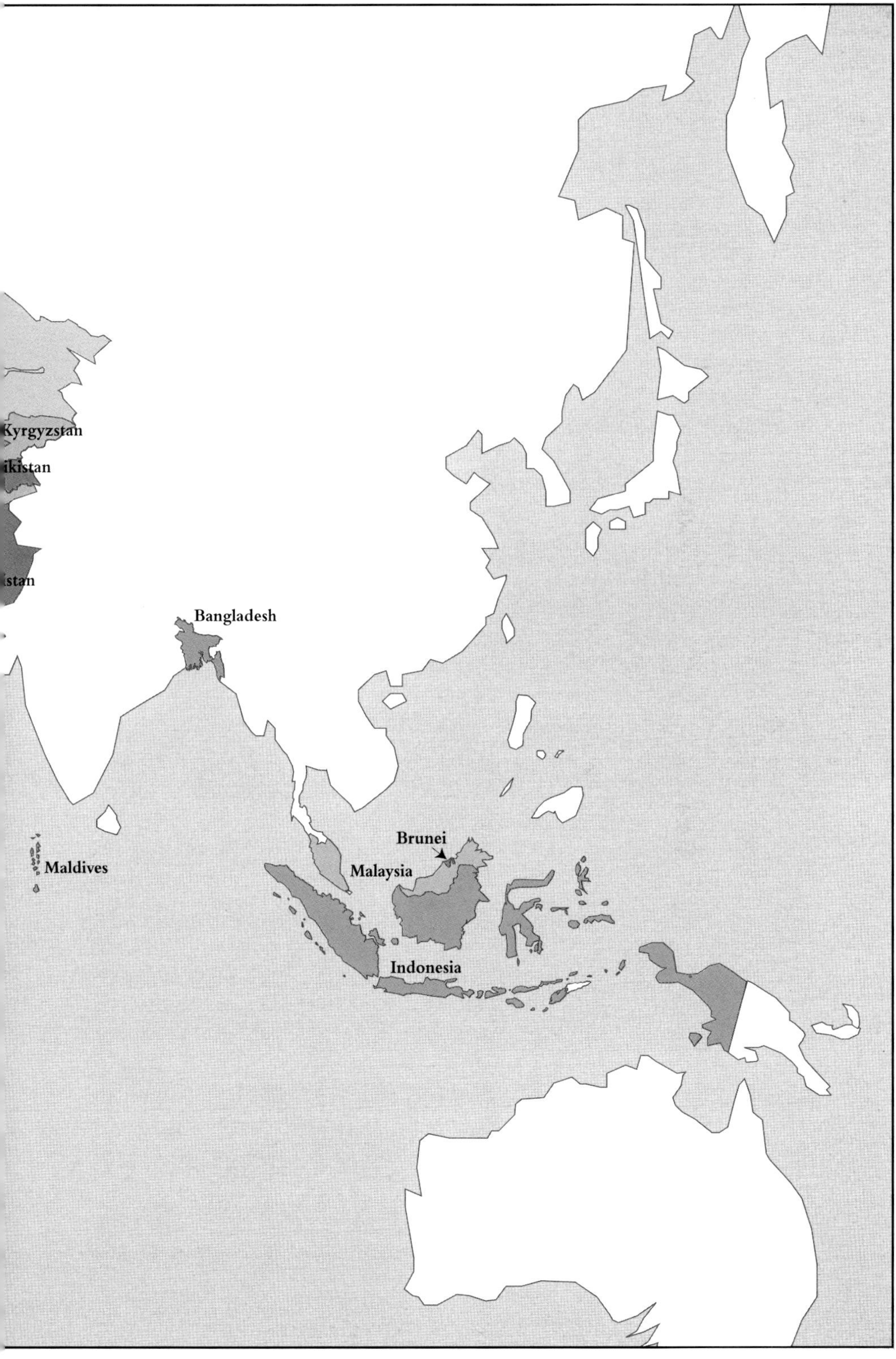
Kyrgyzstan
ikistan
istan
Bangladesh
Maldives
Brunei
Malaysia
Indonesia

Muslim Minority Countries

	Name	*Area (sq. km)*	*Total population (in millions)*	*Proportion of Muslims (%)*	*Number of Muslims*
1	Argentina	2,766,890	37.8	1.5	567,000
2	Australia	7,686,850	19.5	1.4	282,000
3	Belgium	30,510	10.3	3.4	350,000
4	Benin	112,620	6.8	20.0	1,358,000
5	Brazil	8,511,965	176.0	0.3	518,000
6	Bulgaria	110,910	7.9	12.1	956,000
7	Burma (Myanmar)	678,500	50.0	11.5	5,750,000
8	Burundi	27,830	6.4	10.0	637,000
9	Cambodia	181,040	12.0	5.8	700,000
10	Cameroon	475,440	16.2	20.0	3,237,000
11	Canada	9,984,670	31.4	0.9	283,000
12	Central African Republic	622,984	3.6	15.0	546,000
13	China	9,596,960	1,284.3	3.0	38,529,000
14	Congo, Dem. Rep. of	2,345,410	55.2	10.0	5,523,000
15	Congo, Rep. of	342,000	3.0	2.0	59,000
16	Croatia	56,542	4.4	1.2	53,000
17	Cyprus‡	9,250	0.8	18.0	138,000
18	Denmark	43,094	5.4	2.0	107,000
19	Fiji	18,270	0.9	8.0	69,000
20	France	547,030	59.8	10.0	5,977,000
21	Gabon	267,667	1.2	12.0	148,000
22	Georgia	69,700	5.0	11	546,000
23	Germany	357,021	83.3	3.7	3,080,000
24	Ghana	239,460	20.2	30.0	6,073,000
25	Greece	131,940	10.6	1.3	138,000
26	Guyana	214,970	0.7	15.0	105,000
27	India	3,287,590	1,045.8	12.0	125,501,000
28	Israel	20,770	6.0	16.0	965,000
29	Italy	301,230	57.7	1.0	600,000
30	Kenya	582,646	31.1	20.0	6,228,000
31	Liberia	111,370	3.3	20.0	658,000
32	Macedonia	25,333	2.1	30.0	616,000
33	Madagascar	587,040	16.5	10.0	1,647,000

‡ Cyprus is now divided into two separate states: the Muslim majority part is called the Turkish Federated State of Cyprus and the other part is the Republic of Cyprus.

34	Malawi	118,480	10.7	20.0	2,140,000
35	Mauritius	2,040	1.2	16.6	199,000
36	Mongolia	1,565,000	2.7	4.0	108,000
37	Mozambique	801,590	19.6	20.0	3,922,000
38	Nepal	140,800	25.9	4.2	1,087,000
39	Netherlands, The	41,526	16.1	4.7	755,000
40	Philippines	300,000	84.5	5.0	4,226,000
41	Romania	237,500	22.3	0.3	56,000
42	Russia	17,075,200	145.0	19.0	27,456,000
43	Rwanda	26,338	7.4	4.6	340,000
44	Singapore	682	4.5	14.9	663,000
45	South Africa	1,219,000	43.6	2.0	873,000
46	Spain	504,782	40.1	1.1	450,000
47	Sri Lanka	65,606	19.6	8.4	1,644,000
48	Suriname	163,270	0.4	20.0	87,000
49	Swaziland	17,363	1.1	10.0	112,000
50	Thailand	514,000	62.4	10.0	6,235,000
51	Togo	56,785	5.3	20.0	1,057,000
52	Trinidad & Tobago	5,128	1.2	6.0	70,000
53	Uganda	236,040	24.7	16.0	3,952,000
54	Ukraine	603,700	48.4	4.1	2,000,000
55	United Kingdom	244,820	58.8	2.7	1,591,000
56	United States of America	9,629,091	280.6	2.5	7,000,000
57	Vietnam	329,560	81.1	0.1	81,000
58	Yugoslavia	102,350	10.7	19.0	2,025,000
59	Zambia	752,614	10.0	5.0	498,000
60	Zimbabwe	390,580	11.4	1.0	114,000

The total Muslim population of the world is estimated to be over 1,431 million, out of a world population of more than 6,234 million, about 23% of all the people on Earth.

Sources:

1. Figures supplied by the London embassies of some of the above countries in the year 2002.
2. The World Factbook 2002, CIA.
3. International Religious Freedom Report for 2002, US Dept. of State.
4. www.adherents.com (for percentage of Muslims).
5. Muslim World Minorities, Islamabad, 1993 (for percentage of Muslims).

What did you learn? (14)

Key Stage 5 (17–18)

1. Discuss the material and numerical potential of the Muslims in the present day world.
2. Study a map giving the location of Muslim countries in the world and make your own observations in the light of their location and importance
3. *"There is a lot to be desired from the British Muslims in terms of their unity, practice of Islām and contribution to the society they live in"* — Discuss this objectively and subjectively.
4. *"Muslims in the world are almost about 1.3 billion, but they have not been able to use their numerical strength and their material resources for the common good of humanity."* How will you comment on this statement?
5. How do you visualise the future of Muslims in the present day technology-dominated world? Discuss your vision in detail.

Notes for Teachers and Parents

Teaching Islām to young people requires careful planning and skill. Teachers and parents need to be clear about the aims of providing such teaching. The objective is to educate young people in Islām, to enable them to become conscious and practising Muslims.

The Muslims of the U.K. do not yet have a well-organised system of Islāmic teaching, although sincere and dedicated efforts are being made in different parts of the country to provide basic Islāmic education for our young generation.

The *Muslim Educational Trust* has started to make Islāmic teaching organised and systematic. The Trust published a syllabus and guidelines for Islāmic teaching in 1980. The first edition of this textbook, *Islām: Beliefs and Teachings*, was published in October 1980, based on the syllabus.

In the second edition, we incorporated some suggestions for teachers and parents on how to use the book.

A. This book is mainly aimed at school pupil's aged 11–16 and covers briefly the essential aspects of Islām. Younger pupils may not fully understand some of the topics. At the moment, we are not in a position to publish five or six separate books on Islām to cater for the needs of pupils of all age groups. The topics covered in this book have been arranged so that they can be studied progressively as the young people move up the school. The topics near the end of the book will also be useful for pupils aged 17–18 when studied in tandem with other books and resources on those topics.

B. Books on their own cannot work miracles. Dedicated Islāmic teachers are needed to guide the pupils and to explain to them the topics given in the book. Without clarification and explanation, some of the material in the book may not be clear to some pupils. Teachers and parents need to be conscious of this.

C. Teachers and parents should consult other books for more detailed analysis of different topics and guide the pupils accordingly. The select bibliography at the end of this book may be of help in this regard.

D. Correct pronunciation of Arabic words needs care and attention. We must take as much care as possible to see that the pupils pronounce Arabic words correctly. The transliteration guide given at the beginning of the book will be useful. We would request Islāmic teachers and parents to avoid different spellings of Arabic words. Given care and attention, young people will be able to pronounce and spell Arabic words correctly. A few examples of varying spellings and pronunciations should make this point clear:

	Standard	Other commonly-used spellings
i.	*Muḥammad*	*Moḥammed, Muḥammed, Moḥammad, Moḥamad*
ii.	*Ramaḍān*	*Ramadhan, Ramazan*
iii.	*Dīn*	*Deen*
iv.	*Mūsā*	*Mosa, Moosa*

v. *'Ā'ishah* *Ayesha, Aisha*
vi. *'Uthmān* *Usman, Osman*
vii. *Ḥadīth* *Hadis, Hadees*
viii. *Lūṭ* *Loot, Lot.*

It is strongly recommended that the standard spellings be followed.

E. The use of charts, maps, posters, slides and videos of related topics should also be used to help make the teaching interesting and effective. Islāmic teachers should do their best to use them whenever possible.

F. At the end of each topic, we have included questions for different age groups. The use of the exercises will help to deepen the impact of the teaching, and pupils will grasp lessons better this way. The questions also indicate to the teacher how well the lessons have been understood by each pupil.

G. With pupils in year 7, you may find the book *Islām for Younger People* more useful, especially the stories given in it.

H. In years 8 and 9 you should arrange your lessons to incorporate some stories of the prophets.

I. In years 10–12, the pupils should be encouraged to do more extensive research projects and not be limited to the book alone. These should cover the following topics:

i. *Ṣalāh* and its importance in our life.
ii. The role of the Mosque in Islām.
iii. *Al-Ka'bah.*
iv. *Masjīdun Nabī.*
v. *Ḥajj.*
vi. Festivals: *'Īdul Fiṭr* and *'Īdul Aḍḥā.*
vii. *Qur'ān.*
viii. Muslim countries and their resources.

J. For pupils in years 10–12 class discussions on various issues related to growing up in an unislāmic society can also be incorporated to allow pupils to express their ideas and answer any queries.

K. It is the challenging task of the Muslim teachers and parents to make their lessons both interesting and motivating for pupils of all age groups to ensure the knowledge learnt is not just memorised but internalised and therefore practised in their day to day lives. The lessons have to therefore be varied to engage the pupils and not become lectures given by the teachers. It is also the teacher's responsibility to differentiate the teaching according to the ability of different pupils. The questions at the end of each topic vary in difficulty and can be selected to cater for pupil's individual needs.

L. Qur'ānic references are included throughout the book and should be utilised fully in lessons to enable pupils to understand its role as a guide for our lives.

Suggested arrangement of study topics according to age group

Key Stage 3: Year 7 (age 12)

Total no. of lessons for a year: 25

1. Islām: two lessons:
    - i. Meaning and Way of Life
    - ii. Everything in nature is obeying the law of Allāh
2. Purpose of Creation: one lesson
3. Basic Beliefs: one lesson
4. *Al-Īmānul Mufaṣṣal:* one lesson
5. *Tawḥīd:* two lessons:
    - i. Meaning and *Sūratul Ikhlāṣ*
    - ii. Powers of Allāh
6. *Risālah:* two lessons:
    - i. Meaning of *Risālah* and its importance
    - ii. Names of prominent prophets
7. *Ākhirah:* two lessons:
    - i. Death and its implications
    - ii. Day of Judgment
8. *Shahādah:* one lesson: Meaning word by word
9. *Ṣalāh:* one lesson: Names and timings
10. *Wuḍū'*: three lessons:
    - i. Importance, *Niyyah*
    - ii. How to make *Wuḍū'*
    - iii. What makes *Wuḍū'* invalid?
11. *Farḍ Ṣalāh:* one lesson: *Rak'ahs* in each *Ṣalāh*
12. How to perform *Ṣalāh:* seven lessons:
    - i. *Niyyah* and *Subḥanaka*
    - ii. *Ta'awwudh, Tasmiyah* and *Sūratul Fātiḥah* (recitation)
    - iii. Meaning of *Sūratul Fātiḥah*
    - iv. *Sūratul Īkhlāṣ* (meaning and recitation)
    - v. *Ruku', Qiyām, Tasbīḥ* and *Sujūd*
    - vi. *Tashahhud*
    - vii. *Darūd* and *Du'ā'*
13. Lessons of *Ṣalāh:* one lesson

Key Stage 3: Years 8 & 9 (age 13–14)

Total no. of lessons for a year: 25

1. Islām (introduction): one lesson
2. Purpose of Creation: one lesson
3. Mohammedanism is a misnomer: one lesson
4. Basic Beliefs: one lesson: Seven Beliefs and *Al-Īmānul Mufaṣṣal*
5. Grouping of Basic Beliefs: one lesson:
   Tawḥīd, Riṣālah, Ākhirah
6. *Tawḥīd:* two lessons:
   - i. *Sūratul Ikhlāṣ*
   - ii. Powers and attributes of Allāh
7. *Risālah:* two lessons:
   - i. Meaning of *Risālah* and its significance
   - ii. Names of 25 prophets mentioned in the *Qur'ān*
8. *Ākhirah:* two lessons:
   - i. Effect of this belief on human life
   - ii. Death and Day of Judgement (explanation)
9. Basic Duties: six lessons:
   - i. Names of Duties and the meaning and significance of *Shahādah*
   - ii. *Ṣalāh* — names, times, importance
   - iii. *Ṣawm* — meaning and explanation
   - iv. *Zakāh* — meaning and significance with rate
   - v. *Ḥajj* — meaning and important rituals
   - vi. *Jihād* — meaning and explanation
10. Life of *Muḥammad* ﷺ: eight lessons:
    - i. Explanation of verses (33:21) and (21:107) of the *Qur'ān*
    - ii. Birth, Childhood and Business Trip to *ash-Shām*
    - iii. Marriage and Prophethood
    - iv. First revelation (5 verses of *Sūratul 'Alaq*)
    - v. *'Alī's* acceptance of Islām, *'Alī* and the Dinner
    - vi. The Prophet ﷺ on Mount *Ṣafā*
    - vii. Hostility of the *Quraish*
    - viii. *'Umar* accepts Islām

Key Stage 4: Years 10 & 11 (age 15–16)

Total No. of lessons for a year: 25

1. Islām (introduction): one lesson:
   Explanation of the complete code of life
2. Purpose of Creation: one lesson
   Explanation of *'Ibādah* and the verse 51:56 of the *Qur'ān*
3. Three Basic Concepts: three lessons:
   - i. *Tawḥīd* and *al-Qadr*
   - ii. Effect of *Tawḥīd* on human life
   - iii. *Risālah* and *Ākhirah*
4. Basic Duties: four lessons:
   - i. *Shahādah* and its significance
   - ii. *Ṣalāh* and its teachings
   - iii. *Ṣawm* and *Zakāh*
   - v. *Ḥajj* and *Jihād*
5. Life of *Muḥammad* ﷺ: twelve lessons:
   - i. The best example for mankind and the last prophet
   - ii. Birth, Childhood, Teenager and the *Ḥarbul Fijār* and *Ḥilful Fuḍūl*
   - iii. Marriage and Search for the Truth, receiving the Truth
   - iv. Islāmic Movement begins, *'Alī's* acceptance of Islām. *'Alī* and the Dinner
   - v. The Prophet on Mount *Ṣafā*
     Hostility begins
     Emigration to Abbyssinia
   - vi. *'Umar* accepts Islām,
     Boycott and confinement,
     Year of sorrow
   - vii. *Al-Mi'rāj* and *Hijrah*
   - viii. Battle of *Badr*
   - xi. Battle of *Uḥud*
   - x. Battle of *Aḥzāb*
   - xi. Conquest of Makkah
   - xii. Farewell Address and Death
6. Islāmic Personalities: two lessons:
   - i. *Abū Bakr* and *'Umar*
   - ii. *'Uthmān* and *'Alī*

7. Economic and Political System of Islām: two lessons:
    i. Economic System
    ii. Political System

Key Stage 5: Years 12 & 13 (age 17–18)

Total no. of lessons: 25

1. Islāmic way of life: two lessons:
    i. Islām is a complete code of life. Verse 3:19 of the *Qur'ān* and explanation
    ii. Excellence and practicality of Islāmic way of life for all ages
2. Basic Duties of Islām: three lessons:
    i. Basic Beliefs of *Tawḥīd*, *Risālah*, *Ākhirah* and *Shahādah*
    ii. *'Ibādah* — the purpose of life — *Ṣalāh*, *Ṣawm*, *Zakāh* and *Ḥajj*
    iii. *Jihād*, the end result of *'Ibādah*
3. Prophet *Muḥammad's* ﷺ life: seven lessons:
    i. a) The mission of the Prophet ﷺ (61:9)
       b) The last Prophet ﷺ
       c) The best example for mankind
    ii. a) The beginning of the Islāmic Movement
       b) Hostility
       c) *Hijrah*
    iii. a) First Islāmic State at Madīnah
       b) Battle of *Badr*
    vi. a) Battle of *Uḥud*
       b) Battle of *Aḥzāb*
    v. Conquest of Makkah
    vi. Farewell address
    vii. a) Mission Accomplished
       b) The example of the ideal way of life
4. *Sharī'ah*: two lessons:
    i. a) *Sharī'ah* and its meaning
       b) Sources of the *Sharīi'ah*
    ii. a) Six most authentic Books of *Aḥādīth*
       b) *Fiqh*

5. Family Life in Islām: three lessons:
   i. a) Basis of Social Life
      b) Marriage — Basis of Family
   ii. Rights of Women
   iii. Polygamy and Islām
6. Economic System of life: two lessons:
   i. Islām and Economic System
   ii. Basic Features of Islāmic Economic System
7. Political System of Islām: two lessons:
   i. Islām and Politics
   ii. Features of Islāmic Political System

8. Qur'ānic Quotations: two lessons:
   i. Basic Virtues of Life
   ii. Bad Conduct
9. Selected *Aḥādīth:* two lessons:
   i. Basic Duties
   ii. Bad Conduct

Select Bibliography

Only a selection of the many sources consulted during the preparation of this book is given here. Some of these are now out of print.

The Qur'ān: Translation and Interpretation

The Noble Qur'ān — Dr M. Taqī-ud-Dīn al-Hilālī and Dr M. Muḥsin Khān, Riyadh, 1994.

The Holy Qur'ān — 'Abdullāh Yūsuf 'Ali, Madinah, 1991.

The Glorious Qur'ān — M. Marmaduke Pickthall, Karachi, 1973.

Towards Understanding the Qur'ān — Abul A'lā Mawdūdī, Leicester, 1988–99.

The Noble Qur'ān — 'Abdalhaqq Bewley and 'Āisha Bewley, Norwich, UK, 1999.

The Qur'ān — Ṣaḥeeḥ International, Jeddah, 1997.

The Qur'ān in Plain English (part 30) — Iman Torres-al-Haneef, Leicester, 1993.

Mukhtaṣar Tafsīr Ibn Kathīr (3 vols.)
— Ikhtiṣār wa taḥqīq — Muḥammad 'Alī aṣ-Ṣabūnī, Beirut, 1981.

In the Shade of the Qur'ān (vol. 30) — Sayyid Quṭb, translated by A. Ṣalāḥī and A. A. Shamis, London, 1979.

The Qur'ān: Basic Teachings (with Arabic) — T. B. Irving, Khurshīd Aḥmad and Manāzir Aḥsan, Leicester, 1992.

The Qur'ān: Translation & Study (Ajzā' 1–4, 30) — Jamilun Nisā' bint Rafai, London, 1995.

Ḥadīth

Saḥīḥ al-Bukhārī (9 vols.) — Muḥammad bin Ismā'īl al-Bukhārī, translated by M. Muḥsin Khān, Riyadh, 1997.

Saḥīḥ Muslim (4 vols.) — Muslim bin al-Ḥajjaj, translated by A. Ḥamīd Ṣiddīqī, Lebanon, 1972.

Mishkāt al-Maṣabiḥ — Ibn al-Farrā' al-Baghawī, translated by James Robson, Lahore, 1972.

Al-Muwaṭṭa' — Imām Mālik, translated by 'Āisha 'Abdarahmān at-Tarjumana and Ya'qūb Johnson, Norwich, UK, 1982.

Riyāḍ-us-Ṣāliḥeen (vols. 1–2) — Imām an-Nawawī, translated by Dr. Muḥammad Amīn Abū Usāmah al-'Arabī bin Razduq, Riyadh, 1998.

Forty Ḥadīth — Imām an-Nawawī, translated by 'Ezzeddīn Ibrāhīm and Denys Johnson-Davies, Damascus, 1977.

Commentary on Forty Ḥadīth of al-Nawawī — Jamāl al-Dīn M. Zarabozo, Boulder, USA, 1999.

Sīrah

As-Sīratun Nabawiyyah (Arabic) — Ibn Hishām, Beirut, 1975.

At-Tabaqāt (vols. I, V, VI) (Urdu) — Muḥammad ibn Sa'd, translated by 'Abdullāh al-'Amādī, Karachi, 1972.

The Life of Muḥammad — *Sīrat Rasūl Allāh* of Ibn Isḥāq, translated by A. Guillaume, Oxford University Press, 1970.

Muḥammad — Martin Lings, Cambridge, 1983.

The Life of Muḥammad — Muḥammad Ḥusayn Haykal, Trans. Ismā'īl al-Farūqī, Indiana, 1976.

Ar-Raḥeeq al-Makhtum — Saifur Raḥmān al-Mubarakpuri, Riyadh, 1995.

The Life of Muḥammad — Tahia al-Ismail, London, 1988.

Tarīkh (vol. I) (Urdu)	A. Raḥmān bin Khaldūn, translated by Aḥmad Ḥussain Alahabadi, Karachi, 1972.
Sīratun Nabī (Urdu)	Shiblī Nu'mānī, Lahore.
Ḥayātuṣ Ṣahābah (Arabic)	Muḥammad Yūsuf al-Kāndahluwī, Damascus, 1983.
Muḥammad: Man and Prophet	Adil Salahi, Leicester, 2002.
Qaṣaṣul Anbiā' (Arabic)	'Abdul Wahhāb an-Najjār, Cairo, 1966.
Al-Farūq	Shiblī Nu'mānī, translated by Zafar 'Alī Khān, Lahore, 1970.
Abū Bakr	Bahādur Yār Jang, translated by Moinul Ḥaq, Lahore, 1975.
The Glorious Caliphate	S. Aṭhar Ḥusain, Lucknow, 1974.
Tales of the Prophets	A. H. 'Alī Nadwī, translated by E. H. Nadwī, Lucknow, 1976.
Jesus: Prophet of Islām	Muhammad 'Aṭā'ur-Raḥīm and Aḥmād Thomson, London, 1997.
The Prophets	Prof. Syed 'Alī Ashraf, London, 1980.
Brief Lives of the Companions of Prophet Muḥammad	Dr M. A. J. Beg, Cambridge, 2002.

Islam: General

Towards Understanding Islām	Abul A'lā Mawdūdī, Leicester, 1981.
Introduction to Islām	Ḥamīdullāh, London, 1979.
Islām in Focus	Hammūdah 'Abdal 'Aṭī, Kuwait, 1977.
Islām: Its Meaning and Message	Edited by Khurshīd Aḥmad, London 1976.
Ideals and Realities of Islām	S. H. Naṣr, London, 1975.
Islām: Belief, Legislation and Morals	Aḥmad Shalaby, Cairo, 1970.
Ḥajj	'Alī Shari'atī, Ohio, 1977.
Fundamentals of Islām	Abul A'lā Mawdūdī, Lahore, 1978.
Let us be Muslims	Abul A'lā Mawdūdī, Leicester, 1985.

Women in Islām

Woman in Islām	Ayesha B. Lemu and Fāṭima Heren, Leicester, 1976.
Family Life in Islām	Khurshīd Aḥmad, Leicester, 1974.
Purdah and the Status of Women in Islām	Abul A'lā Mawdūdī, translated by al-Ash'ārī, Lahore.
Status of Women in Islām	Gamal A. Badawī, Indiana, 1976.
Polygamy in Islām	Gamal A. Badawī, Indiana, 1976.
The Family Structure in Islām	Hammūdah 'Abdal 'Aṭī, Philadelphia, 1977.
Hijāb (veil): The View from the Inside	Kanla Nakata (Japan), Ruth Anderson (USA), Riyadh, 1995.
The Muslim Woman's Handbook	Huda Khattab, London, 1993.
Women, Muslim Society and Islām	Lamya al-Faruqi, Indiana, 1988.
Gender Equity in Islām	Jamal Badawi, USA, 1995.
The Laws of Marriage and Divorce in Islām	Abul A'lā Mawdūdī, Lahore, 1983.

Islāmic Law and Fiqh

The Lawful and the Prohibited in Islām	Yūsuf al-Qaraḍāwī, translated by Kamal El-Helbawy *et al.*, Indianapolis.
Questions and Answers	Dr. S. M. Darsh. London, 1997.
Islāmic Law and Constitution	Abul A'lā Mawdūdī, Lahore, 1969.
Fiqh-az-Zakāt	Yūsuf al-Qaraḍāwī, translated by Dr. Monzer Kahf, London, 1999.
Fiqh us-Sunnah (vols. 1–5)	As-Sayyid Sābiq, translated by Muḥammad Sa'eed Dabas et al., Indiana, 1986-93

Nailul Awṭar (Arabic) — Muḥammad bin 'Alī bin Muḥammad ash-Shawkānī, Beirut, 1979.

Zadul Ma'ad (Arabic) — Ibn Qayyim, Beirut, 1979.

Islāmic Jurisprudence — (Shafi'ī's *Risālah*) Majīd Khaddurī, Baltimore, 1961.

Sharī'ah, the Way of Justice — Khurram Murād, Leicester, 1981.

Sharī'ah, the Way to God — Khurram Murād, Leicester, 1981.

Sharī'ah: The Islāmic Law — 'Abdur Raḥmān I. Doi, London, 1984.

Human Rights in Islām — Abul A'lā Mawdūdī, Leicester, 1976.

Islāmic Economics

Some Aspects of Islāmic Economy — Nejātullāh Ṣiddīqī, Lahore, 1970.

Islām and the Theory of Interest — Anwār Iqbāl Qureshi, Lahore, 1974.

Social Justice in Islām — Sayyid Quṭb, New York, 1970.

Insurance and Islāmic Law — Muṣleḥuddīn, Lahore, 1969.

Islāmic Economics — M. A. Mannān, Lahore, 1975.

Contemporary Aspects of Economic Thinking in Islām — American Trust Publications, 1976.

Objectives of the Islāmic Economic Order — M. 'Umar Chapra, Leicester, 1979.

The Islamic Welfare State and Its Role in the Economy — M. 'Umar Chapra, Leicester, 1979.

Economic Development in an Islāmic Framework — Khurshīd Aḥmad, Leicester, 1979.

Outlines of Islāmic Economics — AMSS, Indiana, 1977.

Islāmic Economy — Dr. M. Kahf, Indiana, 1978.

Studies in Islāmic Economics — Edited by K. Aḥmad, Leicester, 1980.

Muslim Economic Thinking — Nejātullāh Ṣiddīqī, Leicester, 1981.

Miscellaneous

Encyclopaedia Britannica — London, 1979.

Da'irah Ma'arifi Islāmiyyah (Urdu) — Lahore, 1973–75.

The Oxford Encyclopaedia of the Modern Islāmic World — Oxford University Press, 1995.

The Oxford History of Islām — Oxford University Press, 1999.

The Bible, The Qur'ān and Science — Maurice Bucaille, Indiana, 1978.

What everyone should know about Islām and Muslims — Suzanne Haneef, Lahore, Pakistan.

The Islāmic Ruling on Music and Singing — Abū Bilāl Musṭafā al-Kanadī, Jeddah, Saudi Arabia.

The Muslim Prayer Encyclopaedia — Ruqaiyyah Waris Maqsood, New Delhi, India, 1998.

Islām and the Environment — Harfiyah Abdel Halim, London, 1998.

What does Islām say? — Ibrāhīm Hewitt, London, 1998.

Wisdom of Islāmic Civilisation — Dr. M. A. J. Beg, Kuala Lumpur, 1986.

The Muslims Supplications Throughout the Day and Night — Collected by Siddiqah Sharafaddeen, Jeddah, 1994.

Abortion, Birth Control & Surrogate Parenting — An Islāmic Perspective — Abul Fadl Mohsin Ebrahim, USA, 1989.

The Miracle of Life — Fatima M. D'Oyen, Leicester, 1996.

The Muslim Marriage Guide — Ruqaiyyah Waris Maqsood, 1995.

Sex Education – The Muslim Perspective — Ghulam Sarwar, London, 1996.

Hidayah — Translated by Charles Hamilton, Lahore, 1963.

Glossary

It is difficult to translate Arabic terms into English (or any other language), especially those used in the *Qur'ān* and the *Aḥādīth*. A brief explanation of the meaning of the important Arabic words used in this book is given below. Note that some words in Arabic have 'al' (meaning 'the') at the beginning, e.g. *al-Qur'ān*. In these cases we omit the 'al', e.g. just *Qur'ān*. We retain it, however, in names and phrases. We have also used a phonetic translation, e.g. *an-Nasā'ī* (not *al-Nasā'ī*).

ﷺ	صَلَّى اللهُ عَلَيْهِ وَسَلَّمَ	The Arabic *Ṣallallāhu 'alaihi wasallam*, written after the name of Prophet *Muḥammad* ﷺ, meaning 'peace and blessings of Allāh be upon him.
Adhān	أَذَان	The call to *Ṣalāh*.
Aḥādīth	أَحَادِيث	(sing. *Ḥadīth*) Reports of the sayings, deeds and actions approved by Prophet *Muḥammad* ﷺ.
Aḥzāb	اَلْأَحْزَاب	Meaning the Troops or the Confederates. The thirty-third *Sūrah* of the *Qur'ān* and the name of the third important battle fought by Prophet *Muḥammad* ﷺ.
Ākhirah	آخِرَة	Life after death. It includes the Day of Judgement and the never-ending life after death.
'Alaq	اَلْعَلَق	Something that clings. Also translated as clot of blood or leech. Name of the ninety-sixth *Sūrah* of the *Qur'ān*.
Allāh	اَللّٰه	The proper name of God. Allāh is the Maker of all creatures. He is not just the God of Muslims, but of all human kind.
Āli 'Imrān	آلِ عِمْرَان	The third *Sūrah* of the *Qur'ān* meaning the family of *'Imrān*.
A'māl	أَعْمَال	(sing. *'Amal*) Actions or deeds.
Amānah	أَمَانَة	(also *Amānat*) Meaning trust. (2:283; 4:58; 8:27)
Āmīn	آمِين	The word said after the recitation of *Sūratul Fātiḥah* or any *du'ā'* to Allāh. The word means: 'Accept our prayer, O Allāh'.
al-Amīn	اَلْأَمِين	Meaning 'the Trustworthy', one of the titles of Prophet *Muḥammad* ﷺ.
'Ankabūt	اَلْعَنْكَبُوت	Twenty-ninth *Sūrah* of the *Qur'an*, meaning 'the spider'.
Anṣār	اَلْأَنْصَار	(sing. *Anṣārī*) The Madīnan Muslims who helped Prophet *Muḥammad* ﷺ.
'Aqabah	اَلْعَقَبَة	The place near Makkah where Madīnan Muslims made a covenant with Prophet *Muḥammad* ﷺ.
'Arafāt	عَرَفَات	The plain 25km south-east of Makkah where people gather during *Ḥajj*. (2:198)
Arkānul Islām	أَرْكَانُ الْإِسْلَام	The five pillars (or basic duties) of Islām.
Asadullāh	أَسَدُ الله	Lion of Allah. One of the titles of *Khalīfah 'Alī*.
'Āshūrā'	عَاشُورَاء	The tenth day of the first Islāmic month, *Muḥarram*.
'Aṣr	عَصْر	Name of the *Ṣalāh* after mid-afternoon.
Aws	أَوْس	A tribe of *Madīnah*.

Awsuq	اَوْسُق	(also *Awsāq*, sing. *Wasq*) 5 *Awsuq* are equivalent to 653 kg, the *Niṣāb* for *Zakāh* on agricultural produce.
Āyah	آيَة	(pl. *Āyāt*) A verse of the *Qur'ān*.
Badr	بَدْر	The place 128 km south-west of Madīnah where the Muslims fought their first battle against the infidels of Makkah. (3:13; 8:41)
al-Baihaqī	اَلْبَيْهَقِيّ	Refers to a collection of *Aḥādīth* by *Abū Bakr Aḥmad bin Ḥusain al-Baihaqī*.
Baitul Maqdis	بَيْتُ الْمَقْدِس	The Sacred House situated in Jerusalem, i.e. *Masjidul Aqṣā*.
Baitullāh	بَيْتُ الله	The House of Allāh in Makkah, Saudi Arabia.
Banū	بَنُو	(also *Banī*) This word means 'children of' or 'tribe of'.
Bashar	بَشَر	Meaning 'man'. (18:110)
Basmalah	بَسْمَلَة	(see *Tasmiyah*)
Birr	اَلْبِرّ	Meaning 'righteousness'. The Qur'ānic term refers to all good actions and efforts done to gain Allāh's favour and blessings.
al-Bukhārī	اَلْبُخَارِيّ	Refers to *Ṣaḥīḥ al-Bukhārī*, the most authentic collection of *Aḥādīth* of *Imām al-Bukhārī*.
Darūd	دَرُود	Reciting *aṣ-Ṣalāh 'alan Nabiyy* during *Ṣalāh* or at any other time. This is a Persian word.
Dhikr	ذِكْر	Remembering or praising Allāh.
Dhul Ḥijjah	ذُو الْحِجَّة	Twelfth month of Islamic calendar, when *Ḥajj* is performed every year.
Dīn	دِين	Meaning 'religion', 'way of life', 'judgement'. (1:3; 3:19; 5:3; 107:1; 109:5; 110:2)
Dīnul Fiṭrah	دِينُ الْفِطْرَة	The natural way of life or the religion of nature. (30:30)
Du'ā'	دُعَاء	A supplication to Allāh, or asking Allāh for favour, blessing and mercy.
Fajr	فَجْر	Name of the *Ṣalāh* at dawn.
Faqīh	فَقِيه	A person with a sound knowledge and understanding of Fiqh.
Farḍ	فَرْض	Compulsory duty prescribed by Allāh.
Farḍu Kifāyah	فَرْضُ كِفَايَة	A collective obligation or duty of the Muslims. When some of the Muslims in an area do this, the obligation is discharged. If no one does it, everyone in the area would be considered sinful — e.g. *Ṣalātul Janāzah*.
al-Fārūq	اَلْفَارُوق	The title of *Khalīfah 'Umar* meaning 'the distinguisher between the right and the wrong'.
Fatwā	فَتْوَى	(pl. *Fatāwā*) A ruling on an issue given by a person well versed in the *Qur'ān* and the *Sunnah*.
Fiqh	فِقْه	Literally 'understanding'. The term refers to the science of Islāmic law or jurisprudence.
Fiqhuz Zakāh	فِقْهُ الزَّكَاة	Islāmic laws regarding Zakāh. (Also the name of a book written by Yūsuf al-Qaraḍāwi.)

Fir'awn	فِرْعَوْن	(English: Pharoah) Title of the rulers of ancient Egypt.
Ghair Mu'akkadah (Sunnah)	غَيْر مُؤَكَّدَة	Refers to the *Ṣalāh* performed only occasionally by Prophet *Muḥammad* ﷺ. As opposed to these, there are *Sunnah Mu'akkadah Ṣalāh* which Prophet *Muḥammad* ﷺ performed regularly, e.g. 2 *rak'ahs* of *Sunnah* before *Ṣalātul Fajr.*
al-Ghanī	اَلْغَنِيّ	The title of *Khalīfah 'Uthmān* meaning 'the rich'.
al-Ghurrul Muḥajjalūn	اَلْغُرُّ الْمُحَجَّلُوْن	Meaning 'distinctly bright'. The parts of the body of the Muslims washed during *Wuḍū'* will shine on the Day of Resurrection and angels will call them by this name.
Ghusl	غُسْل	Washing the whole body for *Ṭahārah.* (4:43; 5:6)
Ḥadīth	حَدِيث	(pl. *Aḥādīth*) A report of a saying, deed or action approved by Prophet *Muḥammad* ﷺ.
Ḥāfiẓ	حَافِظ	(pl. *Ḥuffāẓ*) One who memorises the whole *Qur'ān.*
Hājar	هَاجَر	(English: Hagar) One of the wives of Prophet *Ibrāhīm*, and the mother of Prophet *Ismā'īl.*
al-Ḥajarul Aswad	اَلْحَجَرُ الْأَسْوَد	The Black Stone at the southeast corner of the *Ka'bah.*
Ḥajj	حَجّ	The pilgrimage to 'The House of Allah' (*Baitullāh*) in Makkah. One of the five basic duties or pillars of Islām. (2:158, 196–203; 3:97; 5:2; 22:30)
Ḥalāl	حَلَال	That which is lawful (permitted) in Islām.
Ḥarām	حَرَام	That which is unlawful (forbidden) in Islām.
Ḥarbul Fijār	حَرْبُ الْفِجَار	A sacrilegious war which broke out during *Muḥammad's* ﷺ youth when he was between fifteen and twenty years old. It is so called because the war was fought during the months when war was conventionally forbidden.
Ḥawwā'	حَوَّاء	(English: Eve) Wife of *Ādam*, first man and the Prophet of Allāh on earth.
Ḥayā'	حَيَاء	Meaning 'modesty', 'self-respect', 'bashfulness', etc. Refers to the feeling of shame when a bad act is done or something indecent happens.
Hidāyah	هِدَايَة	Guidance from Allāh.
Ḥijāb	حِجَاب	A Muslim woman's veil or head-covering when meeting strangers and going out.
Hijrah	هِجْرَة	The migration of Prophet *Muḥammad* ﷺ from Makkah to Madīnah.
Ḥilful Fuḍūl	حِلْفُ الْفُضُول	Meaning 'The Alliance for the Virtuous'. The charitable organisation which *Muḥammad* ﷺ joined as a young man of Makkah.
Ḥirā'	حِرَاء	Name of the cave in Mount *Nūr* at Makkah where the first revelation of the *Qur'ān* was brought by the angel *Jibrā'īl* to Prophet *Muḥammad* ﷺ.
Hubal	هُبَل	The chief idol of the Makkan people in the pre-Islāmic period of ignorance. It was destroyed when Makkah was conquered by the Muslims.

Ḥudaibiyyah	اَلْحُدَيْبِيَّة	A well-known place 16 km from Makkah on the way to Jeddah.
'Ibādah	عِبَادَة	Translated as 'worship', it refers to any permitted activity performed to gain Allāh's pleasure.
Iblīs	إِبْلِيس	The devil or Satan *(Shaiṭān)* who disobeyed Allāh and swore to misguide humans from Allāh's path.
'Īdul Aḍḥā	عِيْدُ الأَضْحَى	The annual festival of sacrifice between 10–13 *Dhul Ḥijjah.*
'Īdul Fiṭr	عِيْدُ الفِطْر	The annual festival on 1st *Shawwāl*, after a month of fasting in *Ramaḍān.*
Iḥrām	إِحْرَام	The special dress worn by pilgrims during *Ḥajj.*
Iḥsān	إِحْسَان	The highest stage of *Īmān* when a believer obeys Allāh's commands as if he is seeing Allāh, and though he does not see Allāh, he knows Allāh sees him all the time. (16:90)
Ijmā'	إِجْمَاع	Consensus reached by the Islāmic jurists on a matter of Islāmic law. One of the sources of Islāmic *Sharī'ah.*
Imām	إِمَام	The person who leads prayer in a congregation, or a leader.
Īmān	إِيْمَان	Faith or belief.
al-Īmānul Mufaṣṣal	اَلإِيمانُ الْمُفَصَّل	The faith in detail.
Injīl	إِنْجِيل	Gospel. The book revealed to Prophet *'Īsa* (Jesus).
Iqāmah	إِقَامَة	The second call to prayer, made when *Ṣalāh* is about to begin in congregation.
Iqra'	إِقْرَأْ	Meaning 'read', the first word of the *Qur'ān* revealed to Prophet *Muḥammad* ﷺ at cave *Ḥirā'*. (96:1)
'Ishā'	عِشَاء	Name of the *Ṣalāh* at night
Islām	اَلإِسْلاَم	This is the name given by Allāh to the religion for mankind. The word means submission and obedience to Allāh's commands to attain peace in this life and in the *Ākhirah*. It began with the first prophet *Ādam* and was completed at the time of Prophet *Muḥammad* ﷺ.
Isrāfīl	إِسْرَافِيل	Name of the angel who will blow the trumpet signalling the end of this world, the resurrection of mankind and the start of the judgement. (*Qur'ān:* 18:99; 36:51; 23:101; 39:68; *Ṣaḥīḥ Muslim:* vol.1, no. 1694)
Isrā'īl	إِسْرَائِيل	Another name of Prophet *Ya'qūb* (Jacob), hence *Banū* (or *Banī*) *Isrā'īl* meaning: 'The children of *Isrā'īl*'.
I'tidāl	إِعْتِدَال	Returning to the position of *qiyām* after *rukū'*.
'Izrā'īl	عِزْرَائِيل	Name of the angel called *Malakul Mawt* in the *Qur'ān*. (32:11; *Tafsīr Ibn Kathīr*, vol 3, page 73, Beirut 1981).
Jahannam	جَهَنَّم	Hell, the place of eternal suffering.
Jamā'ah	جَمَاعَة	Congregation, when people say *Ṣalāh* as one group.
Janāzah	جَنَازَة	The funeral *Ṣalāh.*
Jannah	جَنَّة	Heaven, the place of eternal bliss. Literally 'Garden', also called Paradise.

Jerusalem	اَلْقُدْس	The city, known in Arabic as *al-Quds*, where *al-Masjidul Aqṣā* is situated. This was the first *Qiblah* of the Muslims. It is the third most sacred place in Islām. It is now under Israeli occupation.
Jibrā'īl	جِبْرَائِيل	The angel (Gabriel) who brought revelation from Allāh. (2:97–98).
Jihād	جِهَاد	One of the important duties in Islām, it means to strive. *Jihād fī sabī lillāh* (Striving for the sake of Allāh) means exerting all our efforts to establish *Ma'rūf* and remove *Munkar* from society in order to gain Allāh's pleasure.
Jinn	جِنّ	Allāh's creatures with free will, created from smokeless fire.
Jizyah	جِزْيَة	The tax levied on non-Muslim citizens of an Islāmic state. (9:29; also *al-Bukhārī*, vol. 4, 384–386)
Jūdiyy	اَلْجُودِيّ	The mount of *Jūdiyy* in Turkey where Prophet *Nūḥ's* ark rested. (11:44)
Jumādal Ākhirah	جُمَادَى الآخِرَة	The sixth month of the Islāmic calendar.
Jumu'ah		(see *Ṣalātul Jumu'ah*)
Ka'bah	كَعْبَة	The first place built for the worship of Allāh, in Makkah. Also called 'The House of Allāh' *(Baitullāh)*.
Kāfir	كَافِر	(pl. *Kāfirūn* or *Kuffār*) A person who does not believe in Islām.
al-Kalimatuṭ Ṭaiyibah	اَلْكَلِمَةُ الطَّيِّبَة	The pure sentence, i.e. the words said in *ash-Shahādah*.
Khaibar	خَيْبَر	An Arabian oasis inhabited by Jews during Prophet *Muḥammad's* ﷺ time, situated 160 km north of Madīnah.
Khalīfah	خَلِيفَة	An agent or vicegerent of Allāh on earth.
Khalīlullāh	خَلِيلُ الله	Friend of Allāh. The title of Prophet *Ibrāhīm*.
Khandaq	اَلْخَنْدَق	Meaning 'trench' or 'ditch'. Refers to the battle of Aḥẓāb or the battle of Khandaq
Khazraj	اَلْخَزْرَج	A tribe of Madīnah during Prophet *Muḥammad's* ﷺ time.
Khilāfah	خِلَافَة	The Caliphate. The rule by a *Khalīfah*.
Khul'	خُلْع	A wife's right to seek separation from her husband under Islāmic law, when the marriage is unsustainable.
al-Khulafā'ur Rāshidūn	اَلْخُلَفَاءُ الرَّاشِدُون	The rightly-guided *Khulafā'* or the four consecutive successors of Prophet *Muḥammad* ﷺ, i.e. *Abū Bakr aṣ-Ṣiddīq*, *'Umar al-Fārūq*, *'Uthmān al-Ghanī*, and *'Alī al-Murtaḍā*.
Khuṭbah	خُطْبَة	The sermon given before *Ṣalātul Jumu'ah*. Usually a lecture about Islām.
Kirāman Kātibūn	كِرَامًا كَاتِبُون	Meaning 'respected scribes'. (82:11) The angels who write down everything man does on earth.
al-Kubrā	اَلْكُبْرَى	Meaning 'the Great' (feminine of *al-Kabīr*). A title of *Khadījah*, the first wife of Prophet *Muḥammad* ﷺ.
Kutubullāh	كُتُبُ الله	The books revealed by Allāh.
al-Lāt	اَللَّات	The idol worshipped by the tribe *ath-Thaqīf* in *Ṭā'if*. It was destroyed by *al-Mughīrah bin Shu'bah*.

Madīnatun Nabiyy	مَدِينَةُ النَّبِيِّ	The city of Prophet *Muḥammad* ﷺ, commonly shortened to Madīnah.
Maghrib	مَغْرِب	Name of the *Ṣalāh* just after sunset.
Makkah	مَكَّة	The city where the *Ka'bah* is located and the birth place of Prophet *Muḥammad* ﷺ. Also called Bakkah in the *Qur'ān*. (3:96)
Makrūh	مَكْرُوه	Those things which are disliked and are reprehensible in Islāmic *Sharī'ah*.
Malā'ikah	مَلاَئِكَة	(sing. *Malak*) Angels.
Malakul Mawt	مَلَكُ الْمَوْت	The angel of death. Also known as *'Izrā'īl*. (32:11)
Mandūb	مَنْدُوب	The word used in Islāmic *Sharī'ah* to mean 'recommended'.
Ma'rūf	مَعْرُوف	Right actions. Its opposite is *Munkar* (wrong).
Marwah	اَلْمَرْوَة	The hillock on the other side of *Ṣafā*. (2:158)
Masjid	مَسْجِد	Literally 'a place of prostration'. A mosque.
al-Masjidul Aqṣā	اَلْمَسْجِدُ الْأَقْصَى	The mosque in Jerusalem which was the first *Qiblah* for Muslims before *al-Masjidul Ḥarām*. (17:1)
al-Masjidul Ḥarām	اَلْمَسْجِدُ الْحَرَام	The mosque in Makkah where the *Ka'bah* is situated.
al-Masjidun Nabawī	اَلْمَسْجِدُ النَّبَوِى	The Prophet's Mosque at Madīnah.
Mikā'īl	مِيكَائِيل	(also *Mīkāl*) The angel who is mentioned in the *Qur'ān*. (2:98)
Millah	مِلَّة	(also *Millat*) Nation or community.
Millatun Wāḥidah	مِلَّةً وَاحِدَةً	One nation.
Minā	مِنَى	A place situated 6.5 km to the east of Makkah.
Mīqāt	مِيقَات	(pl. *Mawāqīt*) Five fixed places from where wearing *Iḥrām* is compulsory for those intending to go on *'Umrah* or *Ḥajj*.
Mi'rāj	اَلْمِعْرَاج	The ascent of Prophet *Muḥammad* ﷺ to Heaven, which happened on 17 *Rajab*. (53:11–12)
Mīrāth	مِيرَاث	Inheritance in Islāmic law.
Mishkāh	مِشْكَاة	Refers to *Mishkātul Maṣābīḥ*, a collection of *Aḥādīth* by *Abū Muḥammad al-Ḥusain bin Mas'ūd* (died 516 AH).
Mu'adhdhin	مُؤَذِّن	The person who calls the *Adhān*.
Mubāḥ	مُبَاح	A term of Islāmic law meaning silent, i.e. neither recommended nor reprehensible.
Muftī	مُفْتِي	One who is qualified to give a *Fatwā* (Islāmic ruling).
Muhājirūn	اَلْمُهَاجِرُون	(sing. *Muhājir*) The migrants. The Makkan Muslims who migrated to Madīnah. Literally, those who make *Hijrah*.
Muḥammad ﷺ	مُحَمَّد ﷺ	The final messenger of Allāh to mankind. He was Muḥammad bin 'Abdullāh.
Mu'min	مُؤْمِن	(pl. *Mu'minūn*) A believer.
Munāfiq	مُنَافِق	(pl. *Munāfiqūn*) Meaning 'hypocrite'. A person who claims to be a believer but does not act according to his beliefs.

Munkar	مُنكَر	Wrong actions. Its opposite is *Ma'rūf* (right).
Muqīm	مُقِيم	A local resident.
Muqtadī	مُقْتَدِي	A Muslim who prays behind an *Imām*.
al-Murtaḍā	اَلْمُرْتَضَى	A title of *Khalīfah 'Alī* meaning 'the one with whom Allāh is pleased'.
Muṣallī	مُصَلِّي	A person saying *Ṣalāh*.
Muṣḥaf	مُصْحَف	A copy of the *Qur'ān*.
Muslim	مُسْلِم	A person who freely and consciously accepts the Islāmic way of life, and sincerely practices it. Also, refers to *Ṣaḥīḥ Muslim*, the authentic collection of *Aḥādīth* of *Imām Muslim*.
Muttaqī	مُتَّقِي	An Allāh-conscious person. A person having *Taqwā* is called a *Muttaqī*.
Muzdalifah	اَلْمُزْدَلِفَة	A place between *'Arafāt* and *Minā* located 11.5 km to the east of Makkah. Pilgrims are required to stay here (called *al-Mash'āril Ḥarām*) on the night of 10 *Dhul Ḥijjah*. (2:198)
Nabiyy	نَبِيّ	(pl. *Anbiyā'*) Prophet.
Naḍīr	اَلنَّضِير	*Naḍīr* was a Jewish tribe in Madīnah.
Nāfilah	نَافِلَة	(pl. *Nawāfil*) Optional.
an-Nasā'ī	اَلنَّسَائِي	Refers to *Sunan an-Nasā'ī*, one of the six most authentic collections of *Aḥādīth*.
Naẓāfah	نَظَافَة	Cleanliness.
Nikāḥ	نِكَاح	Meaning marriage between a man and a woman.
Niṣāb	نِصَاب	The amount of annual savings of a Muslim on which payment of *Zakāh* is compulsory.
Niyyah	نِيَّة	Intention.
Nūr	نُور	Allāh's light. Angels are created from *Nūr*.
Qaḍā'	قَضَاء	Making up for a missed prayer.
Qādisiyyah	اَلْقَادِسِيَّة	A place in Iraq where the Muslim and the Persian army fought a battle in the year 636/637 CE.
Qadr	قَدْر	Meaning 'measure', 'power' or 'destiny'. *Al-Qadr* refers to the foreknowledge of Allāh about all of creation.
Qainuqā'	قَيْنُقَاع	*Banū Qainuqā'* was a Jewish tribe in Madīnah.
Qiblah	قِبْلَة	The direction towards the *Ka'bah* in *Makkah* to which Muslims face during *Ṣalāh*.
Qiyām	قِيَام	Standing upright in *Ṣalāh*.
Qiyās	قِيَاس	Analogy or reasoning in Islāmic *Sharī'ah* on the basis of similar circumstances.
Qunūt	اَلْقُنُوت	The special *du'ā'* said during *Ṣalātul Witr*.

Qur'ān	اَلْقُرْآن	The sacred book of Muslims, the final book of guidance from Allāh, sent down to *Muḥammad* ﷺ through the angel *Jibrā'īl* (Gabriel) over a period of 23 years.
Quraiẓah	قُرَيْظَة	*Banū Quraiẓah* was a Jewish tribe in Madīnah.
Rabī'ul Awwal	رَبِيْعُ الْأَوَّل	The third month of the Islāmic calendar.
Rajab	رَجَب	The seventh month of the Islāmic calendar.
Rak'ah	رَكْعَة	(pl. *Raka'āt*) A 'unit' of *Ṣalāh*, each *Ṣalāh* having two, three or four *rak'ahs*.
Ramaḍān	رَمَضَان	Ninth month of the Islāmic calendar, the month of obligatory fasting.
Rasūl	رَسُوْل	(pl. *Rusul*) Messenger. *Rasūlullāh* means Messenger of Allāh.
Ribā	رِبَا	Interest, which is unlawful in Islām. (2:275–276)
Risālah	رِسَالَة	Messengership. The channel of communication between Allāh and His Messengers, through His angels, books and messengers.
Rūḥ	رُوْح	Soul, which lives on after death. (32:9) Also used in the *Qur'ān* to refer to the angel *Jibrā'īl*. (97:4)
Rukū'	رُكُوْع	Bowing during *Ṣalāh*.
Ṣadaqah	صَدَقَة	Charitable expenditure in Islām. Also used to refer to *Zakāh*. (9:60)
aṣ-Ṣādiq	اَلصَّادِق	One of the titles of Prophet *Muḥammad* ﷺ, meaning 'The Truthful'.
Ṣafā	اَلصَّفَا	The hillock near *Baitullāh* (House of Allāh) from where pilgrims make a fast walk to the hillock of *Marwāh*. (2:158)
Ṣafar	صَفَر	Second month of the Islāmic calendar.
Ṣaḥābah	اَلصَّحَابَة	(sing. *Ṣaḥabī*) Companions of Prophet *Muḥammad* ﷺ.
Saḥūr	سَحُوْر	A pre-dawn meal taken by Muslims during the fasting month of *Ramaḍān*.
Saifullāh	سَيْفُ الله	Sword of Allāh. The title of *Khālid bin al-Walīd*, the famous commander of the Muslim army.
Saiyidatun Nisā'	سَيِّدَةُ النِّسَاء	Leader of the women in *Jannah*. This is the title given to *Fāṭimah*, the youngest daughter of Prophet *Muḥammad* ﷺ.
Sajdah	سَجْدَة	Prostration during prayer.
Sajdatus Sahw	سَجْدَةُ السَّهْو	Prostrations to make up for a mistake made during *Ṣalāh*.
Ṣalāh	صَلَاة	The compulsory prayer, offered at fives set times every day in a particular way.
Salām	سَلَام	Turning the head to the right and left at the end of *Ṣalāh*, saying *Assalāmu 'alaikum wa raḥmatullāh*.
aṣ-Ṣalātu 'alan Nabiyy	اَلصَّلَاةُ عَلَى النَّبِيِّ	The *Darūd* recited after *at-Tashahhud* at the end of a particular *Ṣalāh*.
Ṣalātul Jumu'ah	صَلَاةُ الْجُمُعَة	The special congregational *Ṣalāh* said at midday every Friday.
Ṣawm	صَوْم	Fasting in the month of *Ramaḍān*, one of the five pillars (basic duties) of Islām.

Sha'bān	شَعْبَان	Eighth month of the Islāmic calendar.
Shahādah	شَهَادَة	Testifying that "There is no god but Allāh, *Muḥammad* is Allāh's messenger". The first pillar (basic duty) of Islām.
Shahīd	شَهِيْد	A Muslim who sacrifices his life for Allāh's sake.
Shaiṭān	شَيْطَان	The Arabic word for devils or evil forces from *Jinn*.
Sharī'ah	شَرِيْعَة	Way, path, law, or code of conduct.
Shawwāl	شَوَّال	The tenth month of the Islāmic calendar.
Shirk	شِرْك	Attributing partnership to Allāh. A great sin.
Shūrā	شُوْرَى	Consultation among learned Muslims. (42:38)
aṣ-Ṣiddīq	اَلصِّدِيق	The title of *Khalīfah Abū Bakr* meaning testifier to the truth.
Sīrah	اَلسِّيْرَة	Biography of the life of Prophet *Muḥammad* ﷺ and his companions.
Sujūd	سُجُوْد	Prostrating during *Ṣalāh*.
Sunnah	سُنَّة	(pl. *Sunan*) The example of Prophet *Muḥammad* ﷺ in what he did, said and approved.
		Also, the additional *Ṣalāh* practised by Prophet *Muḥammad* ﷺ.
Sūrah	سُوْرَة	(pl. *Suwar*) A chapter of the *Qur'ān*.
Ta'awwudh	تَعَوُّذ	Saying *A'ūdhu billāhi minash shaiṭānir rajīm*.
Tafsīr	تَفْسِيْر	Detailed explanation of the meaning of the *Qur'ān*.
Tahajjud	تَهَجُّد	Optional *Ṣalāh* between midnight and dawn.
Ṭahārah	طَهَارَة	To be clean and pure.
Takbīr	تَكْبِيْر	Saying *Allāhu Akbar*.
Takbīratul Iḥrām	تَكْبِيْرَةُ الإِحْرَام	Saying *Allāhu Akbar* at the start of the *Ṣalāh*.
Ṭalāq	طَلَاق	A husband's right to divorce his wife in Islāmic *Sharī'ah* when the marriage is not sustainable. (2:228–232; 65:1–7) *Aṭ-Ṭalāq* is the name of the 65th *Sūrah* of the *Qur'ān*.
Talbiyah	تَلْبِيَة	Literally 'response' or 'compliance'. The words *"Labbaik, allāhumma labbaik…"* recited whilst in *Iḥrām* during *'Umrah* or *Ḥajj*.
Taqwā	تَقْوَى	Piety, Allāh consciousness or fear of Allāh.
Tarāwīḥ	تَرَاوِيْح	The special *Ṣalāh* said after *'Ishā'* in *Ramaḍān*.
Tasbiḥ	تَسْبِيْح	Saying *Subḥāna rabbiyal…* (Glorification of Allāh).
Tashahhud	تَشَهُّد	The recitation after two *rak'ahs* and at the end of *Ṣalāh*.
Tashrīq	أَيَّامُ التَّشْرِيق	The three festive days following *'Īdul Aḍḥā* (11–13 *Dhul Ḥijjah*).
Tasmiyah	تَسْمِيَة	Saying *Bismillāhir raḥmānir raḥīm*. Also called the *Basmalah*.
Tawbah	تَوْبَة	Meaning 'repentence'. To ask Allāh's forgiveness for our mistakes and sins. *At-Tawbah* is the name of the 9th *Sūrah* of the *Qur'ān*.
Tawrāh	تَوْرَاة	Torah. The book revealed to Prophet *Mūsā* by Allāh.

Tayammum	تَيَمُّم	Dry ablution, performed when water is scarce, unavailable or when using it would be harmful.
Thanā'	ثَنَاء	Meaning 'praise' or 'appreciation'. Saying *Subḥānaka allāhumma…* after *Takbīratul Iḥrām*.
Thawr	ثَوْر	A mount near Makkah in which there is a cave where Prophet *Muḥammad* ﷺ and *Abū Bakr* took shelter whilst migrating to Madīnah. (9:40)
at-Tirmidhī	اَلتِّرْمِذِيّ	Refers to *Jāmi' at-Tirmidhī*, one of the six most authentic collections of *Aḥādīth*.
Ṭuwā	طُوَى	The name of the sacred valley at *Mount Sinai* where Prophet *Mūsā* received Allāh's message. (20:12)
Uḥud	أُحُد	A mount north of Madīnah where the second battle was fought by Prophet *Muḥammad* ﷺ and the Muslims against the infidels of Makkah. (3:121–128)
Ummah	أُمَّة	Community, nation. (3:110)
Ummiyy	أُمِّيّ	A person who cannot read or write. The *Qur'ān* uses this term to describe Prophet *Muḥammad* ﷺ.
'Umrah	عُمْرَة	The lesser pilgrimage to the *Ka'bah* in Makkah any time of the year. (2:158)
Uswatun Ḥasanah	أُسْوَة حَسَنَة	Meaning 'an excellent example'. The Qur'ānic term refers to Prophet *Muḥammad* ﷺ.
al-'Uzzā	اَلْعُزَّا	The idol of *Banū Shaibān* located at *Nakhlah*. It was destroyed by *Khālid bin al-Walīd*.
Wājib	وَاجِب	Obligatory.
Witr	وِتْر	Literally 'odd' (opposite of even). Refers to the *Ṣalāh* offered after *'Ishā'*.
Wuḍū'	وُضُوء	Washing for *Ṣalāh* in a prescribed way.
Yathrib	يَثْرِب	A pre-Islāmic name of Madīnah. (33:13)
Yawmuddīn	يَوْمُ الدِّين	The Day of Reckoning or of Judgement in the life after death.
Yawmul Ākhir	يَوْمُ الآخِر	The Last Day or the Day of Judgement.
Zabūr	زَبُور	Psalms. The book revealed by Allāh to Prophet *Dāwūd*.
az-Zahrā'	اَلزَّهْرَاء	A title of *Fāṭimah*, the youngest daughter of Prophet *Muḥammad* ﷺ, meaning 'radiantly beautiful'.
Zakāh	زَكَاة	Welfare contribution — a compulsory payment from a Muslim's annual savings, one of the five pillars (basic duties) of Islām. It is an act of *'Ibādah* (worship) and should not be confused with any tax.
Zamzam	زَمْزَم	Literally 'bubbling' or 'abundance of water'. The famous well near the *Ka'bah*, discovered by *Hājar*.
Ẓuhr	ظُهْر	Name of the *Ṣalāh* just after midday.

Index

Purification. *See* Ṭahārah
Pus 44
Q
Qaḍā' 59, 227
Qādisiyyah 128, 227
Qadr 17, 22, 227
al-Qāsim 94, 136
Qatar 205
Qiblah 44, 48, 58, 105, 120, 227
Qiyām 48, 51, 227
Qiyās 154, 227
Qubā' 99, 119
Qubādh II 127
al-Quds. *See* Jerusalem
Qunūt 227
Quraish 33, 80, 81, 82, 89, 92, 110, 130, 131
Qur'ān 11, 24, 27, 31–35, 85, 116, 127, 131, 153, 176–195, 199, 228
R
Rabbis 84
Rabī'ul Ākhir 11
Rabī'ul Awwal 11, 228
Rajab 11, 228
Rak'ah 46, 53, 228
Ram 174
Ramaḍān 11, 38, 47, 72–73, 83, 84, 85, 120, 174, 228
Ramlah bint Abī 'Awf 88
Rasūl 39. *See also* Messengers
Rasūlullāh 228
Relatives 182
Religion 79, 105, 117, 169, 222
Repentance 200
Respected Scribes. *See* Angels: Kirāman Kātibūn
Resurrection 178. *See also* Day of Judgement
Revelation 84, 86
Reward 14
Ribā 105, 120, 165, 167, 167–168, 194, 228
Ridicule 194
Right. *See* Ma'rūf
Risālah 18, 24, 31, 39, 177–178, 196, 228
Roman Emperor 111, 131
Romania 209
Romans 126, 127, 131
Rubber 203
Rūḥ 228. *See also* Soul
Rukū' 51, 58, 228
Rūm 131
Ruqaiyah (daughter of Muḥammad ﷺ) 82, 130, 136
Russia 209
Rustam 128
Rusul. *See* Messengers
Rwanda 209
S
Sacrifice 174
Sa'd bin Abī Waqqāṣ 88, 89, 128, 129, 130
Ṣadaqah 72, 167, 201, 228. *See also* Zakāh
aṣ-Ṣādiq 83, 96, 228
Ṣafā 75, 76, 89, 94, 119, 159, 228
Ṣafar 11, 228
Ṣafiyah bint Ḥuyaiy 94
Ṣaḥābah 125, 228
Saḥīḥ al-Bukhārī 154, 222
Saḥīḥ Muslim 154
Sahl 103
Saḥūr 73, 228
Sa'īd bin al-'Āṣ 33
Sa'īd bin Zaid 93
Saifullāh 128, 228
Saiyidatun Nisā' 137, 228
Sajāḥ bint al-Ḥārith 126
Sajdah 228
Sajdatus Sahw 58, 228
Ṣalāh 38, 40–41, 44, 46–47, 48–55, 76, 87, 104, 117, 119, 129, 153, 161, 170, 187, 196, 197, 228
Salām 136, 200, 228
aṣ-Ṣalātu 'alan nabiyy. *See* Darūd
Ṣalātul Janāzah 35, 59
Ṣalātul Jumu'ah 46, 47, 55, 59, 161, 175, 228
Ṣalātul Witr 56
Salmā 125
Salmān al-Fārisī 109
Satan. *See* Shaiṭān
Saudi Arabia 205
Savings 70
Sawdah 94, 137
Ṣawm 38, 39, 72–73, 76, 105, 117, 120, 129, 153, 161, 174, 196, 228
Senegal 205
Sex. *See* Conjugal relations
Sha'bān 11, 105, 229
ash-Shāfi'ī. *See* Muḥammad bin Idrīs ash-Shāfi'ī
Shahādah 19, 39, 229
Shahīd 107, 229
Shaiṭān 116, 173, 193, 229. *See also* Iblīs
ash-Shām 80, 105, 110, 111, 114, 119, 126, 128, 130
Sharī'ah 153–156, 229
ash-Shawṭ 107
Shawwāl 11, 174, 229
Sheep 71, 174
Shepherd 81
Shi'bi Abī Ṭālib 94, 119, 136
Shirk 149, 229
Shīrūyah 127
Shoes 76
Shūrā 169, 229
Shuraḥbīl bin Ḥasanah 126, 127
Sick 72, 200
aṣ-Ṣiddīq 96, 125, 229
Sierra Leone 205
aṣ-Ṣifāt 22
Silk 201
Silver 70, 71